TOWARD A HAYEKIAN THEORY OF SOCIAL CHANGE

Economy, Polity, and Society

Series Editors: Virgil Storr and Jayme Lemke, Mercatus Center

The foundations of political economy—from Adam Smith to the Austrian school of economics to contemporary research in public choice and institutional analysis—are sturdy and well established, but far from calcified. On the contrary, the boundaries of the research built on this foundation are ever expanding. One approach to political economy that has gained considerable traction in recent years combines the insights and methods of three distinct but related subfields within economics and political science: the Austrian, Virginia and Bloomington schools of political economy. The vision of this book series is to capitalize on the intellectual gains from the interactions between these approaches in order to both feed the growing interest in this approach and advance social scientists' understanding of economy, polity, and society.

This series seeks to publish works that combine the Austrian school's insights on knowledge, the Virginia school's insights into incentives in non-market contexts, and the Bloomington school's multiple methods, real-world approach to institutional design as a powerful tool for understanding social behaviour in a diversity of contexts.

Titles in the series

Toward a Hayekian Theory of Social Change, edited by Peter J. Boettke, Erwin Dekker, and Chad Van Schoelandt

Knowledge and Entrepreneurship in Public Policy, edited by Christopher J. Coyne, Abigail R. Hall, and Eileen Norcross

Social Coordination and Public Policy: Explorations in Theory and Practice, edited by Roberta Herzberg, Gavin Roberts, and Brianne Wolf

Market Process and Market Order: From Human Action, But Not of Human Design, edited by Rosolino A. Candela, Kristen R. Collins, and Christopher J. Coyne

Institutions and Incentives in Public Policy: An Analytical Assessment of Non-Market Decision-Making, edited by Rosolino Candela, Rosemarie Fike, and Roberta Herzberg

Economics and the Public Good: The End of Desire in Aristotle's Politics and Ethics, by John Antonio Pascarella

Culture, Sociality, and Morality: New Applications of Mainline Political Economy, edited by Paul Dragos Aligica, Ginny Seung Choi, And Virgil Henry Storr

Nudging Public Policy: Examining the Benefits and Limitations of Paternalistic Public Policies, edited by Rosemarie Fike, Stefanie Haeffele, And Arielle John

Informing Public Policy: Analyzing Contemporary Us and International Policy Issues through the Lens of Market Process Economics, edited by Stefanie Haeffele, Abigail R. Hall, and Adam Millsap

Exploring the Political Economy and Social Philosophy of Vincent and Elinor Ostrom, edited by Peter J. Boettke, Bobbi Herzberg, and Brian Kogelmann

TOWARD A HAYEKIAN THEORY OF SOCIAL CHANGE

Edited by
Peter J. Boettke, Erwin Dekker, and
Chad Van Schoelandt

LEXINGTON BOOKS

Lanham • Boulder • New York • London

Published by Lexington Books
An imprint of The Rowman & Littlefield Publishing Group, Inc.
4501 Forbes Boulevard, Suite 200, Lanham, Maryland 20706
www.rowman.com

86-90 Paul Street, London EC2A 4NE

British Library Cataloguing in Publication Information Available

Library of Congress Cataloging-in-Publication Data

Names: Boettke, Peter J., editor. | Dekker, Erwin, 1984- editor. | Van Schoelandt, Chad, editor.
Title: Toward a Hayekian theory of social change / edited by Peter J. Boettke, Erwin Dekker, and Chad Van Schoelandt.
Description: Lanham, Maryland : Lexington Books, [2023] | Series: Economy, polity, and society | Includes bibliographical references and index.
Identifiers: LCCN 2023038989 (print) | LCCN 2023038990 (ebook) | ISBN 9781666937138 (cloth : acid-free paper) | ISBN 9781666937145 (ebook)
Subjects: LCSH: Social change. | Economics. | Social sciences—Philosophy. | Hayek, Friedrich A. von (Friedrich August), 1899-1992.
Classification: LCC HM831 .T6856 2023 (print) | LCC HM831 (ebook) | DDC 303.4—dc23/eng/20230908
LC record available at https://lccn.loc.gov/2023038989
LC ebook record available at https://lccn.loc.gov/2023038990

∞™ The paper used in this publication meets the minimum requirements of American National Standard for Information Sciences—Permanence of Paper for Printed Library Materials, ANSI/NISO Z39.48-1992.

Contents

List of Tables and Figures vii

Introduction: Toward a Hayekian Theory of Social Change 1
Peter J. Boettke, Erwin Dekker, and Chad Van Schoelandt

1 Technological Progress as the Only Source of Economic Growth?: F. A. Hayek's Critical Assessment of Growth of Technological Knowledge as a Decisive Factor for Economic Growth 11
Lachezar Grudev

2 Gift-Giving as a Substitution for Monetary Exchange: Evidence from the Potlatch 37
Casey Pender

3 Locating the Artisan in Hayek's Free Civilization 65
Jaime L. Carini

4 The Form of the Farm 89
Samuel Schmitt

5 Friedrich Hayek on Freedom and the Rule of Law in *The Constitution of Liberty* 113
Abigail Staysa

6 Imperfect Laws and Liberties: The English Common Law in Medieval Ireland 131
Craig Lyons

7 Microenterprise Development in the Caribbean: Entrepreneurial Opportunity, Cultural Context, and Emergent Orders 149
Kayleigh Thompson

8 A Tale of Two Crimes: An Inquiry into the Normative Evaluation of Illicit Spontaneous Orders 179
Florian A. Hartjen

9 Hayek on the Origins of Moral Sentiments: Biological versus Cultural Mechanisms for the Evolution and Transmission of Human Morality 213
Edgar V. Cook

Index 229

About the Editors 235

About the Contributors 237

List of Tables and Figures

List of Tables

Table 2.1 Illustration of an OLG Model 46
Table 2.2 Illustration of an OLG Model with a Gift-Giving Norm 49
Table 8.1 Typology of Ordering 184
Table 8.2 Migrant Smuggling vs. Human Trafficking 194

List of Figures

Figure 2.1 A Dance for the Dead at a Cowichan Potlatch 41
Figure 2.2 Potlatch at Alert Bay 43

Introduction

Toward a Hayekian Theory of Social Change

Peter J. Boettke, Erwin Dekker, and Chad Van Schoelandt

SCHOLARS WIDELY RECOGNIZE FRIEDRICH HAYEK as one of the most important economists of the twentieth century (Caldwell 2004; Boettke 2018), and numerous studies explore his work in political philosophy (Gray 1984; Kukathas 1989; Shearmur 1996; Gaus 2011). Despite this, scholars took longer to recognize that Hayek is also one of the twentieth century's major social philosophers (Frowen 1997; Hennecke 2000). In the second half of Hayek's career, he broadened and deepened his research program to include the analysis of subsequent ideological, political, social, legal, and finally cultural change. His contribution combined substantive analysis with methodological reflections about how to analyze change in a complex system. His critique of equilibrium-based analysis, with which he had started his career, grew with his appreciation for evolutionary models of explanation and systems theory (Gaus 2006; Lewis 2014, 2016; Marciano 2009)

At the core, Hayek's work was concerned with social change. As he wrote in his seminal essay "The Use of Knowledge in Society": "Economic problems arise always and only in consequence of change" (Hayek 1945, 523). Hayek believed that social change comes from neither the actions of pathbreaking entrepreneurs upsetting the status quo nor of policymakers steering society in a desired direction. Instead, social change arises from many different individuals interacting in social processes in an institutional setting consisting of interdependent rules. Central to his thinking about social change was Hayek's notion of complex phenomena: a pattern grows more complex with the minimum number of elements necessary to explain it (Hayek 2014d; Lewis 2017). Hayek contrasts complex with relatively simple phenomena to distinguish the social sciences from the more mechanical parts of the natural sciences. He argued that most patterns that social scientists seek to explain are more complex in nature than those that natural scientists seek to explain. This puts epistemic questions central in Hayekian social philosophy: to what extent can we obtain knowledge about complex phenomena, to what extent can we explain them, and to what extent can actors within the system, ranging from entrepreneurial rule breakers to policymakers, influence processes of social change.

Complex phenomena, Hayek argued, come from human action but not from human design (Hayek 2014c). This closely connects to the notion of spontaneous order, complex phenomena that emerge from the interaction of many different elements but, as orders, take on important social significance and in turn shape the behavior of the individuals who operate within such a system. It is in this sense that Hayek's social philosophy seeks to formulate an answer to one of the key problems in the social sciences: the relationship between structure and agency. Contrary to popular belief, Hayek's social philosophy is not atomistic or methodologically strongly individualist (Boettke 2018; Denis 2014; Iorio 2015). Quite to the contrary, Hayek's work over time increasingly begins to analyze legal rules and social norms, the combination of which makes up the "orderly" part of the spontaneous order (Lewis 2015; Lewis and Lewin 2015). An order within which individuals interact.

Arguably, Hayek's social philosophy is limited because, as some of his contemporaries quipped, he does not know the words "for example." This means that much of his social philosophy work is relatively abstract and hard to approach. This might also explain why scholars took a while to fully appreciate his social philosophy's breadth and depth. The current volume seeks to remedy the lack of more practical studies of Hayek's theory of social change by bringing together a number of scholars from different social science disciplines who relate Hayek's theory of social change to empirical phenomena and methodological debates within their respective disciplines.

A Brief Historical Overview of Hayek's Work on Social Change

Hayek's interest in broader social changes started in the late 1930s when he undertook what he called "The Abuse of Reason Project," which sought to examine how and why social science had come to duplicate the methods of the natural sciences and how this had fueled a belief in the possibility that society could be engineered (Caldwell 2004, chap. 11). This project worked on the premise that developments in the social sciences have important long-term effects on political ideologies.

That ideology and social science were intimately connected for Hayek becomes more evident if we read his *The Road to Serfdom* (Hayek 2007) and his opening statement at the founding meeting of the Mont Pèlerin Society (Hayek 1967). There, he makes it clear that he believes that long-term social changes are ultimately driven by changes in ideas. And so, protecting the world from socialism and fascism requires more than fighting their specific proposals; it is necessary to reorient the leading ideas back in a more liberal direction (Dekker 2016).

If we work from a rough periodization of Hayek's work, we can say that he started out as a technical economist. Then his middle period as a political economist would stretch from the Abuse of Reason Project to the *Constitution of Liberty* (Hayek 1960). In this book, Hayek restates the principles of a free society, but the book is particularly remarkable for the way in which Hayek connects the themes of liberty, epistemology, and the importance and significance of social change. He demonstrates that since individual values are heterogeneous and knowledge is dispersed, liberty is primarily important because it generates openness to change. In Hayek's epistemic vision, the discovery of knowledge and the evolution of rules are crucial for social progress, and he defends an open society because it facilitates this social discovery process.

As such, the early chapters of *The Constitution of Liberty* can be understood as a transition in Hayek's oeuvre. These early chapters sketch out a theory of social change emphasizing social interaction and experimentation. Exploring this idea and searching for a social order that can generate endogenous change will become central themes in the later part of his career. The counterpart to this theme is analyzing how planning, legislation from above, and the belief that society can be rationally constructed and reformed prevent this dynamic of endogenous social change and rule formation.

After this transition, the idea of complex phenomena becomes central, and Hayek largely abandons linear theorizing about social change. A linear model was implicitly present in his earlier theory of ideological change, in which he argued that changes in social science lead to changes in political ideologies and finally to (misguided) economic policies. Afterward, he thought about society as a complex system with many simultaneously moving and interacting parts. Hayek applies this model of thinking in two prominent domains.

In *Law, Legislation and Liberty* (Hayek 2021), he studies the evolution of law over the ages and situates his theory of legal change between two rival notions: natural law and legal positivism. In the latter conception, as Hayek exemplified by the legal positivism of his contemporary and fellow Viennese Hans Kelsen, law is whatever the government decides. In this conception, law is the result of political decisions and can be changed through democratic or non-democratic political procedures. The natural law tradition, on the other hand, assumes that there is an underlying natural order that law should seek to discover or approximate. Although liberal thought has traditionally been closely associated with the natural law tradition, Hayek turns away from it. Instead, he proposes law as an evolving set of rules that have been adapted to local circumstances and evolving notions of justice in a decentralized system. Hayek argues that an (idealized) common law system takes this form, in which the existing legal rules, the legal tradition, are important and get applied by many different judges to (slightly) new situations, which allow legal rules to evolve over time in reaction to changing moral standards, new circumstances, and legal disputes that arise.

Around the same time, during the late 1960s, Hayek wrote his important paper "Competition as a discovery procedure" (Hayek 2014a), and one could argue that the notion of a discovery procedure became his dominant way of understanding social change. Hayek argues that liberal institutions facilitate learning through competition, in which many different individuals or groups seek to do better than others. Society gains along the way because the competitive process facilitates learning and discovering new knowledge. For Hayek, the competitive process's major advantage and social development's primary driver are extending knowledge. The knowledge problem (Hayek 1945) is central to his economics and the efficient allocation of resources, but Hayek's later work treats the discovery of new knowledge as the central problem that a society's institutions should solve. Boettke has therefore suggested that one should understand Hayek's approach as epistemic institutionalism, the study of which institutions facilitate social learning (Boettke 2018).

In the final decade of his work, in particular in his last book, *The Fatal Conceit* (Hayek 1988), Hayek uses this way of thinking about social change to study the evolution of cultural norms. He argues that groups within society, and societies, are differentiated by the cultural norms that are shared within them. In the medium or long run, we can think of the interaction between these groups as a competitive process in which the interrelated set of cultural norms competes with each other, and the relatively better set of norms will be imitated by other groups, or the group with better rules might grow faster (Witt 2008).

In conceptualizing both legal rules and cultural norms, Hayek moves away from the model of deliberate rule change and suggests that the rules of social interaction are a by-product, an unintended consequence, of repeated patterns of interaction. Social change thus primarily *emerges* as an unintended by-product of social interaction and changing circumstances rather than as the result of deliberate efforts by entrepreneurs or lawmakers to change the rules. This makes Hayek conclude in quite radical fashion that "man did not adopt new rules of conduct because he was intelligent. He became intelligent by submitting to new rules of conduct" (Hayek 1982, 163). He makes it clear that rule changes are frequently not deliberately designed but instead evolve within social interaction, and more importantly, that the precise functionality of these rules and why they work is often not clear to individuals. In that sense, rules and the social order in which we live contain an organically grown wisdom to some extent beyond the grasp of rational understanding. In this sense, society is not only a complex order in the sense that it is made up of many different interacting elements, but also in the sense that we cannot fully understand why existing rules are useful and how they interact (Hayek 2014b). Any changes in rules might thus lead to truly unintended and unforeseeable consequences.

Some Outstanding Questions for a Hayekian Theory of Social Change

Even from our brief sketch of Hayek's thinking about social change, it becomes evident that there are several important, yet unresolved, outstanding questions.

1. Hayek considers the interdependence of the different spheres of society, such as the spheres of ideas, laws, and cultural norms, as a complex order. But this also raises questions about the nature of this interdependence, whether empirical researchers should expect to find social change originating in one of the spheres, and whether questions of a change's origin even make sense within the Hayekian theory of society as a complex order. At the very least, Hayek warns against identifying simple linear relationships between individual intentions and social outcomes.
2. Contemplating the complexity of society and the interrelationships between interdependent orders leads to questioning the extent to which Hayek's work on legal and cultural change is compatible with his more technical economics. Some scholars suggest that Hayek moved away from his earlier equilibrium-oriented economics, but at the same time, it is undeniable that his economic writings of the 1930s and 1940s contain clear seeds for his later complexity thinking. A similar question should be asked about the position of subjectivism and his methodological dualism, between the subjectivist social sciences and the objectivist natural sciences, and his later distinction between simple and complex phenomena. Should we think of these changes as an evolution in Hayek's thought, from which scholars have yet to fully realize the implications for the specific social sciences? Or are they more fruitfully understood as elaborating on his earlier technical economic work?
3. Hayek's most worked-out theory of change is the evolution of the legal order, in which judges play an important role in applying existing rules

and precedent to decide new cases disputants bring. Obviously, judges will seek to do so considering the cases before them, but it is reasonable to assume that they will also seek to decide with an eye on the whole. One can generalize this basic idea to any other individual acting to achieve something in a specific action situation who might also intend broader social change. Hayek's later work has sometimes been read as downplaying the importance of intentionality and intelligence at the individual level, but examining his account of the evolution of common law clearly shows that this is a misunderstanding. Nonetheless, it is relevant to ask what scope Hayek's theory of social change leaves for deliberate action by entrepreneurs and other key actors aimed at changing rules and the direction of social change more broadly.

4. Spontaneous orders have a positive connotation, but critics note that spontaneous orders could oppress, exclude, or generate stagnation or negative forms of development. Other critics worry that competition requires a more specific institutional framework for it to have generally socially beneficial effects, an institutional framework that is not present when we study the evolution of institutions and rules (Kirzner 2000; Boettke 2014). It is therefore a largely open question under which conditions spontaneous orders lead to socially beneficial outcomes and under which conditions this is unlikely.
5. Hayek identifies a key tension that has shaped social development in recent centuries between the culturally evolved morality of the intimate order and the different morality enabling the extended order that Hayek calls the Great Society. While Hayek is aware that ideological and cultural beliefs could change in the short run, he argues that the most important part of human morality has been formed in a small band or tribe, is egalitarian in nature, and makes relatively sharp distinctions between the morality within and outside the group. This morality clashes with the morality required to enable the widespread division of labor and anonymous social relations that characterize modern societies. A key empirical question is whether it is possible to change these deep-seated moral instincts or whether society must manage this duality.

The chapters in this book seek to resolve these tensions and answer these questions, primarily on the applied level, as they occur in empirical, conceptual, and methodological questions that arise in various social sciences. Some chapters deal with Hayek's own more applied ideas and how they relate to his broader social philosophy. Others apply and consider the usefulness of a Hayekian lens to study processes of social change. Yet others explore partly conceptual questions about what generates change and the extent to which this change tends to be beneficial. The chapters were all written from the starting point that Hayek's social philosophy is worth engaging with and a challenge to most of the dominant approaches in the social sciences.

The chapter by Lachezar Grudev should be situated between the first and second questions. His analysis of the way that Hayek treats technological change in both his technical economics and his broader analysis of social dynamics suggests continuity between the two. It further demonstrates that Hayek was never prone to thinking of technological development as an external phenomenon that impacted the economy, but rather as a consequence of individual plans and social interaction with the institutional order of the free market economy.

The chapter by Casey Pender looks at the evolution of First Nations gift-giving institutions and analyzes the ways these institutions functioned as an alternative to exchange to produce efficient resource allocations in the circumstances of other cultural practices of those within the institutions. The chapter also considers the harms of external suppression of those institutions and the imposition of Western institutions misaligned with local knowledge and norms.

Jaime Carini's chapter investigates the extent to which the direction of social and rule change can be shaped by individuals and communities. She connects the notion of craftmanship as it was developed by Vincent and Elinor Ostrom with Hayek's theory of social change and suggests that the Ostromian notion of agency and crafting provides an important supplement to Hayek's work. In doing so, she explores what a Hayekian theory of entrepreneurship can be, which recognizes the importance of traditions and evolved social practices.

The chapter by Samuel Schmitt does not take creativity as its starting point, but entrepreneurial agents with knowledge of time and place who seek to orient social change based on values they hold dear. He explores to what extent such value-driven change is likely to succeed, whether this can be done bottom-up, or if it also requires a form of directionality at the system level.

Abigail Staysa's chapter explores a related question. She examines the role that the ideal of the rule of law plays in Hayek's legal theory. Staysa brings out key features of Hayek's account by contrasting it with Aristotle's own qualified endorsement of the rule of law. Hayek's ideal of the rule of law is a guiding idea for the kind of changes he proposes on the political and legal level, and so her chapter helps us to better understand the role of ideas and ideals in guiding the direction of legal and policy changes, as well as challenges to Hayek's account. Together, these chapters address questions two and three that we have outlined above.

The chapter by Craig Lyons analyzes the introduction of the rule of law in medieval Ireland by the English. He argues that the imposition of the legal framework, which Hayek praised, led to various adverse outcomes that were caused both by the incomplete application of the common law, which enabled the differential treatment of Irish and English individuals, as well as the refusal to incorporate endogenous legal rules into the English legal framework. His distinction between the discovery of legal principles appropriate to local circumstances and the substance of the rule of law provides relevant nuances to Hayek's theory of legal evolution.

The chapter by Kayleigh Thompson should be read as related to both the third and fourth questions we outlined. Her examination of development projects in the Caribbean addresses the question of change from above and change from below, but it relates these structural social inequalities, in this case gender inequalities. This allows her to analyze to what extent changes reinforce or undermine existing social patterns, which are the result of previous interactions.

The chapter by Florian Hartjen on migrant smuggling and human trafficking examines a form of entrepreneurship within the boundaries of what is legally allowed and morally accepted. His distinction between migrant smuggling, which happens on a mostly voluntary and paid basis, and human trafficking, which happens on an involuntary basis, seeks to identify when spontaneous orders tend to produce or undermine social cooperation, the fourth question above.

Finally, the chapter by Edgar Cook takes up Hayek's theory of cultural evolution and relates it to more recent research in the field of moral psychology. He demonstrates that Hayek anticipated many of the recent developments and links his theory of cultural evolution to the idea of spontaneous orders at different scales. In conclusion, Cook argues that the evidence suggests that moral systems have substantial culturally evolved aspects but that these rest on biologically evolved and shared cognitive systems.

References

Boettke, Peter J. 2014. "Entrepreneurship, and the Entrepreneurial Market Process: Israel M. Kirzner and the Two Levels of Analysis in Spontaneous Order Studies." *The Review of Austrian Economics* 27 (3): 233–247.

———. 2018. *F. A. Hayek: Economics, Political Economy and Social Philosophy*. London: Palgrave Macmillan.

Caldwell, Bruce. 2004. *Hayek's Challenge*. Chicago, IL: University of Chicago Press.

Dekker, Erwin. 2016. *The Viennese Students of Civilization: The Meaning and Context of Austrian Economics Reconsidered*. Cambridge: Cambridge University Press.

Denis, Andy. 2014. "Methodological Individualism and Society: Hayek's Evolving View." In *Austrian Economic Perspectives on Individualism and Society: Moving*

Beyond Methodological Individualism, edited by Guinevere Liberty Nell, 7–20. New York: Palgrave Macmillan US.

Frowen, Stephen F., ed. 1997. *Hayek: Economist and Social Philosopher: A Critical Retrospect*. Basingstoke: Macmillan.

Gaus, Gerald F. 2006. "Hayek on the Evolution of Society and Mind." In *The Cambridge Companion to Hayek*, edited by Edward Feser, 232–258. Cambridge Companions to Philosophy. Cambridge: Cambridge University Press.

———. 2011. *The Order of Public Reason*. New York: Cambridge University Press.

Gray, John. 1984. *Hayek on Liberty*. New York: Basil Blackwell.

Hayek, Friedrich A. 1945. "The Use of Knowledge in Society." *The American Economic Review* 35 (4): 519–530.

———. 1960. *The Constitution of Liberty*. Chicago, IL: University of Chicago Press.

———. 1967. "Opening Address to a Conference at Mont Pèlerin." In *Studies in Philosophy, Politics and Economics*, 148–159. Chicago, IL: University of Chicago Press.

———. 1982. "The Three Sources of Human Values." In *Law, Legislation and Liberty, Volume 3: The Political Order of a Free People*, 153–176. London: Routledge.

———. 1988. *The Fatal Conceit: The Errors of Socialism*. Edited by W. W. Bartley. Chicago, IL: University of Chicago Press.

———. 2007. *Road to Serfdom: The Definitive Edition*. Chicago, IL: University of Chicago Press.

———. 2014a. "Competition as a Discovery Procedure." In *The Market and Other Orders*, edited by Bruce Caldwell, 304–313. The Collected Works of F. A. Hayek Volume XV. Chicago, IL: University of Chicago Press.

———. 2014b. "Rules, Perception, Intelligibility." In *The Market and Other Orders*, edited by Bruce Caldwell, 232–253. Chicago, IL: University of Chicago Press.

———. 2014c. "The Results of Human Action but Not of Human Design." In *The Market and Other Orders*, edited by Bruce Caldwell, 293–303. The Collected Works of F. A. Hayek Volume XV. Chicago, IL: University of Chicago Press.

———. 2014d. "The Theory of Complex Phenomena." In *The Market and Other Orders*, edited by Bruce Caldwell, 257–277. The Collected Works of F. A. Hayek Volume XV. Chicago, IL: University of Chicago Press.

———. 2021. *Law, Legislation, Liberty*. Edited by Jeremy Shearmur. Chicago, IL: University of Chicago Press.

Hennecke, Hans Jörg. 2000. *Friedrich August von Hayek: Die Tradition Der Freiheit*. Düsseldorf, Germany: Verlag Wirtschaft und Finanzen.

Iorio, Francesco di. 2015. *Cognitive Autonomy and Methodological Individualism*. Cham: Springer.

Kirzner, Israel M. 2000. *The Driving Force of the Market: Essays in Austrian Economics*. London: Routledge.

Kukathas, Chandran. 1989. *Hayek and Modern Liberalism*. Oxford: Oxford University Press.

Lewis, Paul. 2014. "Hayek: From Economics as Equilibrium Analysis to Economics as Social Theory." In *Elgar Companion to Hayekian Economics*, edited by Roger W. Garrison and Norman Barry, 195–223. Cheltenham, UK: Edward Elgar.

———. 2015. "Notions of Order and Process in Hayek: The Significance of Emergence." *Cambridge Journal of Economics* 39 (4): 1167–1190.

———. 2016. "Systems, Structural Properties and Levels of Organisation: The Influence of Ludwig Von Bertalanffy on the Work of F. A. Hayek." In *Research in the History of Economic Thought and Methodology, Vol. 34A*, 125–159. Bingley: Emerald Group Publishing Limited.

———. 2017. "The Ostroms and Hayek as Theorists of Complex Adaptive Systems: Commonality and Complementarity." In *The Austrian and Bloomington Schools of Political Economy, Vol. 22*, 35–66. Bingley: Emerald Publishing Limited.

Lewis, Paul, and Peter Lewin. 2015. "Orders, Orders, Everywhere...on Hayek's the Market and Other Orders." *Cosmos + Taxis* 2 (2): 1–17.

Marciano, Alain. 2009. "Why Hayek Is a Darwinian (after All)? Hayek and Darwin on Social Evolution." *Journal of Economic Behavior & Organization*, Darwin, Darwinism and Social Darwinism, 71 (1): 52–61.

Shearmur, Jeremy. 1996. *Hayek and After: Hayekian Liberalism as a Research Programme*. Routledge Studies in Social and Political Thought. London: Routledge.

Witt, Ulrich. 2008. "Observational Learning, Group Selection, and Societal Evolution." *Journal of Institutional Economics* 4 (1): 1–24.

1

Technological Progress as the Only Source of Economic Growth?

F. A. Hayek's Critical Assessment of Growth of Technological Knowledge as a Decisive Factor for Economic Growth

Lachezar Grudev

HAYEK WAS CRITICIZED FOR HAVING never incorporated technological progress into his explanation of business cycles (Klausinger 2012a, 65). I would even add that Hayek did not focus on the impact of technological progress on economic growth. My chapter raises the hypothesis that if Hayek had explicitly employed technological progress in the explanation of these macroeconomic phenomena, such an approach would have diverted the focus from the primacy of the institutional framework for generating socially beneficial outcomes such as economic growth or how interventions can give rise to socially harmful outcomes such as business cycles. This means to neglect the idea that these macroeconomic phenomena actually arise *spontaneously* from the interaction among millions of individuals where the institutional framework performs a fundamental coordination function necessary to bring different and even contradicting economic plans into a mutual agreement, whereas any changes in institutions can affect whether these interactions can promote socially beneficial or socially harmful outcomes.

The different patterns of interaction affected by the institutional framework can help us understand why Hayek promoted the concept of *order* as an instrument of analysis in the social sciences, which makes him a close associate of the Freiburg School of Ordoliberalism (Hayek [1963] 1969, 32; [1967] 1969, 187–189).[1] Thinking in order stands diametrically opposed to the approach employed by modern macroeconomics. The latter is still trapped in the idea developed since Saint-Simon, continued by Karl Marx, and that fascinated Joseph Schumpeter, who believes in the "inevitability of the development of society and of the economic order in a predetermined, non-reversible direction . . ." where "the course of the history follows a law which is as inescapable as a law of nature and like each law, this law can be discovered or at least uncover this law" (Lutz 1966, 8). And this law is generated by some external forces called technological progress.

On the Necessity of Technological Progress and Other Fallacies

The Materialistic Approach

Karl Marx was the most renowned philosopher and economist who identified technological progress as the driving force behind the emergence of macroeconomic phenomena such as economic growth and economic crises. Marx's materialistic understanding of history reduced the course of history to a process generated by general dynamic law, which treated all religious, cultural, and political phenomena as an immediate result of the technological-economic foundation of society. Innovations as an expression of technological progress were inevitable consequences of entrepreneurial activity because entrepreneurs feared their rivals, who had been gaining competitive advantages over them, and thus endangered their existence. In unisono with his understanding of history as an eternal struggle among classes, Marx claimed that if entrepreneurs want to survive the fierce struggle arising from competition, then they should innovate in order to decrease the prices of their products, attract more customers, and at least preserve their level of profits. As a result, innovation was not treated by Marx as a personal option but an existential must: "Innovate, innovate! This is Moses and the prophets" (Marx 1967, 1972; Eucken [1940] 1950, 246–247; Kurz 2008, 265; Hayek 2010, 292–293).

The Austrian economist Joseph Schumpeter considered Marx's description of capitalism as his lifelong challenge. His research program was oriented toward proving Marx's dynamics of capitalism. Schumpeter saw in innovative entrepreneurs the ultimate source for economic growth inherent in capitalism and, at the same time, the essence of its instability, which took the expression form business cycles. The latter reflected a periodic recurrence of economic booms and depressions. Schumpeter tried to prove that the reason for the endogenous movement arose spontaneously and discontinuously, creating wave-like movements representing the cyclical fluctuations:

"Analyzing business cycles means neither more nor less than analyzing the economic process of the capitalist era" (Schumpeter 1939, v). This characterizes the nature of the capitalist system (Rühl 1994; Dal Pont Legrand and Hagemann 2007). Schumpeter defined that a new dynamic economic theory should be developed whose aim is to explain this endogenous movement of the capitalistic economies arising from the inherently antagonistic powers within capitalism. These antagonistic powers were expressed by the conflict between pioneering entrepreneurs and the static proprietor. The pioneering entrepreneurs were supported by commercial banks' credit, with whose help entrepreneurs were able to attract the resource from the static proprietor. The latter were unable to produce anything new and relied on old routines. The introduction of the new innovations generated the boom phase, which attracted further entrepreneurs until complete saturation of the markets was achieved. Afterwards, complete breakdowns and depressions followed (Dal Pont Legrand and Hagemann 2017). Marx and Schumpeter were united by the idea that capitalism would inevitably break down because of its internal contradictions and transform into socialism (Dalton and Logan 2019, 4).

The Modern Macroeconomic Approach

The idea of the inevitable breakdown of capitalism and its transformation into socialism left the research programs of leading mainstream economists, particularly after the transformation of Eastern European economies. However, if a student of economics opens a standard graduate textbook of macroeconomics, he will recognize that technological progress still plays a central role in modern economic theories. Even though these textbooks admit the relevance of "the strength of property rights, the quality of infrastructure, cultural attitudes toward entrepreneurship and work, and so on" (Romer [1996] 2012, 29) as driving forces of economic growth, these textbooks put the weight of explanation of the immense increase in standard of living since the Industrial Revolution on technological progress.

In "A Contribution to the Theory of Economic Growth" (1956), Robert Solow arrived at the conclusion that technological progress had been responsible for this dramatic increase in gross domestic product and thus the standard of living since the Industrial Revolution. At the same time, different rates of technological progress explained why economies varied in their economic growth rates, where technological progress increases the productivity of labor, described as the effectiveness of labor and thus the domestic output. Solow's model debunked the old idea of the relevance of investments and stocks of capital as the driving forces behind economic growth. Thus, Solow provided the basis for the new growth models, which still reflect the cornerstone of modern macroeconomics.

One of the most important empirical implications of Solow's model is that poorer countries should grow faster and catch up with richer economies. The catch-up hypothesis was central to the American textbook of economics until the transformation processes of Eastern Europe. The most eminent example is Paul Samuelson's textbook, which does not question whether the Soviet Union would overtake the US economy but presents it as a matter of time. For Samuelson, the growth rates of both economies are of particular interest for many African and Asian countries because "they are interested in choosing that form of economic organization which will move them most rapidly along the road of development" (Levy and Peart 2009, 9). I interpret that this economic organization refers to this institutional framework, which determines the economic order. Samuelson supposed that even a centrally planned economy could foster stronger economic growth. Later, Samuelson explained why his forecast was not fulfilled.

> In the decade preceding 1970, the United States grew toward the top of its projected range of growth rates. But the U.S.S.R., because of bad weather and crops and shortening of the workweek, seems to have moved lower down on its projected range of growth rates. (1970, 831; citation based on Levy and Peart 2009, 10)

Bad weather, the quality of crops, and political decisions are actually exogenous data for economic theory, something that will be explained later in this chapter. We will also see that these data cannot be responsible for macroeconomic phenomena. Samuelson still believed in the relevance of technological progress as fundamental for faster economic growth rates until the late 1980s, when the economic problems of Eastern European countries were more than obvious. That is why leading macroeconomists were surprised by the breakdown of communism in Eastern Europe and the Soviet Union (Levy and Peart 2009).

Critics stressed that Solow failed to explain the ultimate reason for technological progress, which is responsible for the growth of the effectiveness of labor. Paul M. Romer was among the vehement critics of Solow's growth model. They raised the simple question: if technological progress is responsible for an increase in the effectiveness of labor and thus economic growth, then what generates technological growth (Landmann 2018, 426)? They put the argument forward that Solow actually developed models for growing, which in some way is tautological because he still failed to explain the ultimate engine of growth and assumed technological progress as *deus ex machina* generating economic growth.

Romer's research on endogenous growth gave rise to further development of this branch of economics, which concentrates on how knowledge is generated and accumulated. His models stressed that scientific knowledge is the driving force behind technological progress. So, these models concentrated on how research and development (R&D) added to the existing stock of knowledge. The endogenous growth models developed a production function of knowledge where existing knowledge is considered as an input. But this input does not have the same features as labor and capital, where doubling the latter would double the output. The representatives of endogenous growth theories were aware of the fact that doubling the input "knowledge" would cause the same discoveries, which would not add to the existing stock of knowledge. So, a parameter is introduced to show how the existing stock of knowledge would affect the success of R&D departments in adding knowledge to the existing stock of knowledge. For example, past discoveries and tools can make future discoveries more difficult. As we can see, the endogenous growth theory applies an economic logic to explain how knowledge is generated and how its accumulation is the driving force of economic growth (Romer [1996] 2012, 101–104; The Prize in Economic Sciences 2018).

The economic policy recommendations derived from Romer's theory suggest changes in institutional conditions so that the "production" of knowledge is encouraged. These institutional changes arise from the essence of the production of knowledge, which differs from the production of goods. Machines differ from knowledge because machines, such as labor are rival physical goods that can be excluded from usage by other factories, whereas ideas cannot be excluded. These non-rival goods can easily be used by everybody. Romer defined that these goods can be excluded by technical measures such as encryption or patent law. The institutional framework should cause rivalry and the excludability of ideas because only then would entrepreneurs have an incentive to create new ideas. Romer stressed that the production of ideas is related to rapidly declining costs where the first blueprint produced large fixed costs that, with replication and reproduction, would decrease. As a result, firms generating knowledge should be allowed to set the price above the marginal costs, in order to be compensated for the high research costs. So, the government should provide monopolistic power to these firms through patent law. Romer concluded that markets do not reward innovators properly, which is the reason why too little R&D is conducted. The underprovision of R&D can be solved by subsidies and patent regulations. These patent regulations should, however, be limited in time and space so that other countries may benefit from the new ideas (Romer [1996] 2012, 116–119; The Prize in Economic Sciences 2018; Landmann 2018).

F. A. Hayek's Critical Assessment

As an Economist . . .

We can find several places where Hayek acknowledged the relevance of technological progress in order to increase the productivity of a given organization of production (e.g., Hayek [1936] 2015; Hayek [1961] 2014, 402). However, he formulated that not technological progress per se made societies wealthy, but that wealthy societies were able to encourage technological progress (Hayek [1961] 2014, 402). This narrative can be traced back to Hayek's early capital-theoretical works such as *Prices and Production* ([1935] 1967), where he focused on how the distribution of production factors affects the productivity of the community and thus the flow of consumers' goods necessary to satisfy human wants even if there is no change in technical knowledge (Hayek [1935] 1967, 35–36; [1941] 2007, 111). In his later social-philosophical works, Hayek claimed that this distribution is affected above all by the institutional framework, which in turn determines the efficient use of resources and the increase of the stream of goods (Hayek [1976] 1978, 116–120).

In *The Pure Theory of Capital* ([1941] 2007), Hayek delineated the main difference between the Anglo-American and the Austrian methods of approach to the concept of capital. With different understandings of capital, the economists on both sides of the Atlantic shared different understandings of the relationship between technological progress and technical methods of production. The Anglo-American approach promoted the idea that technological progress uniquely determines the technical methods of production. The Austrian approach assumes that, at given technological progress, changes in the supply of savings can affect the technique of production. Any increase in savings will change the technique of production, which means changes in methods of how resources are used (Hayek [1941] 2007, 68–69; 90). According to Hayek, the understanding of capital as a quasi-homogeneous mass assumed in the same way as other production factors such as labor and land was at the bottom of misunderstanding on the side of Anglo-American economists. This was the reason for their understanding of the unique relationship between technological progress and the technical methods of production. Austrians conceptualized capital as intermediate non-permanent goods, whereby the variation of relationships among these goods is fundamental for the explanation of more complex phenomena such as the business cycle and economic growth (Hayek 1936, 219; Hayek [1941] 2007, 1–5).

The Austrian (aggregate) production function represents a vertical structure where the services of the original means of production (labor and land) are applied in successive stages of production. This process is necessary in order to bring forth consumers' goods accruing at any point in time. The

Austrian production function shows a transformation of physical quantities such as hours of labor and pounds of seeds (input) into pounds of corn (output) (Boulding 1936, 524). The stages preceding the stage of consumers' goods production (the output) produce intermediate (capital) goods. The process is described as a roundaboutness of production because time elapses between the moment when the first original means of production (labor and land) are invested and the moment when the product is ripe for consumption. The proportion between the number of intermediate products that is necessary in order to secure a flow of consumers' goods, that is, the capital stock, and the amount of consumers' goods stands in a specific relationship (Hayek [1935] 1967, 36–40).

Each entrepreneur invests resources in the employment of labor and machines in his production. These resources are those consumers' goods that entrepreneurs exchange against the services of labor and machines. That is why the size of the flow of consumers' goods is not only an indicator of the wealth of the community but also sets the boundaries of saving and consumption in the community. The structure of the investment in community determines the size of the flow of consumers' goods, that is, economic growth, something that Solow debunked with his model. Many economists neglect that the investment procedure on a societal level reflects a coordinated process where each entrepreneurial act represents a chain of the whole investment procedure. This chain of investment acts should be completed so that the flow of consumers' goods is secured (Hayek 1936, 202–203; Hayek [1937] 1975, 75).

Hayek emphasized that the structure of the investment depended on the distribution of production factors (i.e., labor). Economic growth is generated when the structure of investment procedure is changed by varying the distribution of the production factor. This is made possible when the number of intermediate goods (or the stages) preceding the stage of consumers' goods increases, thus raising the stock of capital goods. In order to make possible this higher capitalistic method of production, the resources (i.e., the original means of production as labor and land) should be devoted to production of goods that would satisfy more distant future needs (future consumption) rather than concentrating these resources on the production of goods for immediate satisfaction of needs (current consumption). This intertemporal allocation from consumption to saving means an elongation of production process. This increase in roundaboutness of production, which changes the structure of production, gives rise to a transition from a given capitalistic to a more capitalistic way of production, described as an increase in capital intensity (Hayek [1935] 1967, 90–96; Streissler 1969, 280).

Hayek assumed that there were two possible ways the transition from a less to more capitalistic method of production could be achieved: by increasing either voluntary savings or the money supply (Hayek [1935] 1967, 50). The fundamental message is that a permanent transition is guaranteed only by an increase in voluntary savings, whereas an increase in the money supply would not be able to guarantee this elongation of production process.

The increase in savings or in the money supply gives rise to an increase in the purchase power of enterprises. The changes in purchase power send signals to the economic agents to act in a specific way. Thus, macroeconomic phenomena arise as a result of the actions of individuals who pursue their economic goals as profit or utility maximization (Hayek [1933] 1966, 80–87). Even a given amount of economic growth can only be preserved if all individuals act in a specific way. The capital structure of the economy is not a magnitude that was once brought about and existed forever. The capital structure (the composition of intermediate goods in a vertical model) would only then remain the same and thus preserve a given flow of consumers' goods when entrepreneurs decide to maintain their own machines and equipment. If they find it profitable to reinvest part of the return from the sale of the product in the maintenances of their equipment, then the capital structure of the economy would be preserved, as would the flow of consumers' goods. This depends on the price that entrepreneurs obtain for their product at a given stage of production on the one hand and the prices paid for original means of production and intermediate products from previous stages of production on the other. The difference between prices obtained for own goods and prices of production factors are profits generated by entrepreneurs. In equilibrium, these profits are defined as the natural rate of interest. So, profits, in general, and prices, in particular, govern the direction of production and distribution of consumers' goods among the different stages of production (Hayek [1935] 1967, 48–50).

Prices should be a result of the principle of imputation of the marginal value of a product in order to signal the right information about the scarcity of resources. According to the concept of imputation (described also as the problem of attribution), factors of production are valued according to how they contribute to the value of consumers' goods (Hayek [1926] 2012; Hayek [1941] 2007, 192; White 2015, x–xiii). This explains the inequality in the enumeration of production factors such as different relative wages. It matters whether this inequality arises as a result of spontaneous forces of markets or whether it is the outcome of government interventions. If this unequal distribution is result of the forces of free market, Hayek concluded that this is necessary in order to maintain the flow of consumers' goods and secure a "just" distribution of resources among the different stages of production according to how much they contribute to the value of the consumers' goods. Production and distribution are two entangled phenomena (Hayek [1976] 1978).

If the government coerces any distribution of resources by changing the valuation of production factors in order to create social justice, this would destroy these forces, which are responsible for the higher quantity and better quality of consumers' goods (Hayek [1976] 1978, 128–132). If the government affects the price system with the aim to foster economic growth and secure employment, this intervention will create malinvestment, which provides the basis for an unstable production structure in the economy. The best example of this is an expansive monetary policy when the central bank lowers the monetary interest rate. Such a policy is based on the premise that capital is a homogenous mass and neglects that the different stages of production stand in such a relationship according to how each stage contributes to the flow of consumers' goods. This relationship is valued by the natural interest rate, which, as already said, determines the relationship among prices in the system. The disturbance of the price mechanism is the cornerstone of his business cycle theory: "production is governed by prices, independently of any knowledge of the whole process on the part of individual producers, so that it is only when the pricing process is itself disturbed that a misdirection of production can occur" (Hayek [1933] 1966, 84–85).

Hayek conveyed two relevant messages: economic agents possessed limited knowledge gained during economic activity and behaved according to the signals they received from those prices, which they considered relevant for their economic activity (production and consumption) (see, e.g., Klausinger 1989, 179). The limited knowledge implies that we cannot expect economic agents to be economic experts who, by reading statistics and so on, adapt their plans to the newly acquired information. Individuals would adapt their plans only when they observed this change in data for which they care, such as prices and opportunities to obtain the necessary resources. This leads to the second message about relevant prices, which means that it does not matter when we talk about boom or depression; the realized prices direct the actions of individuals. This was the reason why Hayek criticized all interventions during the Depression because these interventions would not allow the restoration of the information function of prices, which is necessary in order to reestablish communication among members of society and shorten the depression (Hayek [1931] 2012, 185; Klausinger 2012b, 8–9).

The coercive influence on the distribution of flow of consumers' goods was a central topic in Hayek's argument about the inefficiency of centrally administered economies. An immediate result of knowledge problem on the side of planners is their desire to foster the growth of heavy industries by artificially diverting resources for construction of plants and employing labor necessary for this heavy industry (Hunold 1961, 127).[2] He gave as examples the most modern steel mills in India and the labor-saving rayon plant in Spain, where autocratic regimes foster investment in capital goods, as the Soviet Union has been doing since 1917. Hayek denoted these examples as very wasteful investments that, in a coercive manner, divert resources from one group of society to another without creating economic growth (Hayek [1961] 2014, 411). This is an example of the blind belief in technological progress that burns economic growth into an engineering problem, something that misses the coordinating function of the institutional framework. We should not forget that American textbooks promoted the idea of a planned economy as the fastest way to generate growth until the end of the 1980s (Levy and Peart 2009).

Hayek's economic research program continued the economic understanding that was developed in the writings of Francoise Quesnay[3] through Adam Smith and the English Classics until Eugen Böhm-Bawerk. Schumpeter talked about the Quesnay-Ricardo-Böhm-Bawerk model (Machlup 1960, 11). Hayek, who was also a historian of economics (Hayek 2012, 134), not only continued an old tradition, but he based his model on assumptions that were derived from division of labor, the fundamental problem of economics (see particularly Hayek [1925–1929] 2012; Boettke 2018, 83). Solow did not consider the problems arising from division of labor expressed by structure and composition of capital. Solow's growth model did discuss intertemporal allocation as a trade-off between current consumption and future of the community (White 2007, xvi). However, he assumed capital as a homogenous mass, where the interest rate is just the payment for services derived from production factor *capital*, such as wages, which are a payment for production factor *labor*. Based on the Cobb-Douglas production function, where labor, capital, and knowledge (or effectiveness of labor) stand in a mathematical relationship, doubling effective labor and capital would double output, something that was criticized by Hayek by claiming that for the Anglo-American approach, mere duplication of capital gives rise to an increase in output, whereas in the Austrian approach, changes in technique of production only through elongation of production structure can cause an increase in output (Hayek [1941] 2007, 69). Solow developed a "one-sector" growth model where capital is identical with consumption. Only an increase in level of technology can raise the volume of output. Time is assumed in the model only to show the time paths for capital accumulation, labor force growth, and output growth. This is completely different from Hayek's time-consuming production. As already said, it matters that we discuss the structure and composition of capital stock in order to explain business cycle as a phenomenon of disturbance of the coordination mechanism of markets and economic growth as a result of the coordination mechanism (White 2007, xxxii).

Hayek's approach stands diametrically opposed to what Solow and Friedman (1953) had in mind in the context of their model building (Boettke 2012, 310–311). Solow was so preoccupied with modeling what the statistical data conveyed that he neglected the central theoretical problems that previous economists attempted to solve in their research programs. He once admitted that he tried to read *Prices and Production*, but he failed to grasp the central idea: "I thought there's got to be something wrong with the man who could write that" (cited from White 2007, xxxii). Solow claimed that assumptions do not matter so long as the model explains the economic phenomena (Solow 1956, 65). Nobody denies that a model represents an abstract representation of the world, but even the formulation of assumptions necessary to develop a theory occupied many economists for a long time. They knew the dangers to which their colleagues had been exposed when the latter attempted to construct economic models, which ended up as a pure exercise of logic detached from reality (Eucken [1940] 1950, 347–349).

As a Social Philosopher . . .

Such an economist who concentrated his energies and efforts on defining realistic assumptions was Walter Eucken, whose abstraction procedure was instrumental in his research program (Eucken [1940] 1950; Ostrom 1999, 409). Hayek discussed the problems arising from unrealistic assumptions in his methodological essay "Economics and Knowledge" (1937). Hayek identified those logical mistakes that were committed by economists when they tried to explain macroeconomic phenomena (Hayek 1937, 38). They neglected the cleavage between the logic applied to description of individual behavior and the logic applied to the explanation of processes on a societal level. Hayek criticized this approach as a priori, where from the behavior of economic agents, economists deduce propositions on social phenomena taking place on societal level (Hayek 1937, 35). The analysis of behavior of economic agents which is based on *Pure Logic of Choice* can be applied if we want to explain how an economic agent substitutes one good for another and how he acts according to the rules of marginal utility and productivity. Hayek described such kind of thinking as "Economic Calculus" which "is mainly a technique for describing the different structures which the means-ends relations can produce" (Hayek [1961] 2014, 390). But if we move from an individual to a societal level, and if we want to explain the emergence of phenomena on a societal level, then this logic cannot be employed because it fails to explain these social phenomena as results of interaction among thousands of different individuals.

When economists derive from the behavior of economic agents propositions on the dynamics of the economic system, they "silently" introduce assumptions that actually should be explained. Hayek provided an example of how economists explained the emergence of equilibrium. Hayek formulated that an equilibrium on an individual level can easily be explained because this means that economic agents' plans are fulfilled and expectations realized. But when we move on to the societal level, then the silent assumption is that the process of interaction should promote a state of affairs that we call equilibrium. Economists make the mental shortcut by assuming that all economic agents observe the same subjective data (given facts), possess the same demand and supply functions, and so on, and from these assumptions *somehow* equilibrium is achieved without explaining how this took place. Equilibrium is actually a result of interaction, which is defined as an agreement among the interacting individuals who hold different beliefs and follow their own plans. However, the process towards equilibrium should be clarified by economists. This process reflects how individuals adjust their behavior once they learn new facts in order to realize their plans so that agreement among them is achieved. These new facts represent subjective data for economic agents (Hayek 1937, 33–38; Boettke 2018, 82–83).

Hayek emphasized that in the social sciences, the concept of datum (plural, data) lies at the bottom of all problems. Datum means a given fact. However, when economists theorize on economic phenomena, they forget to distinguish between the facts given to the observing economists and the facts given to the acting individuals. Furthermore, Hayek distinguished between data on an individual level—facts given to the acting agent—and data on a societal level—facts given to the community (Hayek 1937, 39). In the first three sections of his essay "Scientism and the Study of Society" ([1942] 2010), Hayek discussed the subjective character of social sciences, which are concerned with individuals who hold subjective beliefs and perceptions that are based on subjective data observed only by the acting agent. But if we move to the societal level, there are data that are given to the whole society whose realization at a given moment is not known to economists and economic agents. Such data could be the state of technological progress or stock of resources (described as finished and semi-finished goods). The economists are allowed to construct models with whose help they can show how technological progress can affect the economic growth of a community. But this represents an advanced chapter of economics if all problems of capital theory are clarified. Only then, economists are allowed to show how economic variables such as prices and wages change when a new invention is introduced (Hayek [1941] 2007).

This is the great cleavage between Hayek's and Romer's research programs. For Hayek, a change in the state of technology is exogenous, or, as Hayek described it, an "independent variable" for economics (Hayek [1961] 2014, 402), whose change is mentally assumed by the economists in order to explain how this change affects the capital structure of the economy. Economists cannot develop any law on which this change is based. In a similar way, Solow criticized the endogenous growth theory:

> . . . there is probably an irreducibly exogenous element in the research and development process, at least exogenous to the economy. . . . There is an internal logic—or sometimes non-logic—to the advance of knowledge that may be orthogonal to the economic logic. This is not at all to deny the partially endogenous character of innovation but only to suggest that the "production" of new technology may not be a simple matter of inputs and outputs. I do not doubt that high financial returns to successful innovation will divert resources into R&D. The hard part is to model what happens then. (Solow 1994, 51–52)

Romer's model postulates that changes in technical knowledge are subject to a general law that can be discovered and modelled based on economic logic, where R&D departments always produce new knowledge, just as firms produce new goods. The more knowledge is generated, the higher the economic growth of this society, and once this knowledge is somewhere generated, the whole society benefits from this newly generated knowledge. The first problem is that scientific knowledge is not just generated as producers' and consumers' goods; it represents the accidental result of research processes, which can be long and exhausting for the researching scientists. In other words, the economist cannot apply an economic logic, as Solow stressed, in order to deduce a priori how research efforts would inevitably add to existing scientific knowledge. What about all the research failures and abandoned projects? Romer's model shared materialistic thinking that society "moves" according to generally recognized law; here, this law is discovered in the production of knowledge.

A further problem is that Romer's model fails to answer the question of how once-created knowledge is distributed to the whole economy. Whether the invention becomes useful for economic agents and the whole community cannot be said a priori which means that a new invention cannot be postulated as cause of *concrete* macroeconomic phenomena (business cycles and economic growth). The main reason for this is that the social scientist pretends to know too much. He pretends to know the subjective data observed by all economic agents. He pretends to know that economic agents immediately acquire the necessary knowledge about the usefulness of the invention, such as an improvement in marginal productivity of labor and efficient use of resources. The social scientist neglects the relevance of all these mechanisms of communication, such as trade exhibitions, newspapers, and advertisements, that should convey information about the relevance of invention. The social scientist forgets that the installment of the new invention reflects a trial-and-error process where the installment of the new machine does not produce the necessary results immediately.

Innovative and discovery activities on the side of economic agents mean changes in subjective data, but three questions arise: Whose data change, how these data change, and what is the cause of this change? I describe innovation as an activity when the entrepreneur concentrates all his efforts and energies in order to produce a means of production that would change the method of production of his trading partners. A crucial assumption is that the product is not exclusively used by the innovator himself, but he has to convince the other market participants of the usefulness of his invention. This is intimately related to the problem of communication of knowledge facilitated by newspapers, advertisements, and so on. If economists characterize innovations as the only responsible factor for economic growth, then, as Hayek stressed, they "silently" assume "a new element of altogether different character" (Hayek 1937, 35). I delineate even three elements. Economists "silently" assume that market participants immediately become aware of the usefulness of these innovations. Economists "silently" assume that market participants adopt the new innovations, which immediately increase their productivity. Economists "silently" assume that once these innovations are adopted, the productive methods of production will immediately increase the productivity of the whole economy and give rise to economic growth. The "silent" introduction of these assumptions is an expression of the pretense of knowledge on the side of economists. Economists developed their theories by imputing extraordinary knowledge into the market participants, as though the latter immediately got the necessary information about the usefulness of the innovation. In this context, the entrepreneurial innovations reflect an example of apriorism in that, from the action of the so-called representative individual, we can say what the result of interaction is.

A discovery procedure denotes an activity where an economic agent realizes how to use the existing resources in a more efficient way. The knowledge acquired during the economic activity is exclusively used by the "discovering" agent. This is because of the essence of the discovery procedure itself. This procedure was not planned by economic agent because he did not explicitly invest resources in the acquisition of knowledge about how to use the existing resources in an efficient way. The discovery procedure arises as a spontaneous result of the economic activity that takes place at a specific time and place (Hayek [1948] 2014, 108–109). The fact that he "discovers" during economic activity makes this kind of knowledge complementary to economic activity (Böhm 1994). That is why the economist cannot state *a priori* whether this efficient way of production, once discovered, can be translated into the production of the other market participants because the production of the latter can be subject to different subjective data or it takes time until they learn *how* to use the recently acquired knowledge (Hayek [1945] 2014, 95). The economist, however, can claim in a priori way that the institutional framework could affect the incentive effects on economic agents to engage in this discovery. Summed up, discovery activity means that the subjective data change during the economic activity because productivity increases as a result of the regular conduct of the same activity, which means an efficient use of resources. Furthermore, the economic agent acquires knowledge of how to adjust to changing circumstances.

The problematic explanation of innovative and discovery activities can lead to normative implications, which would actually destroy the benefits of once-generated knowledge and innovations. If the accumulation of scientific knowledge is treated as the only ultimate goal that serves the needs of society, and at the same time, the individual knowledge acquired by each member of society in order to serve our wants in the most efficient way is "generally regarded with a kind of contempt" (Hayek [1945] 2014, 96), then this induces public opinion to support the idea that science should be deliberately controlled and cultivated in order to serve concrete purpose of community. This neglects the merits of science, which arise from thinking for the sake of thinking and researching for the sake of research. The process of scientific research and the process of inventions cannot be planned and deliberately controlled, which means that efforts are concentrated on activities whose results cannot be predicted. The achievements of science and innovations are results of genius minds who had wished their inventions to help the people, but he does not know whether his invention can change the methods of how people satisfy their needs and how this invention helps them achieve their goals (Polanyi 1941; [1951] 1998, 59–82; 84–86).[4]

Romer's endogenous growth theory stands also in this tradition that scientific knowledge should be accumulated for the needs of society. Such a materialistic understanding of science is the reason for the problematic economic policy where enterprises should be bestowed with monopolistic positions in order to generate these profits, which are necessary to cover the costs of research. But such proposals prevent the dissemination of once-created ideas, something that would help many enterprises improve their production methods or would allow enterprises to produce already invented products at lower costs. An example is Steve Jobs's introduction of the iPhone, a product imitated and produced at lower costs by other companies. A counterexample is the discovery of the COVID vaccine, which was not allowed to be produced by other enterprises that would be able to produce it at lower costs. We should also not forget that in the nineteenth century in Western Europe, poorer readers were able to enjoy books and music sheets at lower prices when books were printed by avoiding all property rights laws. These laws only secured the authors high bonuses, but they restricted the broader audience from accessing these books because of high prices. Readers from small countries such as the Netherlands, Switzerland, Belgium, and Denmark benefited from so-called pirate copies (Figes [2019] 2020, 165–168).

The Institutional Framework as the Ultimate Source of Economic Growth

The concept of order is an instrument of analysis with whose help social scientists can explain social phenomena (Hayek [1973] 1978, 35). Order is a mental reconstruction of the relationship among elements observed in reality, whereby the observing social scientist has to recognize whether the elements constituting this order are "ordered" according to a concrete logic or how their relationship arose spontaneously without a designing mind. In this vein, we distinguish between an order on an individual level and an order on a societal level (Hayek [1967] 2014, 288).[5] On the individual level, order reflects a *pattern of action* of an economic agent, which is a subject of analysis in "Pure Logic of Choice." Here, the elements are ordered according to *the logic* of the planning economic agent. This logic is derived from his knowledge, which he gained during his economic activity. Individuals can choose between many aims, but because of the scarcity of resources and the means available to them, they are able to realize only some aims. The "Pure Logic of Choice" describes the different means-end structures (Hayek [1961] 2014, 381).

On a societal level, order is a *pattern of interaction* among different individuals, where individuals represent the elements constituting the order. On the societal level, however, this "logic" according to which the relationship among the elements is established is not concentrated in a single mind; this "logic" arises spontaneously from the regular reactions of individuals to changing circumstances. In this vein, the order on the societal level becomes *polycentric*, which stands in contrast to *monocentric* order on the individual level (Hayek [1967] 2014, 284; Polanyi [1951] 1998, 210). The order is exactly this complex structure about which Hayek spoke when he stressed that social scientists should rebuild "from the directly known elements the complex and unique structures which we find in the world" (Hayek [1943] 2010, 134).

The economist constructs mentally *the dynamics of order* by "tracing from the changes in the relations between the elements the changes in the wholes" (Hayek [1943] 2010, 134). The mental construction of the dynamics of orders is fundamental to theorize about macroeconomic phenomena such as economic growth and the business cycle. In other words, we should be able to answer the question on an abstract level when the interaction among different individuals creates economic growth or an economic crisis. In this context, the price mechanism plays a key role because it performs a fundamental coordinating and information function. Individuals observe prices and base their plans on those prices. Any change in prices gives rise to a mutual adjustment of plans. For example, individuals decrease consumption or use less of those goods for their own production, whose prices rise. This behavior on the side of economic agents obeys general rules. This regularity in action is necessary so that the order is preserved. If prices convey the "right" information, which means that they are not disturbed by monetary policy and any governmental interventions, then any change in prices would give rise to adjustment of the plan on the individual level so that internal equilibrium is achieved, and on the societal level, this would give rise to mutual adjustment of the large number of the centers constituting the economy (polycentric order) so that the subjective data observed by economic agents correspond to the objective facts given to the economy (Hayek [1945] 2014, 100–104; see also Polanyi [1951] 1998, 173).

Equilibrium and disequilibrium are two different states of order, with whose help the social scientist theorizes whether the interaction among millions of different individuals would promote socially desirable (progress and economic growth) or undesirable outcomes (economic crises and depressions) as unintended consequences of individual action (Hayek 1937, 49). During the process of this interaction, each economic agent is chasing his own end with the help of means that only the agents themselves are aware of and that build expectations about the actions of his trading partners. So, if the spontaneous interaction promotes equilibrium, then the theorizing economist can reconstruct this interaction as an unbroken chain of complementary action-reaction processes where expectations move toward agreement. As already said, the economist is not allowed to take the mental shortcut in explaining equilibrium on the societal level by assuming that each agent behaves rationally, possessing the same demand, supply function, and specific information, because only during the interaction do economic agents realize whether their plans have been based on the right information, on the one hand, and the social scientist can ascertain whether society is in a state of equilibrium, on the other (Hayek 1937, 38; Klausinger 1989).

Furthermore, the outcome of these interactions is not just a snapshot of the observed reality but a process where either economic agents are encouraged to continue their activity as before because their plans and expectations were fulfilled or they try to adjust their plans to the new, changed circumstances once they realized that their plans had been based on the wrong information. The reestablishment of equilibrium depends on the adjustment activity of the elements constituting this order and the relations among these elements. The central task of the economist is to explain how economic agents acquire the necessary knowledge so that they are able to adjust their behavior to changing circumstances so that mutual adaptation of their plans and expectations results and the *equilibrium* of the order is preserved.

This leads to the proposition that equilibrium on the individual level is entangled with equilibrium on the societal level. On the individual level, the plan of each economic agent is realized, and his expectations are fulfilled. But this will only happen at the societal level (order level) when the intertemporal plans among the individuals are so coordinated that individuals hold coherent foresights (Hayek [1967] 2014, 288). So, the Austrian definition of equilibrium as a process differs from the neoclassical (mechanical) understanding of equilibrium as a state of rest. This explains why the idea of equilibrium cannot just be abandoned, as a leading Neo-Austrian like Ludwig Lachmann did (Vaughn 2021, 122–124; 157). The concept of equilibrium is an indispensable analytical concept with whose help the social scientist studies dynamic phenomena such as business cycles, where the economic order is in a state of disequilibrium and the question arises which factors affect the equilibrium restoration. The concept of equilibrium also provides a benchmark for studying how the institutional framework creates an order that secures the coordination of intertemporal plans and minimizes the probability of disappointment on the side of economic agents.

Different institutional frameworks bring about different economic orders. Hayek was on the quest for an institutional framework that promotes a competitive order. This order not only secures better coordination of the dispersed, fragmented knowledge held by economic agents but also provides an incentive for entrepreneurs to discover new methods of production. These methods would be more efficient than the existing ones and thus improve the entrepreneurs' ability to serve the needs of others. These new efficient methods would be reflected by lower costs of production. These changes in costs, which are prices for their trading partners, communicate to them what to do so that they can reestablish their internal equilibrium in order to continue their economic activity. This mutual reestablishment is necessary to preserve the equilibrium of the overall economic order. The resulting prices convey the necessary information, which summarizes information about marginal productivity on the side of suppliers and preferences on the side of demand. This explains that prices are a *spontaneous* result of interaction among market participants, which could not be calculated by using modern insights into equilibrium and marginal utility theory (Hayek [1948] 2014).

Economic orders differ according to how efficiently resources are utilized. The efficiency of utilization depends on how knowledge is communicated and how the economic plans of millions of individuals are coordinated (Hayek [1945] 2014, 93–94). In this vein, Hayek continued the argument of his teacher Ludwig von Mises, who was concerned with the question of which economic order would promote superior outcomes such as efficient use of resources and securing the coherence of intertemporal plans (Mises [1920] 2009; [1922] 1951). The efficient use of resources is intimately related to the productive capacity of a society, which does not exist as an objective fact independent from its institutional framework. In his essay "Scientism and the Study of Society," Hayek continued his criticism developed in "Economics and Knowledge" (1937) that economists theorized as though there were somewhere an extraordinary mind that possessed all integrated and combined knowledge existing in a society. This extraordinary mind had only one logical task—namely, finding the best use of the limited available resources (see also, Hayek [1945] 2014, 93).

If the institutional framework provides privileges to a specific entrepreneurial group as a consequence of intervention, then this gives rise to a concentration of power. Then, it does not matter how much *"discovery"* lies in the activity of these enterprises; the fruits of this discovery would be enjoyed only by a specific group of customers—that is, rather wealthy customers—because privileges would hinder potential market participants from entering markets in order to acquire additional knowledge about how to improve the existing production methods, decrease costs of production, and lower prices of these goods or services so that a broader group of customers can enjoy these goods or services. The privileged entrepreneurs would possess few incentives to concentrate their skills and knowledge in order to adapt their production to the changing circumstances, which are conditions for maintaining the quality of the offered commodities. Such an institutional framework would facilitate a price mechanism that would be under the control of privileged enterprises and not the result of interaction among firms, reflecting the supply side, and households, reflecting the demand side. This state of affairs thwarts the communication function of prices necessary to convey the relevant information about changes in the scarcity of resources, which in turn disturbs the acquisition of knowledge. So, we arrive at the conclusion that the innovative or discovery procedure inherent in entrepreneurial activity is a necessary but not sufficient condition for generating economic growth.

The explanation of phenomena on a societal level, such as economic growth, cannot be attributed to a single source of dynamics, any exogenous forces, or any behavior of economic agents. By mere postulation of technological progress, social scientists and economists make an assumption about a source of dynamics that exists outside of human interaction. This source of dynamics either causes eternal prosperity or the ultimate breakdown, whereby individuals are just subject to this exogenous power that they cannot influence. Such an example is provided by Schumpeter's and Marx's intellectual legacy, which is united by the idea of historicism that Hayek criticized in his essay "Scientism and the Study of Society" ([1942; 1943; 1944] 2010). In this vein, social scientists fail to understand history as a result of interaction of millions of individuals where institutions provide such conditions for the interaction so that they affect the outcome of interaction, but, as Hayek denoted, Schumpeter and Marx belonged to those social scientists who "pretend to be able to arrive by a kind of mental shortcut at a direct insight into the laws of succession of the immediately apprehended wholes" (Hayek [1943] 2010, 136). This mental shortcut represented by technological progress as an inevitable process assumes that either socially desirable outcomes or disasters in human history are inevitable consequences of this eternal process. However, such an understanding of human progress means accepting all catastrophes in the history of humankind as inevitable consequences of these abstract forces. Schumpeter's interpretation of the Great Depression, which he described as a mere phase of capitalism, is such an example. This understanding forgets the relevance of institutions that affect the ability of economic agents to adapt to changing circumstances, something we observed during the last financial crisis when different European countries reacted to the outbreak of the crisis according to their institutional frameworks. But to formulate, as Solow did, that technological progress as always responsible for eternal prosperity would cause the other extremity. Such thinking can provide the basis for wrong political proposals, such as that it does not matter how we intervene in the market mechanism; technological progress is erroneously trusted to always compensate for these interventions.

Conclusion

The mere assumption of technological progress as the engine for economic growth obscures the relevance of the spontaneous forces that give rise to the market process. This can cause wrong economic and political proposals that presuppose the planning tendencies described by Hayek in his "Scientism" essay as engineering thinking. In this chapter, I showed strands in economics that accepted the idea of technological progress and innovations as the driving forces behind economic growth and human progress. The second part of the chapter concentrated on how Hayek would have responded to them. Some of the strands of economics still provide the cornerstone of mainstream economics, which neglects the relevance of institutional frameworks. My chapter claims that if economists characterize innovations as the only factor responsible for economic growth, then, as Hayek stressed, they "silently" assume "a new element of altogether different character" when they explain the causes and essence of this macroeconomic phenomenon (Hayek 1937). In the chapter, I delineated three elements. Economists assume "silently" an extraordinary knowledge on the side of economic agents about the usefulness of the inventions. Economists assume "silently" that once the invention is introduced, this increases immediately the productivity of their economic activity. Third, economists assume "silently" that once the production of one or a group of entrepreneurs becomes more productive, this generates immediate economic growth. But these "silent" assumptions would be absurd in the institutional framework that facilitates a centrally planned economy.

The breakdown of Soviet and Eastern European centrally planned economies was not a result of a lack of innovations and creative minds, that is, a lack of technological progress. János Kornai, the leading expert on centrally planned economies, described how many genius minds, such as the Soviet physicist Abram Joffe; the Polish engineer Jacek Karpinski; the inventor of Rubik's cube, the architect Ernő Rubik; or the floppy-disk inventor, the Hungarian engineer Marcel Jánosi, lived, invented, and discovered under the conditions of planned economy, but their discoveries and inventions remained unknown to their fellow citizens (Kornai 2012, 26–27; Roland 2012, 3–4). Their institutional framework was unable to facilitate the dissemination of information about these innovations. None of the directors managing the state-owned factories cared for these inventions, which could possibly increase the productivity of production. The necessity of these inventions was recognized by entrepreneurs in the USA and Western Europe. So, it was not a lack of a technological framework, but instead, an institutional framework, that was responsible for the inevitable breakdown of the centrally planned economies.

My chapter suggests the concept of order as an analytical instrument with whose help social scientists can theorize economic growth. *Orders are different patterns of interaction.* Hayek and his Freiburg colleague Walter Eucken based their beliefs in competitive order on objective properties such as efficient use of resources and promotion of coherence among individuals' intertemporal plans (Klausinger 1990, 68). Hence, they focused on this institutional framework that facilitates and secures a *competitive* economic order. Only then we can expect economic growth and progress, which are unintentional outcomes of interaction among millions of individuals. Only in an institutional framework that promotes competitive order, one can define entrepreneurial activity as socially advantageous because we are not interested in the discovering qualities of entrepreneurial activity related per se but in whether this discovering or knowledge-accumulating activity is oriented toward serving the needs of *all* consumers. This happens only if new market participants are allowed to enter the market so that their entrance induces incentives on the side of incumbent market participants not only to improve their production procedures but to deploy their knowledge and skills to adapt their production process to the invariable and unforeseen changes in exogenous data. In contrast, any concentration on the technological progress as the source of economic growth would obscure the relevance of institutional framework. Even more, one would fail to grasp that economic growth actually represents "the result of human action, but not of human design."

Notes

1. F. A. Hayek as a close associate of Freiburg School of Ordoliberalism is a crucial argument of Stefan Kolev's research program (Kolev 2015, 2017, 2023).

2. Here, Hunold cited Hayek who at a meeting of Mont Pèlerin Society in Chicago expressed that "Planned economies always have a preference for large industrial units, which is by no means an optimal use of capital in an undeveloped country" (Cited by Hunold 1961, 127, translations mine).

3. Quesnay was considered to write the first macroeconomic model who also described the production process in stages (in Quesnay's language "classes") and the relevance of price for distribution of consumers' goods among the different stages (i.e., classes) (Machlup 1960, 11).

4. I know that the usage of the concept "genius mind" is considered as Un-Hayekian. However, we should distinguish between genius minds as inventors and those "genius minds" to which social scientists erroneously have been assigning many tasks. The first refers to people such as Thomas Edison and Alexander Bell, whose inventions satisfy our wants in a better and efficient way. The second is derived from the plea of socialists that a genius mind should plan the production process and control the price mechanism. Or the more erroneous claim that the institutions that facilitate wealth are also a result of genius mind. This neglects the fact that these institutions are actually a spontaneous result of the interaction process among different individuals. I think that Hayek would have confirmed the existence and relevance of the former, whereas his criticism was oriented against the latter understanding.

5. This chapter recognizes that Hayek distinguished between cosmos and taxis as two different orders: Cosmos arose spontaneously without a designing mind such as society and economy whereas taxis is a result of an organizing mind such as enterprise and organization (Hayek [1973] 1978, 37). But for the purposes of this chapter, I accept Hayek's distinction of order on individual and societal level that he conceptualized in his "A New Look at Economic Theory" 383–384. Here, Hayek continued the distinction that he discussed in "Economics and Knowledge" (1937).

References

Böhm, Stephan. 1994. "Hayek and Knowledge: Some Question Marks." In *Capitalism, Socialism and Knowledge. The Economics of F. A. Hayek Vol. 2*, edited by M. Colonna, H. Hagemann, and O. F. Hamouda, 160–177. Aldershot: Edward Elgar.

Boettke, Peter J. 2012. *Living Economics: Yesterday, Today, and Tomorrow*. Oakland, CA: Independent Institute.

———. 2018. *F. A. Hayek. Economics, Political Economy and Social Philosophy*. Great Thinkers in Economics. London: Palgrave Macmillan.

Boulding, Kenneth E. 1936. "Professor Knight's Capital Theory: A Reply." *Quarterly Journal of Economics* 50 (3): 524–531.

Dalton, John, and Andrew Logan. 2019. "A Vision for a Dynamic World: Reading Capitalism, Socialism and Democracy for Today." MPRA Paper No. 95012. Online at https://mpra.ub.uni-muenchen.de/95012/.

Dal Pont Legrand, Muriel, and Harald Hagemann. 2007. "Business Cycles in Juglar and Schumpeter." *The History of Economic Thought* 49 (1): 1–18.

———. 2017. "Do Productive Recessions Show the Recuperative Powers of Capitalism? Schumpeter's Analysis of the Cleansing Effect." *Journal of Economic Perspectives* 31 (1): 245–256.

Eucken, Walter. [1940] 1950. *The Foundations of Economics: History and Theory in the Analysis of Economic Reality*. London: William Hodge.

Figes, Orlando. [2019] 2020. *The Europeans: Three Lives and the Making of a Cosmopolitan Culture.* Milton Keynes: Penguin.

Friedman, Milton. 1953. *Essays in Positive Economics.* Chicago, IL: University of Chicago Press.

Hayek, Friedrich A. [1925–1929] 2012. "Investigations into Monetary Theory." In *The Collected Works of F. A. Hayek Volume 8: Business Cycles, Part II,* edited by H. Klausinger, 45–140. Chicago, IL: University of Chicago Press.

———. [1931] 2012. "Appendix: Excerpt from a Letter, F. A. Hayek to Gottfried Haberler, December 20, 1931." In *The Collected Works of F. A. Hayek Volume 8: Business Cycles, Part II,* edited by H. Klausinger, 185. Chicago, IL: University of Chicago Press.

———. [1933] 1966. *Monetary Theory and the Trade Cycle.* New York: Augustus M. Kelley.

———. [1935] 1967. *Prices and Production.* New York: Augustus M. Kelley.

———. 1936. "The Mythology of Capital." *The Quarterly Journal of Economics* 50 (2): 199–228.

———. [1936] 2015. "Technical Progress and Excess Capacity." In *The Collected Works of F. A. Hayek Volume 11: Capital and Interest,* edited by L. H. White, 141–155. Chicago, IL: University of Chicago Press.

———. 1937. "Economics and Knowledge." *Economica* 4 (13): 33–54.

———. [1937] 1975. "Investment That Raises the Demand for Capital." In *Profits, Interest and Investment,* 73–82. Clifton, NJ: Augustus M. Kelley.

———. [1941] 2007. *The Pure Theory of Capital.* Chicago, IL: University of Chicago Press.

———. [1942; 1943; 1944] 2010. "Scientism and the Study of Society." In *The Collected Works of F. A. Hayek Volume 13: Studies on the Abuse and Decline of Reason,* edited by Bruce J. Caldwell, 77–166. Chicago, IL: University of Chicago Press.

———. [1945] 2014. "The Use of Knowledge in Society." In *The Collected Works of F. A. Hayek Volume 15: The Market and Other Orders,* edited by Bruce J. Caldwell, 93–104. Chicago, IL: University of Chicago Press.

———. [1948] 2014. "The Meaning of Competition." In *The Collected Works of F. A. Hayek Volume 15: The Market and other Orders,* edited by Bruce J. Caldwell, 105–116. Chicago, IL: University of Chicago Press.

———. [1961] 2014. "A New Look at Economic Theory." In *The Collected Works of F. A. Hayek Volume 15: The Market and other Orders,* edited by Bruce J. Caldwell, 375–426. Chicago, IL: University of Chicago Press.

———. [1963] 1969. "Arten der Ordnungen." In Freiburger Studien: Gesammelte Aufsätze, 32–46. Tübingen: Mohr Siebeck.

———. [1967] 1969. *Studies in Philosophy, Politics and Economics.* Chicago, IL: University of Chicago Press.

———. [1967] 2014. "Notes on the Evolution of Systems of Rules of Conduct." In *The Collected Works of F. A. Hayek Volume 15: The Market and other Orders*, edited by Bruce J. Caldwell, 278–292. Chicago, IL: University of Chicago Press.

———. [1973] 1978. *Law, Legislation and Liberty, Volume 1: Rules and Order*. Chicago, IL: University of Chicago Press.

———. [1976] 1978. *Law, Legislation and Liberty, Volume 2: The Mirage of Social Justice*. Chicago, IL: University of Chicago Press.

———. 2010. *Studies on the Abuse and Decline of Reason: Text and Documents*. Edited by Bruce J. Caldwell. Chicago, IL: University of Chicago Press.

———. 2012. *Hayek on Hayek: An Autobiographical Dialogue*. Chicago, IL: University of Chicago Press.

Hunold, Albert. 1961. "Freies Bauerntum als Programm für Unentwickelte Länder." In *Entwicklungsländer: Wahn und Wirklichkeit*, edited by A. Hunold, 125–138. Erlenbach-Zurich, Switzerland: Eugen Rentsch.

Klausinger, Hansjoerg. 1989. "Hayek and New Classical Economics on Equilibrium Analysis: Some Second Thoughts." *Jahrbuch für Sozialwissenschaft* 40 (2): 171–186.

———. 1990. "Equilibrium Methodology as Seen from a Hayekian Perspective." *Journal of the History of Economic Thought* 12 (1): 61–75.

———. 2012a. *Die größten Ökonomen: Friedrich A. von Hayek (1899–1992)*. Stuttgart: UTB.

———. 2012b. Editorial Introduction. In *Business Cycles, Part II: The Collected Works of F. A. Hayek*, edited by H. Klausinger, 1–48. Chicago, IL: University of Chicago Press.

Kolev, Stefan. 2015. "Ordoliberalism and the Austrian School." In *Oxford Handbook of Austrian Economics*, edited by Peter J. Boettke, and Christopher J. Coyne, 419–444. New York: Oxford University Press.

———. 2017. *Neoliberale Staatsverständnisse im Vergleich*. Berlin: De Gruyter.

———. 2023. "When Liberty Presupposes Order: F. A. Hayek's Contextual Ordoliberalism." Journal of the History of Economic Thought, forthcoming.

Kornai, János. 2012. "Innovation and Dynamism: The Interaction between Systems and Technical Progress." In *Economies in Transition: The Long-Run View*, edited by G. Roland, 14–56. London: Palgrave Macmillan.

Kurz, Heinz. 2008. "Innovations and Profits: Schumpeter and the Classical Heritage." *Journal of Economic Behavior & Organization* 67 (1): 263–278.

Landmann, Oliver. 2018. "Understanding Economic Growth: On the Work of Paul M. Romer and William D. Nordhaus, Nobel Laureates 2018." *ORDO – Jahrbuch für die Ordnung von Wirtschaft und Gesellschaft* 69: 425–434.

Levy, David M., and Sandra J. Peart. 2009. "Soviet Growth & American Textbooks." Available at SSRN: https://ssrn.com/abstract=1517983 or http://dx.doi.org/10.2139/ssrn.1517983.

Lutz, Friedrich A. 1966. "Presidential Address at Mont Pèlerin Society Regional Meeting in Tokyo." Mont Pèlerin Society Records, Box 17, Folder 9, Hoover Institutions Library and Archives.

Machlup, Fritz. 1960. *Der Wettstreit zwischen Mikro- und Makrotheorien in der Nationalökonomie*. Tübingen: J. C. B Mohr (Paul Siebeck).

Marx, Karl. 1967. *Capital, Vol. I.* New York: International Publishers

———. 1972. *Theories of Surplus Value. Part 3.* London: Lawrence and Wishart.

Mises, Ludwig E. [1920] 2009. Economic Calculation in the Socialist Commonwealth. In *Collectivist Economic Planning,* edited by F. A. Hayek, 87–130. Auburn, AL: Ludwig von Mises Institute.

———. [1922] 1951. *Socialism: An Economic and Sociological Analysis.* New Have, CT: Yale University Press.

Ostrom, Vincent. 1999. "Problems of Cognition as a Challenge to Policy Analysts and Democratic Societies." In *Polycentric Governance & Development: Readings from the Workshop in Political Theory and Policy Analysis,* edited by M. D. McGinnis, 394–415. Ann Arbor, MI: University of Michigan Press.

Polanyi, Michael. 1941. "The Growth of Thought in Society." *Economica* 8 (32): 428–456.

———. [1951] 1998. *The Logic of Liberty.* Carmel, IN: Liberty Fund.

Roland, Gérard. 2012. "Introduction." In *Economies in Transition: The Long-Run View,* edited by G. Roland, 1–13. London: Palgrave Macmillan.

Romer, David. [1996] 2012. *Advanced Macroeconomics.* New York: McGraw-Hill.

Rühl, Christof. 1994. "The Transformation of the Business Cycle Theory: Hayek, Lucas and a Change in the Notion of Equilibrium." In *Money and Business Cycle: The Economics of F. A. Hayek Vol. I,* edited by M. Colonna, and H. Hagemann, 168–202. Aldershot: Edwar Elgar.

Schumpeter, Joseph. 1939. *Business Cycles. A Theoretical, Historical, and Statistical Analysis of the Capitalist Process, Vol. I.* New York: McGraw Hill.

Solow, Robert. 1956. "A Contribution to the Theory of Economic Growth." *Quarterly Journal of Economics* 70 (1): 65–94.

———. 1994. "Perspectives on Growth Theory." *Journal of Economic Perspectives* 8 (1): 45–54

Streissler, Erich. 1969. "Hayek on Growth: A Reconsideration of His Early Theoretical Works." In *Roads to Freedom: Essays in Honour of Friedrich A. von Hayek,* edited by Erich Streissler, 245–286. Abingdon: Routledge.

The Prize in Economic Sciences. 2018. NobelPrize.org. Nobel Prize Outreach AB 2022. Tue. 25 October 2022. https://www.nobelprize.org/prizes/economic-sciences/2018/summary/.

Vaughn, Karen I. 2021. *Essays on Austrian Economics and Political Economy.* Arlington, VA: Mercatus Center at the George Mason University.

White, Lawrence H. 2007. "Editor's Introduction." In *The Collected Works of F. A. Hayek Volume 12: The Pure Theory of Capital,* edited by L. H. White, xiii–xxxvi. Chicago, IL: University of Chicago Press.

———. 2015. "Editor's Introduction." In *The Collected Works of F. A. Hayek Volume 11: Capital and Interest,* edited by L. H. White, ix–xxxii. Chicago, IL: University of Chicago Press.

2

Gift-Giving as a Substitution for Monetary Exchange

Evidence from the Potlatch

Casey Pender

When Europeans made contact with the First Nations along the Pacific coast of North America, they soon became aware of the abundance of resources and wealth these many cultures had obtained, along with their flourishing art scene and culture.[1] In fact, it has been estimated that during this time, people living along the coast were better off than the average person living in London.[2]

Having lived along the Pacific for millennia, these coastal societies had developed technologies, institutions, and human capital to cultivate the ocean with incredible efficiency. Hunting seal, catching halibut, oolichan, shellfish, and most of all, salmon, was the primary source of this wealth, though farming of certain root crops and berries, as well as utilizing timber for building homes and boats, also contributed to it (Trosper 2009; Johnsen 2009, 2016).[3] Specialization was able to take place for the production of these goods, and this generated large surpluses that supported dense populations and allowed time for artistic expression in the form of fashion, carving, and performance art (Harkin 2001; Trosper 2009; U'mista Cultural Society 2022).

What is more, they achieved these relatively high standards of living despite not generally using money.[4] This fact is somewhat surprising, as it is often surmised that some form of medium of exchange is required to sufficiently lower the transaction costs of reallocating goods among society (Menger 1892). Moreover, this reduction in transaction costs is thought to allow for specialization in production and diversification in consumption, the likes of which were witnessed along the Pacific Northwest.

This chapter highlights what we can learn from an institution known as the potlatch—a complex gift-giving ceremony traditionally practised by many Indigenous cultures along the North American Pacific Northwest—in its ability to aid in attaining such levels of wealth and well-being without the wide adoption of monetary trade. I argue that one of the benefits of potlatching may have been to generate and maintain records of the past, what can be called social "memory," in a way that utilized local knowledge and culturally specific customs. This memory could have allowed the potlatch, through the gift-giving norms it generated, to be a successful alternative social arrangement to one of monetary exchange.

To highlight how memory, in this sense, allows for social improvements in well-being absent the use of money, I present a simple overlapping generations model where agents live for two periods but only receive perishable goods in the first period and nothing in the second. These types of models have become commonplace within monetary economics and can be used to bring clarity to our understanding of the economic benefits of the potlatch which may otherwise not have been obvious.

With this setup, the optimal reallocation of endowments can only be obtained by adopting one of the following institutions: a gift-giving norm or a monetary standard. Under this setup, gift-giving norms can be feasible so long as agents have knowledge, or memory, of the past actions of individuals. Alternatively, a monetary standard can allow agents to obtain the same outcomes if this memory is incomplete, unreliable, or not readily accessible.

Such models are often used to explain why so many culturally distinct societies, through time and place, have independently evolved institutions to support monetary exchange. Less discussed, however, is the alternative possibility that when memory is imperfect, investments in the creation and maintenance of institutions that improve memory could have the same benefits as adopting a medium of exchange.

Not only did potlatching involve gift giving, but it also involved elaborate feasts as well as theatrics and performance art, including dances and storytelling. By making the event more memorable, these potlatch festivities would have facilitated the knowledge transfer of a record of events to the potlatch guests. First Nations along the Pacific Coast did not utilize written language prior to colonization, so transmitting this type of knowledge, or memory, through written records would not be possible. Investments in mental record-keeping—literally in memory—therefore would likely have been significant to ensure accurate records of all past actions were preserved through time.

Other works have argued that free-riding can be a problem even when social memory is accurate and readily available (Bigoni et al. 2020). To see how the potlatch could have addressed this concern, I outline three additional features of the potlatch that could have helped deter free-riding: trust-building mechanisms, a social credit system, and spiritual beliefs. Trust building would have come from the intimate nature of the Potlatch and the fact that the guests often lived in the host's village for weeks while the festivities took place. Furthermore, as will be discussed in further detail, many Indigenous coastal societies had a fluid social ranking system where one could move up the more goods they gave away. This meant that anyone who tried to free-ride by only accepting gifts but never giving them would have to pay for this with a loss of social status. Lastly, spiritual beliefs and cultural norms around virtue and the need to give evolved alongside the potlatch, which appeared to have acted as cultural or even supernatural sanctions against free-riding.

If this view is correct, however, then the potlatch ban—first put in place in 1885 and increasingly enforced until 1951—likely played a significant role in the tragic reversal of fortunes witnessed among Indigenous coastal communities over the last hundred years. Beginning in the late eighteenth century, trade with the West meant introducing new tools and technologies for production as well as new demand for the goods First Nations along the coast produced. Thus, initially, the new access to fur markets and new inflows of migrant workers along the coast into the fishing, forestry, and mining industries appear to have only accelerated the wealth and levels of artistic achievements among these Indigenous coastal societies (Harkin 2001). However, as the colonization of North America continued and as the Canadian government increasingly forced its institutions, like the potlatch ban, on Indigenous peoples, this economic growth halted and eventually began to decline.

For example, for the Lekwungen people, whose traditional lands are located around what is now Victoria on Vancouver Island, it has been estimated that their per capita income was higher in the 1880s than in the 1980s (Lutz 2009). This chapter, therefore, also touches on the implications of the ban with respect to the model put forth and how, by destroying social memory, the ban would have also limited the reallocation of goods within these societies. Drawing on the institutional economics literature, I argue that despite the ban being put in place over a century ago, it should not be surprising to see it have persistent effects lasting to this day. This is because the potlatch was an institution that drew on local, tacit knowledge, whereas the remaining alternative methods for resource allocation available after the ban did not.

With this, my chapter contributes to three separate strands of research. First, there have been many other works that highlight important economic and governance functions of the potlatch, including creating a stable social and political environment (Allen 1955); acting as a social safety net and a hedge against wealth inequality (Suttles 1960); reducing acts of violence (Codere 1966); acting as a form of disaster insurance (Piddocke 1965); acting as a means for resource conservation (Trosper 2009); proving better matching for "savers" and "borrowers," leading to increased capital investment (Johnsen 2016); and building and maintaining social networks (McAfee 2021). This chapter contributes to this strand of literature by being the first to explore this additional function of the potlatch, as an investment in social memory, specifically as an alternative to monetary exchange. None of these works need to be contradictory, however. In fact, given the complexity of the potlatch and its central role in many societies, it seems likely to have had many functions.

The second literature this chapter contributes to is the branch of monetary economics comparing the ability of money and memory to achieve optimal resource allocation. Many of these works compare gift-giving societies to money-using societies in theory and attempt to flush out the conditions in which either or both can be feasible (Kocherlakota 1998b; Kocherlakota and Wallace 1998; Wallace 2001; Rocheteau and Nosal 2017). To my knowledge, however, none have detailed concrete examples of societies that have used memory instead of money. Providing a real-world example of successful gift-giving societies—those along the Pacific Coast who potlatch—aids in our understanding of how high levels of specialization and wealth can be achieved without the use of monetary exchange.

Finally, this chapter contributes to the literature on institutional development and institutional stickiness. There is a large body of research dedicated to understanding how exogenously imposed institutions from external parties effects local institutions (e.g., Hayek (1978), Ostrom (1990), Boettke et al. (2008), Williamson (2009), Poteete et al. (2010) to name a few). Studying how the potlatch ban affected Indigenous communities through this lens provides a potential case study of how imposing institutions on a group that do not mesh with local customs and norms can have persistent adverse effects.

The remainder of this chapter is organized as follows: Section 2 gives a brief historical overview of the potlatch and the potlatch ban. Section 3 then outlines a standard overlapping generations model to illustrate how money and gift-giving can be a feasible method for achieving optimal resource allocation under the right conditions. Section 4 then outlines how the more ceremonial aspects of the potlatch could have been used to generate such conditions for gift-giving to succeed. Section 5 discusses what this meant for the First Nations once the potlatch was banned. Lastly, Section 6 concludes.

The Potlatch

Before contact with Europeans, people had been living along the coast in the Pacific Northwest for millennia. Discoveries of tools on the Haida Gwaii islands date back 14,000 years, suggesting there have been populations living in what is now British Columbia (BC) for at least that long (Trosper 2009), likely much longer.[5] Today, there are many First Nations cultures along the Pacific coast, all with unique identities, histories, distinct languages, and customs. However, many have a shared institution—the potlatch.

The potlatch is a ceremony usually centered around a feast, dancing, storytelling, and other performances that can last multiple days or even weeks. Within what is now BC, it has traditionally been an institution among the Tsimsian, the Gitxsan, the Nisga'a, the Nuu-chah-nulth, Nuxalk, the Kwakwaka'wakw as well as the Coast Salish and Chinookan peoples (Trosper 2009). In Alaska, the Tlingit, Haida, Tsimshian, and Eyak also host potlatches (Beck 2013).[6] Though many of these groups still potlatch today, for reasons discussed more below, it is less a part of day-to-day life than it was in 1921 and before.

Potlatches have traditionally been hosted for a variety of reasons within these groups, including the celebration of a marriage, the mourning of a death, to give thanks to nature, to settle disputes, or to pass on inheritance of names, property, and social positions, among other reasons (U'mista Cultural Society 2022). Figure 2.1 shows mask dancers at a potlatch sometime between

Figure 2.1 A Dance for the Dead at a Cowichan Potlatch. *Source*: Photo from City of Vancouver Archives; Photo taken by J. S. Matthews; Copyright is in the public domain.

1890 and 1900. Masked dances for the dead were meant to pay respect to the spirits of those recently departed (U'mista Cultural Society 1975).

Given the diversity of motivations for potlatching, their frequency could be quite common. When visiting the Kwakwaka'wakw, for example, anthropologist Franz Boas noted that "there is a small or large potlatch almost every day" (Boas 1966).[7] Though potlatches could take place throughout the year, they tended to be much more common in the winter months between November and March (Barnett 1938). This is because industry and production, primarily salmon fishing, were seasonal, and the summer months were more filled with work. This left time in the winter for larger and longer potlatches (Codere 1966).

The specifics of the ceremony varied through time and depended not only on the reason for the particular potlatch but also on the local culture and customs of the group taking part (Risdale 1997; McAfee 2021). However, one key aspect essential to potlatching was the practice of gift-giving.[8] The host of the potlatch was expected to provide gifts to their guests as thanks for attending and witnessing the ceremony (Allen 1955; Drucker 1967; U'mista Cultural Society 1975).

Thus, regardless of the impetus for potlatching, gift-giving was always a central aspect and the way in which all potlatches concluded. With these emerging gift-giving norms, goods in the communities were primarily redistributed at potlatches. People of lower social rank and without abundances of wealth would often save for years (Lutz 2009) as well as borrow from kin (Johnsen 2016) in order to be able to host a potlatch and gift all that they had acquired or borrowed away.

The gifts that were most common also changed over time with the changing of day-to-day life. For example, in the eighteenth and early nineteenth centuries—before Europeans had sustained contact and developed trade with the First Nations along the coast and on Vancouver Island—some of the most common potlatch gifts reported were furs and skins, as well as elaborate wooden crafts and furniture such as boxes and canoes (Trosper 2009; U'mista Cultural Society 2022). However, once the Hudson Bay Company (HBC) had established a presence in the West, HBC blankets became the most common gift and eventually evolved into the unit of account for many First Nations, in that the value of a gift was denoted by how many blankets the gift was worth (Johnsen 2016). This is not to say that only HBC blankets were gifted at potlatches, however, jewelry, woodwork, dishes and kitchenware, foodstuffs, and oils have also been noted as common gifts during this period (Trosper 2009; U'mista Cultural Society 2022). Figure 2.2 shows gifts being prepared for a potlatch at Alert Bay in 1912.

Another aspect of potlatching that appeared to span most potlatch cultures is that of social status and prestige tied to the ceremony itself. Social structures and potlatching were intimately linked. Potlatch gifts were not

Figure 2.2 Potlatch at Alert Bay. *Source*: Photo from City of Vancouver Archives; Photo taken by J. S. Matthews; Copyright is in the public domain.

distributed equally among guests but were divided by social standing, with the most prestigious attendees receiving the largest gifts (Piddocke 1965).

As noted by Barnett (1938), none of the First Nations along the coast appear to have been organized under any notions of social equality. Instead, elaborate systems of ranking and titles were in place, ranging from chief at the top to enslaved person at the bottom. However, there were so many titles and rankings that it appeared to be a continuous scale with no clear delineation between classes. Furthermore, except for enslaved people, one's position within this social structure was fluid; one could move up or down depending on the success of their potlatching (Piddocke 1965). Prestige was thus tied to one's success in potlatching and how much they could give away (Boas 1966; Trosper 2009; Carlos and Lewis 2016; Johnsen 2016; McAfee 2021). Furthermore, as Risdale (1997, 7) has noted: "the potlatch validated the rights of title which included names of houses and other property of economic and ritual importance, and the right to perform rituals and use feast dishes, carvings, masks and symbols that accompanied those rituals."

The potlatch thus established rights and social status for the hosts, and hosts would, in turn, strive to give away as much as they could afford. The Indigenous peoples of the Pacific coast were not organized centrally. They had no governance structures that would resemble a formal government in the Western sense (Barnett 1938), so potlatching was used to settle disputes and allowed hosts and guests to conduct business on other social and governance issues (Trosper 2009). To use the terminology of Ostrom (2010), despite lacking formal written constitutions, the "rule-in-use" for governing the coastal First Nations was the potlatch. As (Piddocke 1965, 258) summarizes, "The potlatch was, in fact, the linch-pin of the entire system."

The Potlatch Ban

The federal government of Canada—formed in 1867—while unique to the local conditions in many ways, was undeniably under European influence. This included Eurocentric, Christian, and often racist worldviews. Through this lens, the federal government viewed the potlatch as both anti-Christian and anti-European and banned the practice altogether in 1885 (U'mista Cultural Society 1975; Loo 1992; Johnsen 2016).[9] Ostensibly, it was marketed as a paternalistic ban meant to protect Indigenous people from themselves, but under the surface were exorbitant amounts of prejudice and racism, with government officials calling the potlatch "debauchery of the worst kind" (Miller and Lerchs 1978).

At first, the ban was not well enforced. However, updates to the law in 1894 made enforcement of the ban easier for the "Indian agents"—those employed by the federal government and tasked with enforcing and administering the provisions put forth in federal law to govern the First Nations and other Indigenous peoples. Even after the 1894 amendments, for a time at least, potlatching continued, though it became more discrete; the ceremonies were on a smaller scale and no longer commonly went on for weeks at a time (Lutz 2009).

However, as time passed, the enforcement of the ban continually became stricter.[10] Finally, the federal government got word of a large potlatch hosted by Dan Cranmer taking place in Memkoomlish (on Village Island) in late December of 1921. By the end of their investigation, there had been forty-nine federal convictions. As Loo (1992, 127) details:

> Of those convicted, twenty-two were sentenced to two months imprisonment, four to six months, and twenty-three received suspended sentences. The suspended sentences were awarded after each of the recipients signed affirmations to stop potlatching and agreed to turn in

their ceremonial regalia, which consisted mainly of elaborately carved cedar masks, to the Indian agent.

Some of the convictions were for making speeches and gifting canoes, but most were for dancing (U'mista Cultural Society 1975, Loo 1992). Those who received suspended sentences were essentially blackmailed into giving up their most valuable, often priceless, possessions to be placed in museums across the world. These arrests following Dan Cranmer's potlatch were enough to completely disrupt the institution of the potlatch. Though some communities continued to defy the ban, potlatching in secret, this effectively put an end to potlatching in many of these communities.

The federal government finally lifted the ban in 1951; however, by that time, the damage was done.[11] Slowly, since then, potlatching has been returning as part of coastal life. Many First Nations, including the Kwakwaka'wakw have been openly potlatching since the lifting of the ban,[12] as well as communicating with and educating others on the nature of the potlatch (U'mista Cultural Society 1975, 2022).

Money as a Substitute for Memory

While the previous section outlined the potlatch and the accompanying gift-giving norms, this section begins to flesh out the intuition with how monetary theory often thinks about gift-giving and monetary exchange as two distinct solutions to the same problem. Moreover, as will be shown, this idea is tightly linked to the economic concept of "memory."

To begin to see this, take a simple overlapping generations (OLG) model where people live for two periods.[13] When agents are born in the first period, they are "young," and in the next period, they are "old." Thus, for example, a young person born in period 3 is an old person in period 4 (and unfortunately, is a dead person in period 5). Let us further assume that only young people work and earn a bundle of consumption goods, b, whereas old people, being retired, earn nothing. Lastly, let us assume that the goods in b are perishable, so they cannot be saved between periods.[14] The initial endowments of such an economy are depicted in table 2.1.[15]

Assuming all agents want to smooth consumption over time (i.e., they would prefer not to consume all their b when young and therefore have nothing when old),[16] then this society could be made better off if they could come up with some arrangement for reallocating away from the endowments pictured in table 2.1. But is this feasible? Are there opportunities for trade that could make everyone better off?

Young people cannot be made any better off by trading with other young people, for in this model, all young people have the same stuff. Trading some

TABLE 2.1
Illustration of an OLG Model

		Time Period							
		1	*2*	*3*	*4*	*5*	*6*	*7*	…
Generation	0	0							
	1	*b*	0						
	2		*b*	0					
	3			*b*	0				
	4				*b*	0			
	5					*b*	0		
	6						*b*	0	
	…							…	…

Source: Created by Casey Pender
Note: Interior cells depict endowments held.

b for some other *b* leaves you with only what you had in the first place. Old people would like to trade with young people because they want something to consume in old age. However, they have nothing to offer in return. Given this, there is no opportunity for mutually beneficial trade.

However, suppose a social norm could be generated where, in every period, young people always gave a portion of their *b* to the current old generation as a gift. In that case, everyone could enjoy some consumption in both their youth and in old age. In general, so long as everyone followed the rule "if someone wants something I have, I will give it to them as a gift," resources could be allocated in a socially beneficial way. The trick, of course, is how to generate and maintain such a norm.

The first worry with creating such a norm is that of free-riding. Presumably, for such a system to work, one would only want to give gifts to those who follow the rules. Otherwise, people could free-ride, accepting gifts without giving them. Nevertheless, because the current generation of young people was not around when the current older generation was young in the period before, it may be difficult for the young to know if the old had followed the norm in the past. In other words, there is a worry that those who did not give when they were young could nonetheless receive gifts when they are old.

If there was a way to keep track of everyone's past actions—say, if all actions were recorded in a public ledger—then assessing whether or not the person one is contemplating giving a gift to is a rule follower would be relatively easy. But if this type of knowledge were not readily available, making such an assessment would be difficult.

Given that such a ledger would hold information about the past, which agents in the model can access, economists often conceptualize this technology as "memory." With access to the ledger, agents have memory of the past in that they possess knowledge of the past gifts other agents have accepted and given. In a world with such a ledger, or with adequate social memory, it seems at least feasible that gift-giving norms could arise (Kocherlakota 1998b) (after all, agents are motivated to do so as it makes them better off, and memory helps avoid any free-rider problems that would undermine such efforts). To have such memory—the ability to instantly and costlessly access information about the past actions of others—is a strong assumption, however, and one that does not seem overly realistic.

But imagine that instead of relying on memory, everyone who received a gift issued a receipt to the giver. The purpose of this receipt would be to certify that whoever held it had gifted some of their *b* away. Though young people would not have direct knowledge of old people's past actions, they could infer that only old people who held these receipts had followed the gift-giving norm when they were young. Thus, gifts could only be given to those holding receipts, and receipts could always be passed on to gift-givers.

Otherwise worthless tokens—say, a piece of paper with a famous person's face on it—could play the role of such a receipt, and in such a case, we see an economy using money. By definition, this money is neither used for consumption nor production in the model, yet people still accept it as proof of their past good deeds. In this sense, when you buy an apple at the store with cash, it is as though the store owner has gifted you an apple, and you have given them a receipt in return, which they can then use in the future to prove their past goodwill to others. Money, in this sense, is a substitution for memory.

Historically, we have seen many societies evolve institutions surrounding monetary exchange (Menger 1892). Presumably, this is, at least in part, a solution to the problems of imperfect memory.[17] In fact, there is a large body of literature that justifies the widespread adoption of money along these lines (Kocherlakota 1998a, 1998b; Kocherlakota and Wallace 1998; Rocheteau and Nosal 2017; Champ et al. 2022).

While the model outlined in this section relied on "old" and "young" generations having one-shot meetings through time, these basic results do not need to hinge on these specific OLG assumptions. In his seminal paper, Kocherlakota (1998b) showed that money can be an effective substitute for memory in a variety of other model environments.[18]

In general, as Kocherlakota sums up, for money to be socially useful, "there must be limited record-keeping: society cannot costlessly create an accessible record of past events" (Kocherlakota 2002, 58). Yet this would suggest that instead of adopting money, which may have its own costs (i.e., as in Kocherlakota and Wallace (1998)), societies could equally solve this problem of insufficient memory by investing in technologies to better store and transmit knowledge of the past—to improve their memory. In the next section, I argue that the potlatch can be viewed as one such technology.

Memory as an Alternative to Monetary Exchange

The previous section showed how, in a basic OLG framework, we could highlight the usefulness of money as a substitute for memory. Implicit in these models, though less discussed, is that using money itself may come at a cost, and so an alternative solution may be to invest in improving memory.[19] In this section, I argue that many features of the potlatch can be seen as an investment in memory, which allows the related gift-giving norms to be a successful means for the efficient allocation of goods without any heavy reliance on money.

Recall that memory in this context can be conceived of as a ledger that agents can easily refer to observe other individuals' past actions. Prior to contact with Europeans, however, the Indigenous peoples of the Pacific coast traditionally did not utilize written language, and so their ledgers could not have been stored and passed along in physical items like books or spreadsheets. Instead, ledgers would have had to be stored in people's minds, quite literally as memories. Yet the human mind is imperfect; memories fade, and memories can be incorrect. Therefore, additional investment may be required to ensure these mental ledgers' accuracy and resiliency. As such, public displays of giving accompanied by interesting and memorable stories and performance pieces could aid in placing the record of gifts given in the minds of all who attended a potlatch.

To see the intuition behind this idea, assume Jim gives a gift to Barb. Barb should now remember receiving this gift, like a ledger entry in her head. Nevertheless, this ledger entry is not instantly accessible to all other members of society at a low cost. So, on its own, this does not seem like enough memory to feasibly achieve a gift-giving equilibrium. Though if others were to witness Barb receive her gift, a copy of the ledger entry would also be stored in their heads. The more people in attendance, the more closely we have something like the concept of social memory. However, it would not be a single centralized ledger but a distributed network of redundant ledgers in the minds of individuals.

However, as mentioned previously, the human mind is imperfect, so even if many people witness Barb receive a gift, this may not get recorded correctly (or at all) in each witness's mind. However, the fidelity of informational transfer from action to memory likely depends on how memorable the gift-giving act was. In other words, the greater the investment Jim makes in the festivities surrounding his gift-giving to Barb, the lesser the chance of his guests forgetting or misremembering his actions in the future. The overall quality of the distributed network of memory would then be a function of the potlatch's size and the amount of investment put into the festivities and performances.

TABLE 2.2
Illustration of an OLG Model with a Gift-Giving Norm

		Time Period				
		1	*2*	*3*	*4*	...
Generation	0	$(1-\alpha)(b-c)$				
	1	$\alpha(b-c)$	$(1-\alpha)(b-c)$			
	2		$\alpha(b-c)$	$(1-\alpha)(b-c)$		
	3			$\alpha(b-c)$	$(1-\alpha)(b-c)$	
	...				...	...

Source: Created by Casey Pender
Note: Interior cells depict goods held after reallocation from gift-giving.

This idea can be placed within the OLG framework outlined in the previous section. Assume c is the cost of investment in a potlatch that is above and beyond the gifts given away, where $0 < c < b$. As such, c encompasses all the time, effort, and resources put into creating new and interesting performance pieces (songs, dances, stories, *etc.*) to be part of the potlatch festivities. The "young" generation—who now could be better conceptualized as the potlatch host—initially gives away a portion of the goods they own but also pays the cost c to do so publicly and with the accompanying festivities, such that they are left with $\alpha(b - c)$, where $0 < \alpha < 1$ is the proportion of goods that are gifted. The "old" generation—who now could be better conceptualized as the potlatch guests—receive $(1 - \alpha)(b - c)$.[20]

With the institution of potlatching in place, though the initial endowments would look the same as in table 2.1, after the reallocation, resource holdings would be as depicted in table 2.2.

Note that under this arrangement, because of cost c, total lifetime consumption is less than it would have been under the initial endowments (where all of b could be consumed in the first period and nothing in the second). Nevertheless, if the desire to smooth consumption through time is large enough, well-being will increase despite the cost paid. (For intuition, consider whether you would rather eat five pizzas in one day with none for the next four days, or half a pizza daily for five days).[21]

Codere (1966) has noted that despite not having written records of past events, those who partook in potlatch culture that she interviewed could easily remember the exact number of gifts given in potlatches that had taken place going back a century. This would suggest that significant investments had been made in order to ensure that knowledge of these past transactions had been accurately recorded and distributed.

It has been repeatedly noted how potlatch ceremonies often involve (and indeed still involve) stories and songs of past potlatches and history (Allen 1955; Boas 1966; Piddocke 1965; U'mista Cultural Society 2022). Furthermore, Barnett (1938), Boas (1966), Harkin (2001), Trosper (2009), and Lutz (2009) all document the elaborate dances, music, performance pieces, and feasts that were integral to the potlatch. Codere (1966) referred to the gifting given in a potlatch as "dramatic" and Trosper (2009, 23) noted that "all business at feasts and potlatches was conducted in public, with amounts given and received announced to all."

These dramatic dances, songs, stories, and the public nature of the festivities in general, could all, be interpreted as investments in the fidelity of knowledge transfer. As Hunt (2014, 27) has observed: "a number of Indigenous scholars have pointed to stories, art, and metaphor as important transmitters of Indigenous knowledge. Stories and storytelling are widely acknowledged as culturally nuanced ways of knowing, produced within networks of relational meaning-making."

It is not hard to imagine then that the stories and the performance art that were so integral to the potlatch would preserve the knowledge of past events and could have helped propagate this distributed ledger in the minds of individuals.

Given that potlatch guests would thus have been aiding in the maintenance of the overall institution, it should perhaps not be surprising that gifts were often viewed as payment for a service. Gloria Cranmer, daughter of Dan Cranmer, conceptualizes the gifts given as "payments for witnessing the potlatch" (U'mista Cultural Society 1975), highlighting the importance of guests witnessing and remembering the events they saw and took part in. Beck (2013, 77) echoes this sentiment, stating that gifts in the Tlingit and Haida potlatches were given as "tokens of appreciation for the guests' witnessing of these events." Drucker (1967) goes so far as to claim that the primary role of guests at a potlatch "was to witness and validate the proceedings." Allen (1955) sums this up with the notion that potlatches helped to "keep the record straight, so to speak" as "a public ceremony . . . makes an effective record for a people without the written word."

Institutional Response to Free-Riding

In the simple OLG framework outlined above, we see that money is only required when record-keeping is difficult, that is, when memory is poor. On the other hand, this theory suggests that when accurate knowledge of past actions is available, it is sufficient to deter free-riding and allow gift-giving norms to develop. Above, I suggested that many of the more festive aspects of the potlatch could be seen as investments in social memory, ensuring that knowledge of the past is preserved and passed on.

However, some recent research has suggested that such simple OLG models omit some crucial aspects of reality. As such, free-riding can become a bigger problem than theory would predict. For example, using a laboratory experiment, Bigoni et al. (2020) show that free-riding can occur among potential gift-givers/receivers despite having accurate ledgers readily available for participants to access. This implies that the potential to free-ride can undermine gift-giving, even when social memory is relatively high.

The potlatch seems to have been able to overcome this in at least three ways. First, there is literature showing that gift-giving norms lead to an increase in trust. Camerer (1988), Carmichael and MacLeod (1997), and Ruffle (1999) have all shown that repeated gift-giving improves trust within society, and Nowak and Sigmund (2005) have shown that free-riding is low when social trust is high. The intimate nature of the potlatch, the length of time, and the fact that guests would often live in the host's village for weeks while the potlatch was taking place must have aided in such trust-building. Second, as discussed in Section 2, potlatching societies tended to have fluid social ranking systems, which could act to punish free riders. On this point, Johnsen (2016, 74) has noted the "uncanny resemblance" this created to what we think of as credit scores today, implying that free-riders would suffer through reductions in ranking and prestige. Barnett (1938) saw this as well, noting that "to abuse this privilege results in a loss of prestige."

Third, other spiritual and social norms appear to have evolved along with the potlatch, which could have acted as further deterrents to free-riding. Barnett (1938) claims that within the Kwakwaka'wakw worldview, for example, laziness and greed were outright condemned. In contrast, generosity was one of the highest virtues. As such, hoarding goods without the intention to give them away at a later date would have been unthinkable and even "shameful." It is said that at funerals, the songs that honored the dead were not about how much they had accumulated throughout their lives but how much they had been able to give away (Curtis 1915).

With regard to spirituality, anthropologist Marcel Mauss posited that the spiritual "power" seen to be within physical objects among coastal Indigenous belief systems generated a perceived danger of holding onto physical objects for too long, "forcing" them to circulate these objects (Mauss 1954, 41). As Goldman (1975, 123) elaborates, this obligation to give within these societies is in response to "a cosmological conception that postulates and eternal circulation of forms of being" which incentivizes people "to participate in this vital circulation" and builds a moral obligation to give.[22]

Such cultural and spiritual sanctions against hoarding and against receiving gifts without, in turn, giving would undoubtedly have aided a reduction in free-riding. This, when paired with the social memory generated, would have helped sustain the potlatch and its accompanied gift-giving norms as the primary means for redistribution of goods within Pacific Coast society.

The Potlatch: Of Human Creation, but Not of Human Design

Before concluding this section, I wish to caution the reader about the limits of conceptualizing the potlatch as has been done here. Other scholars of the potlatch have criticized Boas for oversimplifying the potlatch and interpreting it through a Western lens (Goldman 1975). Boas' writings on the potlatch, for example, at times imply that gift-giving was done with the expectation that the giver would be able to become a receiver in the future. Indeed, in the OLG model presented here, the "young" only rationally gift to the "old" when they can assume to have the same treatment given to them a period later.

In reality, such motivations appear to be absent, or at least muted, in potlatch culture. As mentioned in Section 4.1, spirituality seems to have provided motivation for gift-giving that cannot be reduced merely to rational self-interest. Anthropologists have tended to agree that what was given to potlatch guests was intended to be true gifts, without any expectation of reciprocity. If this view is correct, it would be inaccurate to ascribe using gifts as a type of loan or capital investment as the prime motivation for hosting a potlatch. To the contrary, as Risdale (1997, 7) puts it, "the ultimate aim was the distribution of wealth and not the accumulation of wealth."

The potlatch is a complex institution that evolved over generations and within different groups of people and was central to life on the Pacific coast. To reduce it to merely a means for generating a public ledger would be a severe mistake. The motivation for the potlatch could be for spiritual or cultural reasons, to improve social status, or any combination of these or other reasons. Nevertheless, even if no potlatch host or guest has ever been motivated explicitly to generate and maintain social memory, as outlined in this chapter, institutional theory suggests that the institution could have been performing these social functions nonetheless.

To elaborate on this further, as Menger (1963) long ago pointed out, institutions are often "the unintended result, as the unplanned outcome, of specifically individual efforts of members of a society." Hayek (1960, 1978, 1980, 1990) has picked up on this theme, outlining how people often follow rules without a complete understanding of the social benefits (or costs) that general abidance by those rules generates. In other words, the social effects of institutions are not only often unplanned by those who live under the institutions but are often not well understood or even wholly unknown by those who live under these institutions as well.

As Boettke (1990) eloquently summarizes this position, "though the complex structures of society are the composite of the purposive behavior of individuals, they are not the result of conscious human design." Like the institutions that support monetary exchange in other societies, the institutions that support social memory—like the potlatch—can arise without anyone who lives under the intuition explicitly understanding or aiming for the ends it ultimately achieves. Just as Alchian (1950) pointed out, rational choice theory, properly understood, is not so much about imposing motivations on people; it is more a shorthand merely to help us predict market outcomes. As Leeson (2021) puts it, just as screwdrivers often perform many functions that they were not designed to do (like, say, opening paint cans), it is equally the case that many institutions perform important social functions that they were not designed to do.

Likewise, interpreting the potlatch *as if* it were designed to maintain a ledger of past actions may help us understand some of the economic functions it performed without literally imposing motivations on anyone. Thus, though this simple OLG framework allows us to view the potlatch as an institution which maintains a social memory of the past and ultimately allows for the level of specialization and wealth that was observed, we need not, nor should we, make any claims about the actual motivations of those involved.

The Effects of the Potlatch Ban on Social Memory

If this assessment of the potlatch as an institution for improving social memory is correct, then two major events were likely to affect memory negatively and, therefore, the overall wealth and well-being along the Pacific Northwest. The first major event is the spread of disease after contact with Europeans. Because the Indigenous peoples of the Pacific coast did not engage in written language, incredible amounts of knowledge must have been lost when European disease ripped through their societies, wiping out massive swaths of the population before they could pass their histories and memories onto the surviving generations.[23] Thinking of the social memory of past potlatches as being decentralized and distributed through the minds of individuals, which in network terms act as "nodes," the sudden erasure of the majority of nodes would undoubtedly destabilize the network.

The second was the potlatch ban itself. By forcing Indigenous people to cease potlatching by law, it is possible they also destroyed the institution that had allowed these societies to have sufficient memories of the past to maintain gift-giving norms.

E.K. DeBeck was a defense lawyer who worked to end the potlatch ban. His father had been an Indian agent in Alert Bay between 1903 and 1906, and so E.K. grew up for a time seeing potlatch culture firsthand (BC Archives 1974). Later in his life, in an interview in 1974, he explained the damage the potlatch ban created as he saw it:

> . . . not having any written language, it was their only method of putting things on record and perpetuating them and other contracts. In fact, everything in their lives was based on that, their whole culture depended on being able to keep things on record. It was [recording] their position in their families, it was births and deaths and marriages and the transfer of property. All the things we have . . . They [the government] deprived the Indians of doing any of these things . . . which broke down their whole structure of organisation. (U'mista Cultural Society 1975)

Such a viewpoint corroborates the thesis I have outlined in this chapter: that the potlatch, in part, was such an essential piece of coastal life because of the social memory it created and maintained. The memory function of the potlatch seems evident, and the destruction of that memory function would have therefore limited their ability to efficiently allocate resources. If the potlatch was the lynchpin of coastal society, then the potlatch ban would have pulled the pin out.

Institutional Stickiness and the Potlatch Ban

One could argue that although the potlatch ban was morally objectionable and even economically disruptive in the short run, it is unlikely to have been the cause of stagnation or declines in wealth in the long run. Recall that money can function as a form of memory when record keeping is unavailable, and so because European colonization of North America brought along money with it, Indigenous peoples could have switched to monetary exchange once the ban took away their social memory.

However, such an argument would overlook the difficulty involved in such an institutional transition. As has been well noted by Hayek (1990), for institutions to be successfully adopted, they need to match the underlying values and culture of those living under the rules. Having evolved organically alongside spiritual beliefs and local conditions, the potlatch would have meshed well with such underlying values and culture.

By contrast, it is unlikely that having monetary exchange imposed by outsiders would have the same harmony. Institutions exogenously imposed by those with different cultures and worldviews are unlikely to be successful, even when those imposing the institution mean well (Boettke et al. 2008;

Williamson 2009). In general, others have already noted how those exogenously imposing institutions on a group/culture to "solve" one problem often underestimate the vast interconnectedness the institutions they aim to replace have with other aspects of social life (Ostrom 1990; Lansing 1991). For example, Lansing (1991) has argued that institutions aimed at making traditional water management in Bali more efficient failed precisely because those imposing the new institutions were unable to account for the social/cultural meanings attached to the traditional institutions they attempted to replace. It is plausible, then, that even if the potlatch ban was well intended, successfully replacing the potlatch with monetary exchange would have been perhaps more difficult than the federal government could have anticipated. What is worse, looking at the evidence provided in Section 2 on the motivation for the potlatch ban, here we have a clear case where those imposing the institution were not well-intentioned.

Gloria Cranmer outlined that when learning and participating in the potlatch, "discipline was strict . . . there were detailed rules governing one's behaviour during the ceremonies" (U'mista Cultural Society 1975). "Indigenous knowledge," according to Hunt (2014), is situated and "place-specific," and accordingly, "no guidebook or PowerPoint, no essay or instructional video" could pass along the local, tacit knowledge required to master the detailed rules required to potlatch. This suggests that a vast amount of human capital would have needed to be built up and passed down through the generations to maintain such an institution. To assume a foreign institution could successfully replace potlatching without such an accumulation of human capital would be to assume away the importance of such place-specific, tacit knowledge in maintaining social rules.

Therefore, given that the institutions to support monetary exchange that originally developed in Europe did not align with local knowledge, Indigenous customs, and worldviews, we have reason to believe such institutions could not easily fill the void left by the disappearance of potlatching (and therefore gift-giving) after the ban. Furthermore, this provides a plausible avenue by which the potlatch ban could still be affecting the wealth and well-being of the First Nations along the Pacific Coast a century after the ban was put in place.

Along similar lines, Feir et al. (2022) have argued that the extinction of the bison in the late 1800s has had persistent effects still seen today due to the institutions the Canadian government imposed on Indigenous societies previously reliant on the bison. They argue that bison hunting requires high levels of human capital through the accumulation of place-specific, tacit knowledge. Once colonization accelerated the bison extinction, the federal government tried to impose agriculture on these societies—a profession that did not mesh with their underlying culture, knowledge, and skills—which led to massive reductions in their wealth and well-being.[24] While more research would need to be done to prove this definitively with respect to the potlatch, if this hypothesis is correct, the potlatch ban would have been much more than a racist and morally objectionable law. It would have also contributed to the destruction of the primary economic system under which much of the Pacific Northwest traditionally operated.[25]

Conclusion

When thinking about a world without a government monopoly on money creation, Hayek once mused: "As soon as one succeeds in freeing oneself of the universally but tacitly accepted creed that a country must be supplied by its government with its own distinctive and exclusive currency, all sorts of interesting questions arise that have never been examined" (Hayek 1990, 13).

One such interesting question is whether a currency is needed at all in order to achieve specialization in production and diversity in consumption. In this chapter, I have suggested that institutions around gift-giving among the First Nations along the Pacific Northwest—the potlatch—allowed them to achieve precisely that.

To make such a claim, I presented a simple OLG model in which optimal resource allocation can only occur if agents either have access to knowledge of past actions, "memory," or have access to transferable but otherwise useless tokens, "money." Thus, it was shown that, in theory, if a society has adequate memory, it can achieve the same resource allocations through gift-giving norms as a society that engages in monetary exchange.

From there, I argued that the more festive elements of potlatching, dancing, storytelling, and so on may have functioned as investments in social memory, which could have aided in the maintenance of their gift-giving norms. This could help explain the high standards of living observed before the twentieth century, despite not using money generally.

Such a diversity of harmful and oppressive policies, regulations, and laws have been imposed on Indigenous peoples in the United States and Canada by colonizing governments, so it would be impossible only to attribute the economic hardships they have faced to a single law. Residential schools, restricted access to credit, and the wiping out of resources all most certainly played a part, to name a few. Nonetheless, in this chapter, I have further argued that the potlatch ban, for many groups in the Pacific Northwest, must be counted among the many genuinely awful government policies of the last 150-plus years. Moreover, as was pointed out in the Introduction, elsewhere it has been suggested that the potlatch had many other economic functions beyond the ones highlighted here. Thus, the potlatch ban may not have only destroyed social memory but also their methods for resource conservation, insurance, deterrence of violence, financial intermediation, and capital investment.

Lastly, drawing on the institutional economics literature, I hypothesized that Western institutions imposed on Indigenous societies were never likely to be successful rules for governance because they did not align with the local tacit knowledge and cultural norms. This could have aided in the persistent adverse effects of the ban continuing long after the ban was lifted.

Notes

1. Acknowledgements: I would like to thank everyone involved with the Mercatus Center and who helps organize the colloquia for the Adam Smith Fellowships. I am very grateful for getting to be a part of this program, and I appreciate all the hard work that goes into making this fellowship possible. I have been able to get helpful feedback from many great people on this chapter, which I am incredibly grateful for, including Donn Feir, Jonathan Eaton, Jordan Lofthouse, Matt Soosalu, the editors of this volume, Peter Boettke, Erwin Dekker, and Chad Van Schoelandt, as well as Kayleigh Thompson, Craig Lyons and all the other contributors to this volume. I also want to thank my PhD supervisors at Carleton, Pat Coe and Chris Gunn for helpful discussions on this work (and for being patient with me while I worked on this instead of my dissertation). Lastly, I would like to thank the U'mista Cultural Society for their online presence dedicated to educating people about the history of the Potlatch in Kwakwaka'wakw culture. Any errors in this chapter are most certainly my own.

2. Carlos and Lewis (2011) estimated that the average Cree living around Hudson's Bay in the nineteenth century was at least as materially well-off as the average Londoner, though this depends on how one weights various goods. For example, "the native diet would have far exceeded that of the best paid workers in England" and their clothing "likely compared favourably to that of the English middle-class clothing . . . Indeed, the high level of decoration of Cree clothing itself is indicative of relatively high living standards. It shows also that the Cree had time for such creative endeavours" (Carlos and Lewis 2011). Yet they also note that in terms of housing and luxury goods, Londoners on average we better off relative to the Cree.

Feir et al. (2022) have noted that the Plains peoples were some of the tallest in the world, at least in part because their protein-rich diet was one of these best in the world at the time. They note that "the bison peoples were some of the wealthiest peoples in North America and arguably as well off as their European counterparts."

Given that it is estimated that the peoples along the Pacific Northwest were better off materially than both the Cree and the Planes peoples, vastly exceeding other First Nations residing in what is now Canada in terms of not only necessities but luxury goods, leisure time, and art culture (Trosper 2009; Johnsen 2016; Carlos and Lewis 2016; Hageman 2021), it can be inferred that they were at least as well off, if not better off, than the average Londoner.

3. For example, Indigenous groups along the coast developed selective breeding methods. They were known to delay fishing once the salmon run had started. They also developed weirs which allowed them to be selective in which fish they kept. Along with the weir, they had developed other fishing techniques such as nets, spears, baits, and traps. Human capital accumulation was immense, with a deep understanding of salmon breeding and lifecycles. They had techniques for transporting fish eggs from one stream to another, and satellite imaging has recently shown evidence that the streams and water flow had also been consciously manipulated (Williams 2006). They had also developed methods for extracting fish oil, which could aid in preserving other foods and was widely traded with the people in the interior (Piddocke 1965; Trosper 2009).

4. There is evidence that some monetary exchange occurred before European contact. For example, Le Dressay et al. (2010) note the use of dentalium shells as a medium of exchange along the Pacific Coast. However, as will be discussed throughout this chapter, the primary method for resource allocation was not indirect trade via monetary exchange but through gift-giving. As Trosper (2009) puts it, the gift-giving norms "dominated the organization of economic exchange." After the colonization of B.C. by Europeans, many Indigenous people began accepting money—in the form of Canadian currency—for their labor, and they integrated into the labour force. However, even still, much of this money was not used for exchange but was saved to be gifted at future Potlatches (Lutz 2009).

5. Anthropologists believe that the first peoples to live along the Pacific Northwest came from Siberia over an exposed land bridge between 25,000 and 100,000 years ago during the Ice Age (Hageman 2021).

6. Since modern North American borders were not created with input from Indigenous peoples, many of these groups are now split between the United States and Canada as their traditional lands span modern borders. For example, the Haida and Tsimsgian both currently have a population in both BC and Alaska, and the Coast Salish and Chinook traditional lands not only encompass parts of BC but the states of Oregon and Washington in the United States as well.

7. He then lamented that the occurrence of near-daily potlatches "of course interrupts my work" (Boas 1966).

8. The word "potlatch" comes from Chinook Wawa—the language of trade that was used along the Pacific Coast—and translates, perhaps not surprisingly, to "to give" (U'mista Cultural Society 2022).

9. This ban came through the "Indian Act"—the body of Canadian federal law used to govern over the First Nations, Inuit, and Métis living within Canadian borders and which throughout history has explicitly aimed at eliminating Indigenous culture (see e.g., Truth and Reconciliation Commission of Canada (2015)).

10. This was the work of one Duncan Campbell Scott, who was the Deputy Superintendent of the Canadian Department of Indian Affairs. Johnsen (2016, 10) has detailed Scott's racism as outright disdain for Indigenous peoples:

His views on Indian policy were draconian by today's standards, and perhaps by any. In his words, "[t]he happiest future for the Indian race is absorption into the general population . . . and this is the object of the policy of our government. In 1920 he declared that "our objective is to continue until there is not a single Indian in Canada that has not been absorbed into the body politic, and there is no Indian question, and no Indian department." Largely insulated from broader political forces, at least on the Indian question, he had considerable autonomy. He came down hard on the potlatch and persisted at it for 14 years until his retirement.

11. As a matter of fact, the ban simply disappeared from the Indian Act in 1951; there was never a formal repeal (U'mista Cultural Society 1975).

12. It took almost twenty years after the lifting of the potlatch ban before Kwakwaka'wakw households felt comfortable to openly potlatch again without fear of being arrested (U'mista Cultural Society 2022).

13. A similar illustration of an OLG model can be found in Handa (2008) and Champ et al. (2022).

14. Similar OLG models have been used in economics, at least since Samuelson (1958). The setup presented here, however, is largely a simplified version of what is presented in Wallace (1980).

15. One may take notice that in table 2.1 there is a generation zero, showing that at the beginning of this world there was an "old" generation alive that was never young. This may seem like an odd construction; however, it is a necessary quirk of the model for some of the possible equilibrium's to take place. This essentially boils down to the initial "young" having someone to give to.

16. Strictly speaking, we want agents in this OLG model to have preferences that are complete and transitive and to have utility functions that satisfy $U'(b) > 0$, $U''(b) < 0$.

17. Other reasons for societies adopting money that have been given are to reduce search costs in finding suitable trading partners (Menger 1892; Kiyotaki and Wright 1993; Pender 2022), and to reduce uncertainty about the future (Keynes 1936; Kiyotaki and Moore 2019).

18. In particular, Kocherlakota (1998*b*) shows that the same general results can be obtained when substituting an OLG environment for either a Turnpike environment like that of Townsend (1987) or a random matching environment such as the one in Trejos and Wright (1995).

19. Some papers that have thought about the effects of investing in memory include Kocherlakota and Wallace (1998) and Luther and Olson (2013).

20. Presumably the guest would also receive some utility from getting to witness and take part in the festivities, but adding this would only complicate the model, which is meant to be simple for ease of illustration. Furthermore, increasing the payoffs for the "old" or the "guests" would only strengthen the general point that utility can be increased with gift-giving norms, even when such norms have a maintenance cost.

21. More formally, this point can be illustrated with the commonly used utility function $U =$ In the no-gift equilibrium, $C1 = b$ and $C2 = 0$, if we let, say, $b = 100$ then utility in this case is 10. However, in the gift-giving equilibrium $C1 = \alpha(b - c)$ and $C2 = (1 - \alpha)(b - c)$, if for illustrative purposes we assume $\alpha = 0.5$ and $\beta = 0.9$, then so long

as $c - 44.5$, utility will be higher than 10 despite the total lifetime consumption being lower. This means that in this case, even if 44% of total resources were devoted to memory improvement instead of consumption, meaning that total lifetime consumption falls from 100 to 66, it would still make people better off. The result is even more dramatic when the standard log utility function is used.

22. Trosper (2009) and Johnsen (2009, 2016) have argued that spiritual and moral sanctions of this type also contribute to the conservation of salmon populations. Among the Plains people, Benson (2006) argues that spiritual sanctions were used to contribute to the conservation of bison.

23. Carlos and Lewis (2016) estimate that 80% to 90% of the Indigenous population in what is now Canada was lost to disease spread by Europeans.

24. Feir et al. (2022) further argue that bison hunting requires many of the same skills and same knowledge as cattle ranching. However, a series of government policies discouraged those previously reliant on bison from entering into the ranching industry, thus further perpetuating the long-term effects of the bison extinction.

25. Johnsen (2016) makes a similar conclusion. He posits that potlatching provided many of the functions of fractional reserve banking, including increasing the "money supply" and reducing the transaction costs of investment. He therefore concludes that the Potlatch ban would have had similar effects on the coastal First Nations as the Great Depression did for Americans. While this point is also unproven, it could be viewed as complementary to the hypothesis put forth here.

References

Alchian, Armen A. 1950. "Uncertainty, Evolution, and Economic Theory." *Journal of Political Economy* 58 (3): 211–221.

Allen, Rosemary A. 1955. "The Potlatch and Social Equilibrium." *Davidson Journal of Anthropology* 2 (1): 233–244.

Barnett, Homer G. 1938. "The Nature of the Potlatch." *American Anthropologist* 40 (3): 349–358.

BC Archives. 1974. "E. K. 'Ned' DeBeck Interview." https://search-bcarchives.royalbcmuseum.bc.ca/e-k-ned-debeck-interview-oreilly-1974.

Beck, Mary G. 2013. *Potlatch: Native Ceremony and Myth on the Northwest Coast.* Portland, OR: Alaska Northwest Books.

Benson, Bruce L., and Terry L. Anderson. 2006. "Property Rights and the Buffalo Economy of the Great Plains." In *Self-Determination: The Other Path for Native Americans*, edited by Thomas E. Flanagan, 29–67. Stanford, CA: Stanford University Press.

Bigoni, Maria, Gabriele Camera, and Marco Casari. 2020. "Money Is More than Memory." *Journal of Monetary Economics* 110: 99–115.

Boas, Franz. [1966] 1975. *Kwakiutl Ethnography*. Edited by Helen Codere. Chicago, IL: University of Chicago Press.

Boettke, Peter J. 1990. "The Theory of Spontaneous Order and Cultural Evolution in the Social Theory of F. A. Hayek." *Cultural Dynamics* 3 (1): 61–83.

Boettke, Peter J., Christopher J. Coyne, and Peter T. Leeson. 2008. "Institutional Stickiness and the New Development Economics." *American Journal of Economics and Sociology* 67 (2): 331–358.

Camerer, Colin. 1988. "Gifts as Economic Signals and Social Symbols." *American Journal of Sociology* 94: S180–S214.

Carlos, Ann M., and Frank D. Lewis. 2011. *Commerce by a Frozen Sea*. Philadelphia, PA: University of Pennsylvania Press.

———. 2016. "Native American, Exchange, and the Role of Gift-Giving." In *Unlocking the Wealth of Indian Nations*, edited by Terry Anderson, 39–60. Lanham, MD: Lexington Books.

Carmichael, H. Lorne, and W. Bentley MacLeod. 1997. "Gift Giving and the Evolution of Cooperation." *International Economic Review* 38 (3): 485–509.

Champ, Bruce, Scott Freeman, and Joseph H. Haslag. 2022. *Modeling Monetary Economies*. 5th ed. New York, NY: Cambridge University Press.

Codere, Helen F. 1966. *Fighting with Property: A Study of Kwakiutl Potlatching and Warfare, 1792–1930*. Seattle WA: Seattle: University of Washington Press.

Curtis, Edward S. 1915. "The Kwakiutl." In *The North American Indian. Vol. X. The Kwakiutl*. Norwood, MA: Plimpton Press.

Drucker, Philip, and Robert F. Heizer. [1967] 2021. *To Make My Name Good: A Reexamination of the Southern Kwakiutl Potlatch*. Berkeley, CA: University of California Press.

Feir, Donn L., Rob Gillezeau, and Maggie E. C. Jones. 2022. "The Slaughter of the Bison and Reversal of Fortunes on the Great Plains." Working Paper 30368: 56. http://www.nber.org/papers/w30368.

Goldman, Irving. 1975. *The Mouth of Heaven: An Introduction to Kwakiutl Religious Thought*. Hoboken, NJ: Wiley-Interscience.

Hageman, Anya, and Pauline Galoustian. 2021. *Economic Aspects of the Indigenous Experience in Canada*. Kingston, ON: Queens University Press.

Handa, Jagdish. 2008. "The Benchmark Overlapping Generations Model of Fiat Money." In *Monetary Economics*. London: Routledge, 717–745.

Harkin, Michael E. 2001. "Potlatch in Anthropology." In *International Encyclopedia of the Social and Behavioral Sciences*, edited by Neil J. Smelser, and Paul B. Baltes. Vol. 17: 11885–11889. Oxford: Pergamon Press.

Hayek, Friedrich A. 1948. *Individualism and Economic Order*. Chicago, IL: University of Chicago Press.

———. 1960. *The Constitution of Liberty*. Chicago, IL: University of Chicago Press.

———. 1978. *Law, Legislation and Liberty, Volume 2: The Mirage of Social Justice*. Chicago, IL: University of Chicago Press.

———. 1991. *The Fatal Conceit: The Errors of Socialism*. New York, NY: Routledge.

Hunt, Sarah. 2014. "Ontologies of Indigeneity: The Politics of Embodying a Concept." *Cultural Geographies* 21 (1): 27–32.

Johnsen, Bruce D. 2009. "Salmon, Science, and Reciprocity on the Northwest Coast." *Ecology and Society* 14 (2): 43.

———. 2016. "The Potlatch as Fractional Reserve Banking." In *Unlocking the Wealth of Indian Nations*, edited by Terry Anderson, 61–83. Lanham, MD: Lexington Books.

Keynes, John M. 1936. *The General Theory of Employment, Interest, and Money*. New York, NY: Macmillan.

Kiyotaki, Nobuhiro, and John Moore. 2019. "Liquidity, Business Cycles, and Monetary Policy." *Journal of Political Economy* 127 (6): 2926–2966.

Kiyotaki, Nobuhiro, and Randall Wright. 1993. "A Search-Theoretic Approach to Monetary Economics." *The American Economic Review* 83 (1): 63–77.

Kocherlakota, Narayana. 1998a. "The Technological Role of Fiat Money." *Federal Reserve Bank of Minneapolis Quarterly Review* 22 (3): 2–10.

———. 1998b. "Money Is Memory." *Journal of Economic Theory* 81 (2): 232–251.

———. 2002. "Money: What's the Question and Why Should We Care About the Answer?" *American Economic Review* 92 (2): 58–61.

Kocherlakota, Narayana, and Neil Wallace. 1998. "Incomplete Record-Keeping and Optimal Payment Arrangements." *Journal of Economic Theory* 81 (2): 272–289.

Lansing, Stephen J. 1991. *Priests and Programmers: Technologies of Power in the Engineered Landscape of Bali*. Princeton, NJ: Princeton University Press.

Le Dressay, Andre, Normand Lavallee, and Jason Reeves. 2010. "First Nations Trade, Specialization, and Market Institutions: A Historical Survey of First Nation Market Culture." *Aboriginal Policy Research Consortium International (APRCi)* 10: 109–132.

Leeson, Peter T. 2021. "Harmful Magic, Helpful Governance." *Current Anthropology* 62 (1): 17–18.

Loo, Tina. 1992. "Dan Cranmer's Potlatch: Law as Coercion, Symbol, and Rhetoric in British Columbia, 1884–1951." *Canadian Historical Review* 73 (2): 125–165.

Luther, William J., and Josiah Olson. 2013. "Bitcoin Is Memory." *Journal of Prices and Markets* 3 (3): 22–33.

Lutz, John S. 2009. *Makuk: A New History of Aboriginal-White Relations*. Vancouver: UBC Press.

Matthews, James S. [1955] 2012. *Conversations with Khahtsahlano, 1932–1954*. Toronto: City of Vancouver. http://archive.org/details/ConversationsWithKhahtsahlano1932-1954.

Mauss, Marcel. [1954] 1990. *The Gift*. Translated, Edited, and with a Forward from Mary Douglas. New York, NY: Routledge.

McAfee, Rosaleen. 2021. "Sculptures of Stolen Marble." In *Culture, Sociality, and Morality: New Applications of Mainline Political Economy*, edited by Paul Dragos Aligica, Ginny Seung Choi, and Virgil Henry Storr, 109–130. Lanham, MD: Rowman and Littlefield.

Menger, Carl. 1892. "On the Origin of Money." *The Economic Journal* 2 (6): 239–255.

———. 1963. *Problems of Economics and Sociology*. Champaign and Urbana, IL: University of Illinois Press.

Moore, Robert G. 1978. "The Historical Development of the Indian Act: Technical Report." Report to Canada. Indian and Northern Affairs Council, August 1978.

edited by Ron Maguire and John Leslie. https://publications.gc.ca/collections/collection_2017/aanc-inac/R32-313-1978-eng.pdf.

Nowak, Martin A., and Karl Sigmund. 2005. "Evolution of Indirect Reciprocity." *Nature* 437 (7063): 1291–1298.

Ostrom, Elinor. 1990. *Governing the Commons: The Evolution of Institutions for Collective Action*. Cambridge: Cambridge University Press.

———. 2010. "Beyond Markets and States: Polycentric Governance of Complex Economic Systems." *American Economic Review* 100 (3): 641–672.

Pender, Casey. 2022. "Preferential Attachment and Carl Menger's Theory of the Endogenous Emergence of a Medium of Exchange." *Cosmos and Taxis: Studies in Emergent Order and Organization* 10 (4 and 5): 47–60.

Piddocke, Stuart. 1965. "The Potlatch System of the Southern Kwakiutl: A New Perspective." *Southwestern Journal of Anthropology* 21 (3): 244–264.

Poteete, Amy R., Marco A. Janssen, and Elinor Ostrom. 2010. *Working Together: Collective Action, the Commons, and Multiple Methods in Practice*. Princeton, NJ: Princeton University Press.

Risdale, F. 1997. "A Discussion of the Potlach and Social Structure."*The University of Western Ontario Journal of Anthropology* 3 (2): 7–15.

Rocheteau, Guillaume, and Ed Nosal. 2017. *Money, Payments, and Liquidity, Second Edition*. Cambridge, MA: The MIT Press.

Ruffle, Bradley J. 1999. "Gift Giving with Emotions." *Journal of Economic Behavior and Organization* 39 (4): 399–420.

Samuelson, Paul A. 1958. "An Exact Consumption-Loan Model of Interest with or without the Social Contrivance of Money." *Journal of Political Economy* 66 (6): 467–482.

Suttles, Wayne. 1960. "Affinal Ties, Subsistence, and Prestige among the Coast Salish." *American Anthropologist* 62 (2): 296–305.

Townsend, Robert M. 1987. "Economic Organization with Limited Communication." *The American Economic Review* 77 (5): 954–971.

Trejos, Alberto, and Randall Wright. 1995. "Search, Bargaining, Money, and Prices." *Journal of Political Economy* 103 (1): 118–141.

Trosper, Ronald L. 2009. *Resilience, Reciprocity and Ecological Economics: Northwest Coast sustainability*. New York, NY: Routledge.

Truth and Reconciliation Commission of Canada. 2015. *Honouring the Truth, Reconciling for the Future: Summary of the Final Report of the Truth and Reconciliation Commission of Canada*. Library and Archives Canada Cataloguing in Publication. www.trc.ca.

U'mista Cultural Society. 1975. "Potlatch . . . A Strict Law Bids Us Dance." British Columbia Arts Council: Moving Images Distribution. https://movingimages.ca/products/potlatch-a-strict-law-bids-us.

U'mista Cultural Society. 2022. "Living Tradition, The Kwakwaka'wakw Potlatch on the Northwest Coast." https://umistapotlatch.ca/potlatch-eng.php.

Wallace, Neil. 1980. "The Overlapping Generations Model of Fiat Money." In *Models of Monetary Economics*, edited by J. H. Karaken, and N. Wallace. Minneapolis, MN: Federal Reserve Bank of Minneapolis. https://www.minneapolisfed.org/~/media/files/pubs/books/models/cp49.pdf?la=en.

———. 2001. "Whither Monetary Economics?" *International Economic Review* 42 (4): 847–869.

Williams, Judith. 2006. *Clam Gardens: Aboriginal Mariculture on Canada's West Coast*. Vol. 15. Transmontanus.

Williamson, Claudia R. 2009. "Informal Institutions Rule: Institutional Arrangements and Economic Performance." *Public Choice* 139 (3): 371–387.

3

Locating the Artisan in Hayek's Free Civilization

Jaime L. Carini

NESTLED WITHIN A VOLUME TITLED *Essays on Individuality* (Morley [1958] 1977) is a contribution by F. A. Hayek ([1958] 1977), "The Creative Powers of a Free Civilization."[1] Hayek's original plan for this chapter was his soon-to-be-published book project, *The Constitution of Liberty* (Hayek [1960] 2011). While preparing the book for publication, Hayek participated in a "Symposium on Individuality and Personality" that took place in Princeton, New Jersey, in September 1956. Flush with postwar concerns, this symposium presented "the problem of man's freedom in the face of modern society's seemingly irresistible urge to socialize and regiment the thought and action of the individual," and the scholars invited to respond to this problem were those who expressed a commitment to "individual privacy, responsibility, and self-determination" in their scholarship (Morley [1958] 1977, 11–12). The papers discussed at this symposium ranged across disciplines but centered on the common theme of individuality. Hayek's ([1958] 1977, [1960] 2011) chapter contributes to both volumes by locating the individual in a free civilization, whose cultural forces shape individual experience.

The title of Hayek's book, *The Constitution of Liberty*, harkens back to the watershed moment in Anglican constitutional history: the creation and signing in 1215 of the *Magna Carta*, deemed "Constitutio Libertatis" ("The Constitution of Liberty") by thirteenth-century cleric and jurist Henry Bracton (Hayek [1960] 2011, 236). In relating a constitution to freedom, Hayek follows Bracton in acknowledging that a people's laws and customs are entangled in the type of cultural evolution that yields a free society, emerging from the struggle for limited government. "The Creative Powers of a Free Civilization" forms the second chapter in Hayek ([1960] 2011), depicting freedom as an artifact of civilization rather than the product of human design. Yet, an ontological characteristic of an artifact is that it emerges from human design and artisanship. This fact reveals tension in Hayek's work arising from the intersection of two seemingly conflicting mental models: cultural evolution, which forms emergent orders, and individual design. This tension also raises important questions about the teleological nature of human action and spontaneous orders.

The Bloomington School of political economy, developed by Vincent and Elinor Ostrom, emphasizes the role of intentional human design in complex orders. Thus, Bloomington School scholarship on artisanship and artifacts, with its claims that there are legitimate forms of human design, enables us to begin resolving this tension and answering these questions. I posit that the Bloomington School's understanding of the artisanship-artifact relationship enables us to assert that artisanship is one form of human action and to begin developing the metaphor of the artisan, which can be imported from the Bloomington School into Hayek's scholarship. Thus, the individual in Hayek's free civilization can be considered an artisan who imagines and realizes individual plans and, in consort with others, fashions institutions and constitutions.

My work in this chapter, by identifying and working to resolve this tension, follows the theme of a recent volume published by the Mercatus Center, *Hayek's Tensions* (Haeffele, Stein, and Storr 2020), and extends previous work on Ostromian artisanship (Aligica 2018; Carini 2021; V. Ostrom 1994, 1997; Sabetti 2011). I assume, as do Boettke and Coyne (2005) and Lewis (2017, 2020), that there is room in emergent orders for methodological individualism. This goes for the various forms of the theory of spontaneous orders developed by Hayek as well as the theory of complex orders crafted by the Ostroms. I also adopt McGinnis's (2005) position that a spontaneous order only seems as such when one scrutinizes it from the outside rather than from within. Hayek ([1944a] 2018) articulates a similar approach to studying the growth of the mind and human knowledge, advocating that we study "human Reason . . . by its patient exploration from the inside, by actually following up the processes in which individual minds interact" (151). To look at the inner workings of a spontaneous order necessarily requires us to speak to the particularities of individual reasoning and acting in a localized time and place (Hayek [1945] 2014; V. Ostrom 1994).

In the first section, I describe the components of Hayek's free civilization, including the artifactual nature of civilizations and the process by which civilizations produce artifacts. I outline Bloomington School artisanship and locate the artisan in Hayek's free civilization in the second and third sections, concluding with future avenues for research generated by this chapter.

Hayek's Free Civilization

In *The Constitution of Liberty* (Hayek [1960] 2011), Hayek advances his research agenda by formulating an idealistic philosophy of a free civilization, which Ronald Hamowy deems Hayek's "most ambitious and important" social-theoretical work (2011, 10, 22). Civilization is the arena within which human action occurs, and human action is executed by individual actors. Hayek considers civilization akin to urban life and the city the heart of civilization, "the source of nearly all that gives civilization its value and which has provided the means for the pursuit of science and art as well as of material comfort" ([1960] 2011, 467). Hayek's reference to civilization, taken as the urban life of the city, could very well be early twentieth-century Vienna. Interwar Vienna, with its remnants of the Habsburg Empire, offered Viennese elite like Hayek a rich intellectual, artistic, and social culture through participation in various *kreise* (Dekker 2016, 27–29).

The original title of *The Constitution of Liberty* was *The Creative Powers of a Free Civilization*, a title that Hayek then used for the second chapter of *The Constitution of Liberty*. "Creative powers" refers to the dynamic process of cultural evolution, generated by individuals who act (actors), that manifests as an emergent order. An emergent order is the resultant pattern of human behavior that we can see if we analyze a cross-section of cultural evolution at any given point in time with a research tool like the diagnostic framework developed by Elinor Ostrom and her colleagues, the institutional analysis and development (IAD) framework (E. Ostrom 2005). In this Hayekian sense of ordered human behavior, many elements of culture—including ecologies, institutions, and rules, such as constitutional rules—are emergent orders that can be considered artifacts of civilization. Hayek's ([1960] 2011) free civilization is another example of an emergent order resulting from cultural evolution, within which various orders of action are nested (Hayek [1967a] 2014; Gaus 2006). Also nested within a free civilization are such institutions as law, language, and markets, as well as ecologies like freedom.

Hayek ([1960] 2011) acknowledges that freedom and liberty have various meanings, pointing us toward one common definition: the state of being free (or as free as possible) from coercion (57–59). In its somewhat quixotic presentation of a free civilization, Hayek's initiative fulfilled what he perceived as a need for an imaginative liberal intellectual adventure that countered the utopias offered by socialism (Hayek [1949] 2009, 236–237; see also Dekker 2016, 97). Other scholars temper this idealism by accounting for the complex reality of coercion and offering ways "to civilize conflict" (V. Ostrom 1994, 252; see also E. Ostrom 1990; V. Ostrom 1997; Viner 1961). In Hayek's estimation, a free civilization is comprised of individuals and becomes possible when the relationships between (1) one individual and other individuals as well as (2) individuals and the cultural institutions of language, law, and markets are allowed to develop organically, without exogenous interference (Dekker 2016, 97, 187; Hayek [1960] 2011). Therefore, Hayekian actors use laws and customs in their efforts to live together rather than to dominate one another. These observations lead Hayek to claim two things: civilization results from human action, and civilization generates artifacts that also arise from human action but not from human design. Hayek's claim that civilization results from human action can be rephrased this way: civilization is an artifact of human action. We can thus examine the artifactuality of free civilization and freedom as an artifact of civilization.

The Artifactuality of a Free Civilization

Civilization can be considered an artifact, as Hayek ([1960] 2011) explicates in his chapter "The Creative Powers of a Free Civilization."[2] He writes,

> In a sense it is true, of course, that man has made his civilization. It is the product of his actions or, rather, of the action of a few hundred generations. This does not mean, however, that civilization is the product of human design, or even that man knows what its functioning or continued existence depends upon. (Hayek [1960] 2011, 74)

Hayek asserts several things. First, civilization develops over a long period of time, "a few hundred generations," which is a length of time so expansive that it surpasses human comprehension. Second, civilization results from human action, which Hayek considers endogenous to the system, rather than human design, conceived by Hayek as exogenous coercion. Third, elements of civilization remain unknowable to humans, in large part because the conditions of civilization are constantly in flux. Therefore, the dynamic process that produces the emergent order of civilization is cultural evolution, which consists of time, human action, and dispersed knowledge.

Institutions facilitate both human action and knowledge exchange. The growth of knowledge is a hallmark of a Hayekian free civilization, characterized by the exchange of knowledge between individuals that allows each person to "transcend the boundaries of his ignorance" (Hayek [1960] 2011, 73). Institutions, therefore, enable an individual to benefit from knowledge he does not possess and to coordinate his actions with people he does not know. A civilization that facilitates relationships between individuals who do not know each other is an abstract, open society (Popper 1950), and individuals in Hayek's civilization are governed by abstract, emergent rules that are general enough to apply to everyone (Hayek [1960] 2011, 221). The individual in Hayek's civilization thus possesses limited, imperfect knowledge and must maintain an open mind to adapt to changes in his conditions (i.e., culture) as they arise.

John Dos Passos, whose chapter "A Question of Elbow Room" was included in Morley ([1958] 1977), observes, "Individuality is freedom lived" ([1958] 1977, 19). Dos Passos posits that individuality arises when a person has "been able to develop his own private evaluations of men and events" as well as "to make himself enough elbow room in society" (ibid.). Like Hayek, Dos Passos notes the importance of a person's environment and institutions to the development of his individuality. In a free civilization, individuals bump into each other as they make elbow room for themselves, which can create discord. Tolerance for one another helps us minimize and resolve such discord (Bowlin 2016). Additionally, institutions and social norms (such as traditions) are tools that ameliorate the social tensions that arise from our bumping into one another, enabling individuals to adapt to their respective environments by facilitating human action (Hayek [1960] 2011, 78).

This process of working out individual freedom through adaptation is the same piecemeal process as that of working out civilization (Hayek [1960] 2011, 131–132; Popper 1950). Hayek terms this process "discipline," asserting, "Freedom was made possible by the gradual evolution of *the discipline of civilization which is at the same time the discipline of freedom*" (1979, 163; emphasis in the original). Here, Hayek ties the artifactual nature of freedom to human action, worked out endogenously within a system. He also reiterates his point that freedom is an artifact of civilization by clarifying that freedom results from human action (i.e., discipline) rather than exogenous design, human or supernatural (cf. Mises [1949] 2007, 28–29). Michael McGinnis clarifies that the "lack of planning" associated with a spontaneous order, like freedom or civilization, only appears as such to an analyst who is "looking at the system from the outside" (2005, 168). Such systems are too complex to be designed by a single person or entity. McGinnis continues: "From the inside, each of these jurisdictional units contains creative individuals who have acted to design and implement these multiple units of governance in order to pursue their own goals and resolve their disputes more effectively" (ibid.) To put it in Bloomington School terms, spontaneous orders contain nested "action arenas," each with a localized context within which the individual acts.

Freedom as an Artifact of Civilization

Hayek ([1960] 2011) begins his chapter "Freedom, Reason, and Tradition" with this statement: "Though freedom is not a state of nature but an artifact of civilization, it did not arise from design" (107). Almost twenty years later, in the third volume of *Law, Legislation, and Liberty*, Hayek similarly claims, "*Freedom is an artefact of civilization* that released man from the trammels of the small group, the momentary moods of which even the leader had to obey. Freedom was made possible by the gradual evolution of *the discipline of civilization which is at the same time the discipline of freedom*" (1979, 163; emphasis in the original). In both publications, Hayek's statements about freedom grapple with artifactuality, design, human action, and spontaneous order.

Hayek's claim is informed by the historical and contemporary sources he compiled for *The Constitution of Liberty*—located in the epigraphs and footnotes to each chapter—which he deemed "an anthology of individualist liberal thought" ([1960] 2011, 41). We will not complete a thorough archaeology of the knowledge located in this anthology. Instead, we will consider two key scholars, Alexis de Tocqueville and Adam Ferguson, whose writings directly influenced Hayek's assertion, "Freedom is an artifact of civilization" ([1960] 2011, 107; 1979, 163), and its surrounding contexts. The epigraph to "Freedom, Reason, and Tradition" (Hayek [1960] 2011) comes from Tocqueville's ([1835] 2010) *Democracy in America*, Volume One, while the opening sentence of this same chapter adopts phrasing from Ferguson's ([1767] 1995) *An Essay on the History of Civil Society*. By engaging with these passages from Tocqueville ([1835] 2010) and Ferguson ([1767] 1995), Hayek connects freedom and its opposite—coercion via despotism—to various types of political institutions.

Tocqueville's volume contains an extended chapter on the advantages of democracy to American society, from which Hayek) extracted the epigraph to "Freedom, Reason, and Tradition." This epigraph includes two sentences on the challenges of learning to be free, translated from Tocqueville's French as "the apprenticeship of liberty" (Hayek [1960] 2011, 107). The text in Tocqueville ([1835] 2010) that surrounds these sentences describes the superficial appeal of despotism when considered a panacea to life's misfortunes. I cite here the passage in full, from the modern translation by James T. Schleifer rather than the translation that Hayek consults. Tocqueville observes:

> There is nothing more fruitful in wonders than the art of being free; but there is nothing harder than apprenticeship in liberty. It is not the same with despotism. Despotism often presents itself as the repairer of all the

> misfortunes suffered; it is the support of legitimate rights, the upholder of the oppressed, and the founder of order. Peoples fall asleep amid the temporary prosperity that it brings forth; and when they awaken, they are miserable. Liberty, in contrast, is usually born amid storms; it is established painfully in the midst of civil discord, and only when it is already old can its benefits be known. ([1835] 2010, 393)

Tocqueville thus juxtaposes despotism with the hard apprenticeship of liberty springing from democracy in the American context. Despotism is an easy investment that yields immediate results. Liberty requires much sacrifice—pain, civil discord, and delayed gratification—before it begins to bear fruit.

Hayek continues to infuse "Freedom, Reason, and Tradition" with Tocquevillian sentiments in the opening paragraph, linking two things: (1) freedom to institutions and (2) the advantages of freedom to the study, theorization, and improvement of liberty and a free society. He writes:

> Though freedom is not a state of nature but an artifact of civilization, it did not arise from design. The institutions of freedom, like everything freedom has created, were not established because people foresaw the benefits they would bring. But, once its advantages were recognized, men began to perfect and extend the rein of freedom and, for that purpose, to inquire how a free society worked. This development of a theory of liberty took place mainly in the eighteenth century. It began in two countries, England and France. The first of these knew liberty; the second did not. Hayek ([1960] 2011, 107–108)

Hayek, having devoted *The Road to Serfdom* (Hayek [1944b] 2007) to despotism, develops in "Freedom, Reason, and Tradition" two of Tocqueville's claims about the art of liberty. First, liberty is an apprenticeship, or, as Hayek (1979) writes, a discipline. Second, the benefits that come from apprenticing in liberty and developing "institutions of freedom" lag behind these actions (Hayek [1960] 2011, 107). Hayek follows Tocqueville in acknowledging these delayed benefits and emphasizing the processual nature of freedom. He then extends Tocqueville by suggesting that a delay in the enjoyment of freedom's benefits means that there was a lack of foreknowledge about these benefits on the part of those who advanced institutions of freedom. Hayek thus advocates for an understanding of freedom that is evolutionary rather than constructionist.

Part of Hayek's reluctance to ascribe any level of teleology to the process that yields institutions of freedom stems from his integration of Ferguson ([1767] 1995) with Tocqueville ([1835] 2010). Ferguson makes a similar observation as Tocqueville about the processual nature of governance: "Men, in general, are sufficiently disposed to occupy themselves in forming projects and schemes: but he who would scheme and project for others, will find an opponent in every person who is disposed to scheme for himself' ([1767] 1995, 119). Unlike Tocqueville, Ferguson perceives this process to be emergent, "from the instincts, not from the speculations, of men" (ibid.), claiming that people simply do not and cannot know in advance what the consequences of their governance decisions will be. Ferguson then states that "establishments," which include legal, social, and governance institutions (Hill 2006, 97–98, 114), are "the result of human action, but not the execution of any human design" (Ferguson [1767] 1995, 119).

Ferguson uses different types of artisanship as metaphors for various governance types. When Ferguson writes that men in general make plans for themselves and that some men try to impose their designs upon others, he distinguishes between two types of design. The first is design that is endogenous to a system, as when individuals scheme for themselves, while the second is design that is exogenous to a system, which occurs when a person attempts to coerce others. The first can be thought of in terms of individual agency and self-governance, and the second as despotism. Ferguson's description of design thus acknowledges that humans are intrinsically designers, a characteristic that Vincent Ostrom develops in his political theory. The metaphors of design and artisanship can thus prove useful when undertaking comparative political economy.

Hayek integrates much of Ferguson's approach to emergent orders into his own political theory, emphasizing two points. First, Hayek iterates Ferguson's statement, rewording it as "the results of human action but not of human design" (Hayek [1960] 2011, 74; [1967b] 2014, 293). Second, Hayek incorporates Ferguson's understanding of spontaneous orders as emerging from human action. Third, Hayek includes Ferguson's notions of endogenous and exogenous design in *The Constitution of Liberty*, but he modifies Ferguson. Instead of describing both forms of plan-making in terms of design, as Ferguson does, Hayek uses the word "making" to refer to the type of human action that produces a civilization, which is the type of action that is simultaneously the "discipline of freedom" and the "discipline of civilization." In the Hayekian worldview, designing a civilization is a metaphor used to describe rule by fiat, whatever the form of government. Hayek thus establishes a distinction between making a civilization and designing a civilization, using the two approaches as metaphors for governance systems. Making a civilization occurs in real time, with creativity, discovery, and execution collapsing into nearly synonymous actions. This is the activity of self-governance, which involves trial and error, room for making bad choices, and the opportunity to learn from and improve upon past experiments. Designing a civilization suggests that there are chronological distinctions between creativity and execution, and thus divisions of labor between the designer and the executor, with the executor carrying out the will of the designer.

Ferguson's statement, along with Hayek's ([1960] 2011) use of it, applies to the societal level of analysis, or what he calls "the multitude" ([1767] 1995, 119). At the individual level, Ferguson acknowledges the human inclination to imagine and execute designs, making observations that contextualize both his famous phrase and several passages throughout Hayek ([1960] 2011). Ferguson writes, "Men, in general, are sufficiently disposed to occupy themselves in forming projects and schemes: but he who would scheme and project for others, will find an opponent in every person who is disposed to scheme for himself" ([1767] 1995, 119). Some individuals attempt to dominate other people, yielding two potential responses, according to Ferguson. While some may acquiesce to subordination, others may opt to resist. In both cases, the circumstances of time and place shape the outcomes of "establishments and measures" far more than the schemes of an individual designer (ibid.).

In these passages from Hayek, Ferguson, and Tocqueville, institutional development is connected to human limitations and individual liberty to the individual right to resist subordination. The locus of liberty thus circumscribes the parallel processes of domination and resistance, shaping the "establishments," governments, and conditions that result from human interaction. These are the processes that Tocqueville refers to as "civil discord" ([1835] 2010, 393), yielding what Hayek describes as "that condition of men in which coercion of some by others is reduced as much as is possible in society" ([1960] 2011, 57). In Hayek's scholarship, freedom, considered an artifact of civilization, results when individuals reduce coercion through legal and market processes.

Individuals as Entrepreneurs

Hayek's esteem for the cultural institutions of language, law, and markets (Dekker 2016, 187–189) reflects those of the Austrian tradition. The market forms the arena within which individuals work out their freedom, supported by (1) legal institutions favorable to private property and (2) formal and informal norms comprised of rules derived from common understandings and uses of language. This is why Mises ([1949] 2007) and Schumpeter ([1942] 2010)—and later, Kirzner (1985)—deem the individual an entrepreneur. The Misesian entrepreneur is a teleological actor, "the driving force of the whole market system," who combines various factors of production (Mises [1949] 2007, 249). The Schumpeterian entrepreneur similarly drives the marketplace through innovation as an economic leader, whose "function . . . is to reform or revolutionize the pattern of production" (Schumpeter [1942] 2010, 117).

The Kirznerian entrepreneur remains alert so as to discover entrepreneurial opportunities (Kirzner 1985, 1999).

Across all three variations of the Austrian entrepreneur, teleology is a defining characteristic, as the entrepreneurs work towards specific ends. Buchanan and Vanberg (1991) critique the Kirznerian entrepreneur for being limited in creativity and open-endedness by this teleological focus on the future discovery of "something knowable out there, to be discovered sooner or later" (178), conditioned by Kirzner's use of the equilibrium framework. They then offer an alternative position, influenced by Shackle's theories of indeterminacy with regards to human choice (Kirzner 2014, 127), which is that entrepreneurial activity involves making creative choices "yet to be made" that will shape the future (Buchanan and Vanberg 1991, 178). Creativity, in Buchanan and Vanberg's assessment, is completely open-ended, with each choice providing an infinite number of potential follow-up choices.

Given the Austrian School's robust theory of entrepreneurship, it may come as a surprise that Hayek rarely uses the term "entrepreneur" to describe market actors.[3] Hayek instead calls the actor in *The Constitution of Liberty* an individual. If individual choice, creativity, and agency are keys to an open society, then we can consider an alternative metaphor for the Austrian individual: the artisan. This metaphor permits us to consider a wider range of mental processes that people engage in as they accomplish their goals, both individually and in coordination with one another. This metaphor also makes it possible to consider domains and institutions outside the market context and to observe how people behave with great consistency at all levels, ranging from mundane to abstract.

The scholarship of Vincent and Elinor Ostrom offers us insights into the nature of artifacts, human design, and the artifactuality of institutional design. The Bloomington School's investigation into how people live and work together helps us make sense of the open society as it is constructed piecemeal (Hayek [1960] 2011, 131–132; Popper 1950). Finally, the Ostroms' concept of the creative artisan—who in various contexts is a political analyst, citizen-practitioner, and academic researcher (V. Ostrom 1994, 253)—differs from that of Buchanan and Vanberg's creative entrepreneur. Like the Austrian entrepreneurs, the Ostromian artisan is a teleological actor who works to realize specific results, such as making a coffee table or a constitution. Yet, an artisan remains open to creative discoveries and bears a problem-solving attitude, which enables her to adapt to problems that arise as she pursues her end goals. These character traits allow us to consider the artisan as a more nuanced metaphor of the individual who interacts in a free civilization as conceptualized by Hayek.

Co-productive human activity—specifically that of the Tocquevillian "art and science of association" that acknowledges the processes of contestation and restraint—is implied in Hayek's use of the term "civilization." This co-production is akin to a team of artisans working together in a workshop. Freedoms of all types, taken together as an artifact of civilization, are thus influenced by human craftsmanship. The metaphor of the Ostromian artisan, who produces artifacts through working out ideas with creativity, modifies that of the Austrian entrepreneur: the artisan, as an agent, possesses a mind that enables her to imagine possible futures or future artifacts, to choose which she prefers, and to engage the artisanal process to realize some semblance of her imagined reality. Artisanship provides a way to understand how humans shape their social contexts, either individually or together, endogenously rather than exogenously.

Bloomington School Artisanship

Bloomington School scholarship, developed by Vincent and Elinor Ostrom, illuminates the teleological questions inherent in Hayek's assertion that freedom is an artifact of civilization. As we have seen, Austrian scholars addressed these questions of teleology, rooted in agency and decision-making, by identifying the individual as an entrepreneur. Vincent Ostrom advanced the notion that entrepreneurs are artisans by describing human agency in all sorts of arenas, from public entrepreneurship and political engagement to academic collaboration. Both Ostroms addressed the question of how people work together through diverse institutional arrangements to solve economic and political puzzles. Elinor Ostrom continued to investigate collective action (understood as collaboration with some coercion) in non-market, non-state contexts for the duration of her career. Bloomington School artisanship thus includes the artisan and the artifact, concepts that enable us to nuance Hayek's argument that spontaneous orders are shaped from within by the aggregate designs of individuals.

The Ostroms address design head-on by acknowledging man's propensity to shape his immediate circumstances. Complex orders in the Bloomington School tradition contain artisans who fashion artifacts for various purposes. Vincent Ostrom developed the Bloomington School's theory of artisanship to study complex orders comprised of "political phenomena" ([1976] 2012, 14). Though Vincent Ostrom began the process of developing and formalizing his theory in his personal correspondence (Aligica 2018) and scholarly output (V. Ostrom [1976] 2012, 1980, 1997 he had been working out these ideas years before—indeed, for his entire career (McGinnis 2005)—as evidenced by an earlier publication (V. Ostrom 1964) and a 1965 letter to a colleague (as quoted in Dekker and Kuchař 2021, para. 17). Artisanship, according to the Ostroms, is located in a plethora of contexts, including academic and civic realms.

Bloomington School artisanship presumes that "artisans create artifacts" (V. Ostrom 1980, 309). Therefore, artisanship is comprised of three components: (1) artisans, (2) artisanal tasks and processes, and (3) artifacts. We can locate each component in an example from Vincent Ostrom (1997), a coffee table that he and Elinor Ostrom co-produced for their home while working with master woodworker Paul Goodman in his workshop. Vincent Ostrom describes how he (and Elinor) constructed this coffee table:

> Building a coffee table with a cabinetmaker involved the use of present means to achieve some future apparent good that began as a concept—fiction of the mind—and was worked through using two odd boards cut from black walnut trees. The cut edge of one, a piece of slab wood, became the surface of the table. A konky knot had to be removed and filled with a wedged replacement. Another gnarled and splintered board was used to construct a set of legs. The curves used to shape the legs were later used to construct a lamp from blond-colored gumwood, which is now located in a corner opposite the coffee table. Principles of heterogeneity and complementarity were used to put together pieces of furniture that serve both utilitarian [useful] and aesthetic purposes in the ecology and economy of a household. (V. Ostrom 1997, 206)

In this example, there are three artisans: Vincent, Elinor, and Paul. Artisans possess agency and rationality, which means that they are thinking individuals. The artisanal process is comprised of several tasks that occur across time to get from "present means" to "some future apparent good." This is the process by which artisans engage shape natural materials with their minds and hands. The artifact is the coffee table, the result of the artisans exerting the artisanal process on natural materials.

Artisans

The artisan is the individual who creates an artifact by working through an artisanal process and, thus, possesses several characteristics critical to artisanship. She has rationality and agency, which are dynamic characteristics that can ebb and flow as the artisan develops them or leaves them be. The rationality of the artisan is located in the artisan's mind and includes several operations, such as thinking and creating, designing, decision-making, and adapting important constituents of the creative process. Design, in fact, is inherent to human beings and can be used for good or ill. Rationality presumes individuality, with the artisan bringing her own personality and values to the artisanal process. By agency, we mean that the artisan is in a state of action or exerts power to produce an effect.

The creative process changes when multiple artisans work together, as the artisans contribute heterogeneous types and various levels of expertise to their collaboration. Some artisans possess greater knowledge about a process, while others contribute more elbow grease.

An artisan who collaborates with other artisans requires some degree of freedom, or what Dos Passos ([1958] 1977) describes as "elbow room." An artisan must also possess a host of moral virtues with which to engage her fellow artisans, as individuals who collaborate often present different perspectives, informed by various types and levels of expertise, that may need to be reconciled (Poteete, Janssen, and E. Ostrom 2010). Because of their differences, artisans sometimes disagree. This disagreement leads them to engage in contestation, a communicative process through which artisans speak and listen to one another to discern a compromise about how to proceed.

Finally, artisans are experts with intimate knowledge about their areas of expertise who work with apprentices. Elinor Ostrom describes the prowess of Paul Goodman, with whom she and Vincent Ostrom apprenticed:

> One of the reasons we called this place a workshop instead of a center was because of working with Paul [Goodman] and understanding what artisanship was. You might be working on something like a cabinet and thinking about the design of it, and thinking this idea versus that idea, and then Paul could pick up a board and say, oh, you shouldn't use this one because it will split. He could see things in wood that we couldn't. So the whole idea of artisans and apprentices and the structure of a good workshop really made an impression on us. (Leonard 2009)

We can see from Elinor Ostrom's story that experts possess knowledge that nonexperts do not, such as being able to "see things in wood" that remain mysterious to nonexperts. Additionally, experts convey this knowledge to their collaborators and apprentices to avoid bad outcomes like split boards or to produce good outcomes like the Ostroms' coffee table. In Bloomington School artisanship, a "good workshop" contains "artisans and apprentices," each making their own contribution to the artisanal process and the final artifact.

Artisanship

Artisanship is the creative process exerted by the artisan to create an artifact. Artisans begin with a mental vision of the artifact—in Vincent Ostrom (1997), the concept of a coffee table—and execute that vision with raw materials, here "two odd boards cut from black walnut trees" (ibid., 206). Sometimes fashioning an artifact involves adapting the raw materials to their new purpose, which is what Vincent Ostrom did when he replaced the "konky knot" with a wedge (ibid., 206). One adaptation might not be enough for an artifact as complicated as Vincent's coffee table, which could only be achieved with lots of adaptations to the raw materials he works with so that the final product bears elements of the natural materials and elements of the artisan's craftsmanship.

To be adaptative, an artisan must be open to discovery, and she must be willing to negotiate with others throughout the course of the project. When designing their coffee table, Vincent and Elinor Ostrom had to come to an agreement about how to make the legs for the table. The Ostroms depict for us how contestation proceeds in this interview from Barbara Allen's (2012) documentary. The italicized text identifies the salient parts of this process:

Elinor: "That was our first table that we ever made."

Vincent: "And we had a *long, long argument* about how to make the legs for the table.

Elinor: (laughs)

Vincent: "And *we finally worked out that.* And after we worked out that, as the basis of making the legs, we used the same design to make the lamp over in the corner."

Elinor: "The square versus circle argument. I don't know which one of us wanted square legs and which wanted round, but *we kept, back and forth,* and so we have square with round inside." (chuckles)

Vincent: "And flat pieces of wood."

Elinor: "So, it's a little like polycentricity that we are able to get some things on the outside and other things on the inside." (chuckles) "So, we're kind of pleased with those legs."

Contestation sometimes begins with conflict, such as the Ostroms' lengthy argument about what kinds of legs they wanted. Because each wanted something different—square legs or round legs—they had to reconcile their artistic design as they worked things out. This process of working things out took time and effort as the Ostroms kept at it, going "back and forth" until they came to a decision. Long after completing the coffee table, Elinor Ostrom admits to forgetting who preferred which style of legs, focusing the story on the final product. In an elegant compromise, the coffee table legs were squared on the outside and rounded on the inside. (In reality, the coffee table legs incorporate both preferences. Visitors to the Ostrom Workshop, where the coffee table resides, can see that some legs are square with round inside and other legs are square with round outside.) Elinor Ostrom's forgetfulness displays charity towards others, a quality that is necessary when engaging in collaborative efforts.

Artifacts

Artifacts are the final products of artisans working through artisanship. The raw materials and the artisan's imagination form the inputs, and the artisan's elbow grease transforms these inputs into the output, that is, the artifact. As such, artifacts are "created by human beings . . . to serve human purposes" (V. Ostrom 1980, 309). Though not every person is intentional about every decision he makes, as Randall Dipert (1993, 67–68) notes, the act of fashioning artifacts requires us to make choices. Hayek (1948), for instance, advocates for the importance of studying choice from the perspectives of both mathematical logic and causal effects. Thus, artifacts are records of human intentionality, uniting the physical characteristics of the artifact with the artisan's preferences and choices (V. Ostrom 1980, 309–310). Artifacts, whether material or immaterial, consequently embody fact and value (V. Ostrom [1976] 2012, 14).

As embodiments of fact and value, artifacts are intertwined with the causal forces of social processes. Complicated relationships between artifact makers and users, material artifacts, and human contexts consequently arise. In their passages on culture, both Hayek ([1960] 2011, 75) and V. Ostrom (1997, 206) incorporate archaeological thought, with Hayek citing Leslie White (1949) for his assertion that culture influences people more than people influence culture and Ostrom utilizing the phrase "science of culture."[4] We can gain additional insight into the relationships between material artifacts, human behavior, and social processes from archaeologist H. Martin Wobst (2006), who connects artifacts to human action and social processes as Hayek and Vincent Ostrom do. Like Hayek, Wobst presumes that social processes are always at work, and Wobst shares Vincent Ostrom's position that artifacts oftentimes result from desired changes in an artifact user's local conditions. Wobst limits his observations to material artifacts, but Hayek and the Ostroms show us that these observations are equally applicable to immaterial artifacts.

Wobst (2006) emphasizes that social processes can be shaped by artifacts. He uses the term "artifactual interference" to describe artifacts as "designs to construct something that is different from what would be if things were left alone" (59). Artifacts, therefore, result from and can shape human action. Artifacts, as "*products* of human behavior" (Wobst 2006, 58; emphasis Wobst; see also V. Ostrom 1980), function as interventions into the present rather than the future, change the objectionable and retain the agreeable, and emerge from contested aspects of the social world (Wobst 2006, 59). In Ostromian and Hayekian terms, respectively, this means that artisans make or refashion an artifact at the present time to change or retain something specific about their localized context, with this primary action producing a secondary effect of shaping social processes now and in the future.

According to Wobst (2006), material artifacts modify the social order; "that is, they are designs to change aspects of the social world that are considered objectionable, or to keep aspects from changing that are considered agreeable" (59). The Ostroms assert that immaterial artifacts like institutions, for example, also change or preserve facets of this social order, joining Hayek and Tocqueville in acknowledging that such change or preservation is worked out through the hard discipline that comes with the art and science of association. Finally, Wobst notes, "A given social context, in its artifactual traces, is an amalgam of such [artifactual] interferences" (59). In Hayek's civilization, the amalgamation of tools not only refers to "material implements," but also includes the immaterial implements of traditions and institutions (Hayek [1960] 2011, 78–79). This is the collected inheritance of civilizational growth that occurs across the span of a few hundred generations.

Where immaterial artifacts like institutions are concerned, political analysts must therefore be aware that amalgamation, such as that which occurs in the institutions and civilizations they study, complexifies their analysis. As we examine artifacts, whether material or immaterial, we must also consider the amalgamation of fact and value that artifacts accumulate. Vincent Ostrom elsewhere deems fact and value as "natural fact" and "artifact" ([1976] 2012, 14), drawing parallels with Searle's "brute fact" and "institutional fact" (1969, 50–52). As a material artifact, the Ostroms' coffee table possesses both types of facts. Its natural, brute facts are its physical attributes, while its institutional facts are the human values and aesthetic choices added to the physical attributes. Immaterial artifacts, such as a constitution, similarly bear traces of human value and meaning.

While constitutional development occupied the scholarship of both Vincent Ostrom and Hayek, Vincent Ostrom drew upon his empirical work as a consultant for the natural resources article of the Alaska Constitution, deeming this work "one of the most enlightening experiences in my life" (Vincent Ostrom interview; quoted in Allen 2011, 37). Vincent Ostrom consequently adopted the position that constitutions are constructed via the methods of artisanship. A constitution might be notated with physical materials and techniques, such as putting pen to paper, but it is primarily fashioned by the artisan from institutional facts—language, rules, and tacit knowledge—rather than physical facts (V. Ostrom 1994, 129–130). When consulting for the natural resources article of the Alaska Constitution, Vincent Ostrom worked with a three-member subcommittee to articulate and fashion "specific formulations" of language (V. Ostrom 2011, 49), generating the beginnings of a lexicon at the subcommittee's request (Allen 2011, 41).

Words used to formulate constitutions can be thought of as bricolage, that is, in terms of amalgamation. For instance, they are inherited symbols that point towards shared (and often previously acquired) concepts and meanings as well as informal and formal norms that form the context, or ecology, within which language is situated (V. Ostrom 1994, 130). Furthermore, words and language are used to construct rules and, thus, rule-ordered relationships (E. Ostrom 2005, 20, 181). The shared knowledge that words refer to makes it possible for individual artisans to communicate with one another. Vincent Ostrom (1994) further asserts, "If we are unwilling to stipulate the theory we are using, or to say how different conceptualizations about the nature and constitution of order in human societies are articulated in both an explanatory and a juridical language, our words lose their meaning" (130). I take this to mean that we must be willing to acknowledge and discuss our differences with one another, as well as to engage in contestation about our different conceptions if words are to retain their meaning.

The Bloomington School's understanding of the artisanship-artifact relationship helps us locate the artisan in Hayek's free civilization and to understand how the individual artisan works together with other individuals and, by means of the organic processes of cultural evolution, shapes emergent orders from within.

Locating the Artisan

Locating the artisan in Hayek's free civilization becomes possible when we recognize that the Ostromian artisan grapples with many of the same issues as those faced by Hayek's individual. They both live in cultural contexts shaped by the particularities of time and place and engage in a Tocquevillian apprenticeship of liberty. Just as the Hayekian individual overcomes the limitations of his own knowledge by using knowledge belonging to others, so too can the Ostromian artisan, who lacks some of the knowledge she needs to craft an artifact, surmount this dearth by seeking mentorship from an expert or collaborating with colleagues. Hayek's individual lives in a state of being that is free (Hayek [1960] 2011), while the Ostroms' artisan inhabits an "ecology and economy" (V. Ostrom 1997, 206). Finally, the Hayekian individual must engage in the disciplines of freedom and civilization, while the Ostromian artisan undertakes a hard apprenticeship in liberty.

Both Hayek ([1967b] 2014) and Vincent Ostrom ([1976] 2012) acknowledge the Humean conceit that design is inherent to human nature. Artisans make artifacts, whether furniture for homes or constitutions for political orders. Artifacts, therefore, are records of human choices and values, pointing toward how these choices and values shape social processes (Wobst 2006; V. Ostrom 1980). Hayek, though acknowledging that people construct constitutions and governments and pointing to the American example as the model for constitutional process, chooses to emphasize the cultural emergence of legal and political institutions, particularly in the latter part of his career. Conversely, the Ostroms stress the artifactual nature of cultural processes such as making social and political institutions, explicating the agency of the artisan who lives in an ecology of social and cultural change. Where Hayek adopts the norm that constitutional-level rules emerge from spontaneous order, following Scotch Enlightenment thought, the Ostroms observed from their empirical and applied work that constitutional-level rules could be altered by humans as needed.[5] The artisan fashions artifacts, knowing that artifacts are, as Wobst (2006) asserts, "designs to construct something that is different from what would be if things were left alone, that is, without artifactual interference" (59). In Bloomington School scholarship, a constitution is an artifact designed to contribute to the "ecology and economy" of freedom (V. Ostrom 1997, 206). A constitution thus encodes the traditions and values of the political order of a specific time and place and shapes the cultural ecology surrounding that order.

Artifacts contain emergent and created elements, as Hayek and Vincent Ostrom both acknowledged, so we can examine these artifacts for human intelligibility (Hayek [1960] 2011, 107; V. Ostrom 1980, 315). Much about the materials that an artisan uses to craft an artifact remains a mystery, lost to the annals of history, especially when one constructs with bricolage, using materials that are an amalgam of fact and value. Words, for instance, carry meanings that are passed from one generation to the next through learning and use. Those of us who use words—such as "democracy" and "state"—with their present meanings may intend something different from the original creators of those words, with the original meaning obscured by the ravages of time. Thus, these words may appear emergent to us. These same words have artisanal qualities, taking on additional meanings as they are defined and re-defined by successive generations of wordsmiths. Understanding the emergent and constructed properties of words and institutions becomes critical to forming constitutions and political orders.

It has been posited that the Austrian individual who operates in the marketplace adopts one of two positions: (1) a mental posture of discovery or (2) an attitude of creativity. The first relates to a teleological posture of discovering something that exists, while the second is associated with a nondeterministic position of creating something completely new (Kirzner 1985; Buchanan and Vanberg 1991). The Ostromian artisan pursues a third course that avoids this "either/or" binary, developing an inclusive mental model that allows for "both/and" with regards to discovery and creativity. Robert Nisbet, in his presidential address to the American Sociological Association, articulates such inclusivity this way: "Whatever the differences between science and art, it is what they have in common that matters most in discovery and creativeness" (1962, 67). Similarly, Bloomington School "institutional analysts and designers were just as much artisans as they were scientists," as Cole and McGinnis (2015, 31) assert. These artisan-analysts use multiple levels of analysis to examine both the exogenous spontaneous order from the perspective of the analyst looking from the outside in and the many endogenous designs that one perceives from inside the order.

Thus, the Ostromian artisan maintains a delicate balance between present hopes and future potentialities as he pursues and realizes goals and aims, negotiating the tension between teleology and open-endedness. Because this process occurs over time, the realization of a goal must occur at some future point after the artisan has conceptualized it. In this scenario, all sense of direction simply cannot be avoided. Thus, the artisan maintains a delicate balance between making adaptations to present needs, as when Vincent replaced the "konky" knot with a wedge, and working towards a future goal, such as producing a coffee table.

Nisbet goes on to suggest that the mental processes involved in scientific exploration are the same as those in artistic creativity, emphasizing discovery, experience, and imagination over formulaic data analysis (1962, 70–71). An inclusive mental model that accounts for discovery and creativity supports the work of human actors, as Vincent Ostrom highlights:

> This is a challenge facing not only artisans but also entrepreneurs and administrators: how to bring ideas into operation. The society that is open to more diverse ways of assembling heterogeneous elements and achieving effective complementarities is the one that allows for greater productive potentials. (1994, 253)

Conclusion

In positing that the individual in Hayek's *The Constitution of Liberty* is an artisan, my argument moves through multiple layers of analysis, ranging from the mundane to that of civilization. In doing so, I draw upon a long Bloomington School tradition of considering artisanship an inherent human characteristic that is at work in various processes, from fashioning coffee tables to designing constitutions. The artisanal process that Vincent Ostrom outlines is the same no matter what artifact is being produced, even though many elements of the process—the materials, tools, and techniques used—may differ. Therefore, the Bloomington School notion of the artisan can be imported into Hayek's free civilization, showing us how the Hayekian individual is shaped by cultural evolution, and then, in turn, shapes emergent orders from the inside.

Throughout this chapter, I have touched upon many related and important issues that deserve further investigation, naming but a few here. For instance, there are connections between (1) localized changes and societal evolution and (2) impersonal evolution and personal artisanship. I also have not delved fully into intentionality and directionality, which are inherent to artisanship, and even my description of the Bloomington School artisan is only the beginning of a project that aims to more completely flesh out the mental models and moral sentiments of artisans. Remaining still is an explication of the necessity of freedom for the artisanal process, as well as a discussion of the effects of cultural evolution upon an artifact and the impacts of creative artisanship upon a free society. Finally, there are open questions about the distinction between what we can and cannot understand, as well as the extent to which we can analyze complex systems before the level of complexity eludes our comprehension.[6]

In *The Constitution of Liberty*, Hayek explores the relationship between liberty, civilization, and institutions. A free civilization is a place where people, through learning and imitation, have developed institutions that enable them to live together. Hayek's exploration of liberty is a study of the emergence of Western civilization. Specifically, Hayek undertakes a comparative analysis of Anglican liberty, which includes both the United Kingdom and the United States, and Gallican liberty ([1960] 2011, 109). Hayek accomplishes much by relating a constitution to a free civilization. A constitution, especially one that is written, encodes the doctrines and principles of individuals who live together in freedom. Hayek ties the notion of cultural evolution to a constitution of liberty. If cultural evolution is what makes civilization possible, and civilization in turn generates freedom, then a constitution encodes a portion, at least, of what makes civilization possible. This enables us to assert that a constitution is an artifact made by artisans that encodes elements of the cultural evolution from whence a free civilization emerges.

Notes

1. Many wonderful mentors and colleagues have dialogued with me about my chapter. I thank my colleagues and editors in the Adam Smith research sequence, my fellow workshoppers at the Ostrom Workshop, and respondents and participants attending the 2022 Public Choice Society meeting and the 2022 Mini-Conference at the Ostrom Workshop. I am grateful to Justus Enninga for encouraging me to add entrepreneurship to my work on artisanship. Special thanks are due to these Workshop artisan-mentors: Paul Dragos Aligica and Roberta Herzberg for addressing my questions about constitutional design, Aurelian Craiutu for referring me to Jacob Viner's scholarship, Daniel Cole for reviewing and commenting on a draft of this chapter, and Eduardo Brondizio and Daniel Cole for advising me during my 2021–2022 Ostrom Fellowship project. Parts of this chapter have emerged from that project, so it seems fitting to finish this chapter as we celebrate the Ostrom Workshop's fiftieth anniversary.

2. Daniel Cole offered me this astute perspective: "There is no brute fact of civilization."

3. I am grateful to Erwin Dekker for this observation.

4. Eduardo Brondizio informed me about the anthropological origins of the term "science of culture."

5. Roberta Herzberg graciously provided me with this insight.

6. Michael McGinnis brought these fascinating questions to my attention.

References

Aligica, Paul Dragos. 2018. "Artefactual and Artisanship: James M. Buchanan and Vincent Ostrom at the Core and Beyond the Boundaries of Public Choice." In *James M. Buchanan: A Theorist of Political Economy and Social Philosophy*, edited by Richard E. Wagner, 1105–1129. Cham, CH: Palgrave Macmillan.

Allen, Barbara, ed. 2011. *The Quest to Understand Human Affairs: Natural Resources Policy and Essays on Community and Collective Choice, Volume 1.* Lanham, MD: Lexington Books.

Allen, Barbara. 2012. "The Artisanship and Science of Institutional Design." https://vimeo.com/59852942.

Boettke, Peter J., and Christopher J. Coyne. 2005. "Methodological Individualism, Spontaneous Order, and the Research Program of the Workshop in Political Theory and Policy Analysis." *Journal of Economic Behavior and Organization* 57 (2): 145–158.

Bowlin, John R. 2016. *Tolerance among the Virtues.* Princeton, NJ: Princeton University Press.

Buchanan, James M., and Viktor J. Vanberg. 1991. "The Market as a Creative Process." *Economics and Philosophy* 7 (2): 167–186.

Carini, Jaime. 2021. "Artisanship, Artifact, and Aesthetic Fact." In *Culture, Sociality, and Morality: New Applications of Mainline Political Economy*, edited by Paul Dragoş Aligica, Ginny Seung Choi, and Virgil Henry Storr, 83–108. Lanham, MD: Rowman & Littlefield.

Cole, Daniel H., and Michael D. McGinnis. 2015. "Introduction to Volume 1." In *Elinor Ostrom and the Bloomington School of Political Economy, Volume One*, edited by Daniel H. Cole, and Michael D. McGinnis, 25–35. Lanham, MD: Lexington Books.

Dekker, Erwin. 2016. *The Viennese Students of Civilization: The Meaning and Context of Austrian Economics Reconsidered.* Cambridge: Cambridge University Press.

Dekker, Erwin, and Pavel Kuchař. 2021. "The Ostrom Workshop: Artisanship and Knowledge Commons." *Revue d'économie politique* 131 (4): 637–664.

Dipert, Randall R. 1993. *Artifacts, Art Works, and Agency.* Philadelphia, PA: Temple University Press.

Dos Passos, John. [1958] 1977. "A Question of Elbow Room." In *Essays on Individuality*, edited by Felix Morley, 17–50. Indianapolis, IN: Liberty Fund.

Ferguson, Adam. [1767] 1995. *An Essay on the History of Civil Society.* Edited by Fania Oz-Salzberger. Cambridge: Cambridge University Press.

Gaus, Gerald F. 2006. "Hayek on the Evolution of Society and Mind." In *The Cambridge Companion to Hayek*, edited by Edward Feser, 232–258. Cambridge: Cambridge University Press.

Haeffele, Stefanie, Solomon M. Stein, and Virgil Henry Storr, eds. 2020. *Hayek's Tensions: Reexamining the Political Economy and Philosophy of F. A. Hayek*. Arlington, VA: Mercatus Center at George Mason University.

Hamowy, Ronald. 2011. "Introductory Essay." In *The Collected Works of F. A. Hayek, Volume 17: The Constitution of Liberty: The Definitive Edition, by F. A. Hayek*, 1–22. Edited by Ronald Hamowy. Chicago, IL: University of Chicago Press.

Hayek, F. A. [1944a] 2018. "Scientism and the Study of Society." In *The Collected Works of F. A. Hayek, Volume 13: Studies on the Abuse and Decline of Reason: Text and Documents*. Edited by Bruce Caldwell. The Collected Works of F. A. Hayek. Carmel, IN: Liberty Fund.

———. [1944b] 2007. *The Collected Works of F. A. Hayek, Volume 2: The Road to Serfdom: Text and Documents: The Definitive Edition*. Edited by Bruce Caldwell. Chicago, IL: University of Chicago Press.

———. [1945] 2014. "The Use of Knowledge in Society." In *The Collected Works of F. A. Hayek, Volume 15: The Market and Other Orders*, edited by Bruce Caldwell, 93–104. Chicago, IL: University of Chicago Press.

———. 1948. *Individualism and Economic Order*. Chicago, IL: University of Chicago Press.

———. [1949] 2009. "The Intellectuals and Socialism." In *The Collected Works of F. A. Hayek, Volume 10: Socialism and War: Essays, Documents, Reviews*, edited by Bruce Caldwell, 221–237. Indianapolis, IN: Liberty Fund.

———. [1958] 1977. "The Creative Powers of a Free Civilization." In *Essays on Individuality*, edited by Felix Morley, 259–289. Indianapolis, IN: Liberty Fund.

———. [1960] 2011. *The Collected Works of F. A. Hayek, Volume 17: The Constitution of Liberty: The Definitive Edition*. Edited by Ronald Hamowy. Chicago, IL: University of Chicago Press.

———. [1967a] 2014. "Notes on the Evolution of Systems of Rules of Conduct." In *The Collected Works of F. A. Hayek, Volume 15: The Market and Other Orders*, edited by Bruce Caldwell, 278–292. Chicago, IL: University of Chicago Press.

———. [1967b] 2014. "The Results of Human Action but Not of Human Design." In *The Collected Works of F. A. Hayek, Volume 15: The Market and Other Orders*, edited by Bruce Caldwell, 293–303. Chicago, IL: University of Chicago Press.

———. 1979. *Law, Legislation and Liberty, Volume 3: The Political Order of a Free People*. Chicago, IL: University of Chicago Press.

Hill, Lisa. 2006. *The Passionate Society: The Social, Political and Moral Thought of Adam Ferguson*. Dordrecht, NL: Springer.

Kirzner, Israel M. 1985. *Discovery and the Capitalist Process*. Chicago, IL: University of Chicago Press.

———. 1999. "Creativity and/or Alertness: A Reconsideration of the Schumpeterian Entrepreneur." *The Review of Austrian Economics* 11 (1/2): 5–17.

———. 2014. "Buchanan and the Austrians: A Tale of Two Bridges." *The Review of Austrian Economics* 27: 119–128.

Leonard, Mike. 2009. "What a Prize." *Times-Mail*, December 5. https://www.tmnews.com/story/news/2009/12/05/what-a-prize/48095907/.

Lewis, Paul G. 2017. "The Ostroms and Hayek as Theorists of Complex Adaptive Systems: Commonality and Complementarity." In *Advances in Austrian Economics, Volume 22: The Austrian and Bloomington Schools of Political Economy*, edited by Paul Dragoș Aligica, Paul G. Lewis, and Virgil Henry Storr, 35–66. Bingley, UK: Emerald.

———. 2020. "Tensions and Ambiguities in Hayek's Social Theory." In *Hayek's Tensions: Reexamining the Political Economy and Philosophy of F. A. Hayek*, edited by Stefanie Haeffele, Solomon M. Stein, and Virgil Henry Storr, 85–114. Arlington, VA: Mercatus Center at George Mason University.

McGinnis, Michael D. 2005. "Beyond Individualism and Spontaneity: Comments on Peter Boettke and Christopher Coyne." *Journal of Economic Behavior and Organization* 57 (2): 167–172.

Mises, Ludwig von. [1949] 2007. *Human Action: A Treatise on Economics*. Edited by Bettina Bien Greaves. Indianapolis, IN: Liberty Fund.

Morley, Felix, ed. [1958] 1977. *Essays on Individuality*. Indianapolis, IN: Liberty Fund.

Nisbet, Robert A. 1962. "Sociology as an Art Form." *The Pacific Sociological Review* 5 (2): 67–74.

Ostrom, Elinor. 1990. *Governing the Commons: The Evolution of Institutions for Collective Action*. Cambridge: Cambridge University Press.

———. 2005. *Understanding Institutional Diversity*. Princeton, NJ: Princeton University Press.

Ostrom, Vincent. [1956] 2011. "Clarifying the Meaning of Article VIII: Natural Resources, as Adopted by the Alaska Constitutional Convention, in 1956." In *The Quest to Understand Human Affairs: Natural Resources Policy and Essays on Community and Collective Choice, Volume 1*, edited by Barbara Allen, 46–56. Lanham, MD: Lexington Books.

———. 1964. "Culture, Science, and Politics." In *The Making of Decisions: A Reader in Administrative Behavior*, edited by William J. Gore and James W. Dyson, 85–92. New York: Free Press of Glencoe.

———. [1976] 2012. "David Hume as a Political Analyst." In *The Quest to Understand Human Affairs: Essays on Collective, Constitutional, and Epistemic Choice, Volume 2*, edited by Barbara Allen, 3–30. Lanham, MD: Lexington Books.

———. 1980. "Artisanship and Artifact." *Public Administration Review* 40 (4): 309–317.

———. 1994. *The Meaning of American Federalism: Constituting a Self-Governing Society*. San Francisco, CA: ICS Press.

———. 1997. *The Meaning of Democracy and the Vulnerability of Democracies: A Response to Tocqueville's Challenge*. Ann Arbor, MI: University of Michigan Press.

Popper, Karl R. 1950. *The Open Society and Its Enemies*. Rev. ed. Princeton, NJ: Princeton University Press.

Poteete, Amy R., Marco Janssen, and Elinor Ostrom. 2010. *Working Together: Collective Action, the Commons, and Multiple Methods in Practice*. Princeton, NJ: Princeton University Press.

Sabetti, Filippo. 2011. "Constitutional Artisanship and Institutional Diversity: Elinor Ostrom, Vincent Ostrom, and the Workshop." *The Good Society* 20 (1): 73–83.

Schumpeter, Joseph A. [1942] 2010. *Capitalism, Socialism and Democracy*. London: Routledge.

Searle, John R. 1969. *Speech Acts: An Essay in the Philosophy of Language*. Cambridge: Cambridge University Press.

Tocqueville, Alexis de. [1835] 2010. *Democracy in America, Volume I*. Edited by Eduardo Nolla. Translated by James T. Schleifer. Indianapolis, IN: Liberty Fund.

Viner, Jacob. 1961. "Hayek on Freedom and Coercion." *Southern Economic Journal* 27 (3): 230–36.

White, Leslie. 1949. *The Science of Culture: A Study of Man and Civilization*. New York: Farrar, Straus.

Wobst, H. Martin. 2006. "Artifacts as Social Interference: The Politics of Spatial Scale." In *Confronting Scale in Archaeology: Issues of Theory and Practice*, edited by Gary Lock and Brian Leigh Molyneaux, 55–64. New York: Springer.

4

The Form of the Farm

Samuel Schmitt

At every turn, liberalism is harried by growing criticism.[1] The crux of many of these critiques is how market-oriented liberalism treats the environment.[2] These critics argue that liberal, market-oriented societies conceive of human beings as separate from and supreme over nature (e.g., Berry 2003; Milbank and Pabst 2016; Deneen 2018). In their view, this conception of the person leads to the destruction of environmental resources, the disruption of ecosystems, and the end of traditional, tightly-knit communities. Even advocates of a market-oriented society sometimes admit the environment is not liberalism's strong suit (Klein 2021).

At the same time, several theorists have bridged the work of F.A. Hayek into environmentalist arguments, showing the promise of Austrian approaches to environmental policy (Pennington 2005; Shahar 2017). I take this task to a critical, constructive case—the traditional, small farm. Rather than start with their differences, I investigate the similarities between ideas of knowledge, order, and institutions in the writing of Hayek and agrarian theologian Wendell Berry (1934–present). Berry is influential amongst contemporary critics of liberalism and plays a key role in the alternative agriculture movement. Perhaps to the surprise and chagrin of both parties (tree- and market-huggers alike), I bring Berry and Hayek together to create a novel and persuasive account of liberal humility toward the environment.

Crucially, investigating Berry and Hayek enables us to see how Hayekian-style arguments lead to a reassessment of farming practices. The Berry-style small farm has advantages over sprawling industrialized agriculture as a matter of *epistemic institutionalism* (Boettke 2018). Just as Hayek rejected central economic planning, Berry rejects industrialized agriculture. Seen through the lens of Hayekian complexity theory, Berry's arguments about the scale and quality of farming are compatible with a liberal political economy. Despite Berry's (2003) rejection of the free market, industrialized agriculture, and the strangeness of his commitment to traditional farming in modern life, we can weave Berry and Hayek together to a great degree—though not completely. *Pace* critics of liberalism, bringing Hayek and Berry together provides pro tanto reason to prefer small, traditional farms to industrialized farms and remove regressive subsidies. Further, I reject the idea that separating humans from nature necessarily leads to wayward human manipulation of creation; it does not. One need not reject liberal theory to endorse Berry-style commitment to place and farming practices. In fact, we can do so for reasons familiar to the liberal political economy found in Hayek.

This merely shows that Berry-style commitments to place and traditional farming are *compatible* with a liberal political economy. Berry's thick normative vision is not required by liberal political economy; his religious and philosophical commitments to place, people, and sacral treatment of the land put more substantive constraints on farming practice than Hayek-friendly epistemic arguments alone. However, there is still space for developments in this direction within liberal society and liberal theory.

The chapter proceeds as follows. I first provide some idea of the objections to markets as they relate to environmental policy. Then, I shift to Hayek and recent Hayekian arguments that address concerns for the environment. These arguments focus on environmental policy and resource management rather than the structure and practice of farming itself. However, the Hayekian policy arguments highlight a crucial fact: the importance of institutions that improve our ability to learn about the environment (i.e., property and exchange through markets).

Next, I draw on Wendell Berry's thought as it relates to local knowledge, the pretense of industrialized agriculture, and the need for institutional arrangements that enhance the farmer's knowledge of the land, love for it, and interest in its overall health. When the farmer's plan outstrips their knowledge or ability to care, Berry predicts the same sort of errors that Hayek predicts in planning. Hayek's critique of planning and Berry's critique of industrialized agriculture are then synthesized to undercut support for regressive subsidies. Despite Berry's rejection of the free market, his views fit well with Hayekian arguments against subsidy. I then introduce elements of Berry's thought that go beyond epistemic defenses of traditional farming practices and scale. For Berry, the scale of the farm is limited by the knowledge of the farmer and their care for it. However, it is also limited by religious commitments to steward God's creation and to love one's neighbors—human, animal, vegetable, living, dead, and yet to come. Against criticisms of liberalism (e.g., Deneen

2018), I see these commitments as compatible with a market society, even if they are unconventional.

Is there any reason to believe Berry-style farms can be successful in comparison to industrialized forms of agriculture? Granted, we should not radically transition industrialized agriculture to small farms; a rapid transition would likely result in disaster. Instead, as goes the logic of market society, more people should experiment with Berry-style methods of farming, and more consumers should test and support their value. This is so both for the ethical, religious reasons Berry suggests in his broader corpus and for liberal, economic reasons—we can vote with our wallets. While the proportion of small commercial farms is shrinking in comparison to large commercial farms, noncommercial small farms are steadily on the rise (Hoppe et al. 2010). Religiously motivated small farms and commitment to place are possible (i.e., already present) in a market-oriented liberal society.

One Non-Liberal Criticism

Though critics disagree on exactly who is responsible for the change (some say Bacon; others say Duns Scotus or Ockham), there is agreement that liberalism incorrectly redefines human beings outside of and above nature. Rather than limited, creaturely beings who rely upon and are constrained by nature, liberalism counsels liberation from natural constraint and mastery of the environment for human ends. While other critics discuss this point (e.g., Milbank and Pabst 2016), the most popular recent critic along this line is Patrick Deneen (2018).

While the focus of Deneen's argument is on liberalism's redefinition of *human* nature, he sees an accompanying liberal impulse to master the natural world in the name of material wealth, thereby expanding the liberal freedom of consumer choice. Ancient cultures evolved forms of knowledge about character and care for the earth that were embodied in rational practices and traditions. The liberal project, on Deneen's account, releases the individual from these constraints, eliminating the *environmentally* conservative impulse in favor of confidence in science and innovation. As he puts it:

> Our carbon-saturated world is the hangover of a 150-year party in which, until the very end, we believed we had achieved the dream of liberation from nature's constraints. We still hold the incoherent view that science can liberate us from limits while solving the attendant consequences of that project. (2018, 15)

The solution, as Deneen sees it, is "more local forms of self-government by choice" (2018, 41). Whatever the merits of Deneen's argument, its tone and frustrations have become popular in our time.[3]

By this standard, Hayek's account of the relationship between human beings and nature is mixed at best. When comparing the natural and social sciences, Hayek uses the following metaphor:

> While at the world of nature we look from the outside, we look at the world of society from the inside; while, as far as nature is concerned, our concepts are about the facts and have to be adapted to the facts, in the world of society at least some of the most familiar concepts are the stuff from which that world is made. (2014, 92)

Here, Hayek seems to think human beings are somehow "outside" the world of nature and can objectively observe and study it. Hayek also deems natural science simpler than social science (2010, 45). But to see Hayek as endorsing a simple distinction between social and natural science is mistaken. The key distinction is not between natural and social science but between simple and complex.

Hayek's comments elsewhere indicate a degree of humility toward the complexity of phenomena in the natural sciences, especially in biology (2014, 362–372). For Hayek, biology presents challenges of complexity similar to those in economics: there are details too dispersed and too intricately interrelated for any one mind to ascertain and manipulate. Sciences of this kind can do little better than formulae whose values cannot be filled in; we can learn relationships but cannot hope to control them.

Perhaps Hayek sees human beings as separate from nature—something illiberal critics like Deneen will abhor. However, Hayek's reverence for the complexity of biological phenomena points us both in the direction of Hayekian innovations in environmental theory *and* toward Wendell Berry's defense of small farming as an institutional answer to the problem of ecological complexity. This suggests it is possible to maintain a separation between humans and nature *and* a complexity-motivated impulse against "mastery" over nature.[4]

Hayek and Hayekian Environmentalism

As Hayek acknowledged and as several of his inheritors argue, the complexity of biology and ecology calls for the same approaches that complexity in the economic sphere suggests—markets. What is Hayek's argument for markets?

Here, the key term is *epistemic institutionalism* (Boettke 2018). For Hayek, the problem of economic coordination is *as much* a problem of the division of knowledge as it is a problem of the division of labor (2014, 72). How does any one person know which materials to use in the production of a consumer good? Which substitutes should they use if their normal materials are scarce? To whom should they sell their product? How many should they make? How should the product be shipped? Should the company switch its focus? How can they rely on cooperating entities to ship the needed materials? These questions and a million like them plague the economist—indeed, they plague anyone who attempts to answer questions of coordination in a sufficiently large society. Well, these questions *did* plague theorists.

Hayek's insight was that certain institutions, namely the "competitive entrepreneurial market process of discovery and learning" (Boettke 2018, 12), which is enabled by private property and exchange, generate prices. In this view, price is not a representation of moral worth or labor input. Instead, it is a form of coded information related to scarcity (Hayek 1945; Pennington 2005). Because of the institutions of private property and free exchange, individuals may buy and sell items on the open market. Their willingness to buy or sell at specific price points is based on their subjective evaluation of the relevant facts, of which perhaps only they are aware or *could be* aware.

In fact, price and the market process don't just transmit extant information; they help create information that would otherwise not exist (e.g., the going price of iron ore). Price makes it so locally bound knowledge, like the availability and speed of shipping, can be translated into a cheaper price for the potential buyer. The buyer doesn't need to know all the details of *why* one shipping option is cheaper; they only need to see the difference in price amongst alternatives.

Here, the point is that the institutions of competition, property, and free exchange enable prices to emerge as coded information—knowledge—about far-flung places or difficult-to-understand matters (e.g., I know next to nothing about how to make a tire, but I can compare prices at local auto shops). What makes these institutions preferable to a centrally planned economy is that they make *better* use of and enable the creation of economically relevant knowledge; the claim is that these liberal, market institutions are preferred to alternative institutions, not that they attain some absolute standard of perfection. While readers of this volume are, no doubt, familiar with the general argument against planning compared to market competition, the importance of markets in environmental policy *and* the similarities between Hayek and Berry are easier to see through key passages of Hayek's Nobel address.

Hayek's worry (2014, 362–372) is that economists have come to see themselves too much as natural scientists do: "It seems to me that this failure of the economist to guide policy more successfully is closely connected with their propensity to imitate as closely as possible the procedures of the brilliantly successful physical sciences" (2014, 362). The trouble with approaching economics in this scientistic way is that the market and, for example, objects colliding in space are not analogous avenues of inquiry. For the physicist, enough of what matters to the analysis *can* be ascertained, measured, and accounted for. For the biologist, ecologist, and economist, the needed facts are so dispersed that they are confronted with challenges of "essential complexity" (2014, 365).

A system is complex if it can only be understood in terms of a relatively large number of variables and can only be predicted or sufficiently manipulated if the specific content of those variables can be filled out (Hayek 2014, 365). While the physicist has a challenging task when analyzing various physical forces in the outcome of a collision, the theorist of biology, economics, or ecology is faced with a virtually *impossible* task when asked to *predict the outcome* of a complex system. Instead, the work of the theorists of complex systems is limited to pattern predictions; they can discern the *kind* of event that might result rather than the exact state of affairs. They may understand the relationship between variables but not the definite outcome (2014, 367).

If the economist-cum-policy advisor (or worse, dictator) attempts to predict and control events in the economy as the physicist assists in the launch of a rocket, the results may be disastrous—this is the pretense against which Hayek warned. Here, it is worth quoting Hayek at length:

> To act on the belief that we possess the knowledge and the power which enable us to shape the processes of society entirely to our liking, knowledge which in fact we do *not* possess, is likely to make us do much harm. In the physical sciences there may be little objection to trying to do the impossible; one might even feel that one ought not to discourage the over-confident because their experiments may after all produce some new insights. But in the social field the erroneous belief that the exercise of some power would have beneficial consequences is likely to lead to a new power to coerce other men being conferred on some authority. Even if such power is not itself bad, its exercise is likely to impede the functioning of those spontaneous ordering forces which, without understanding them, man is in fact so largely assisted in the pursuit of his aims. (2014, 371)

When human beings attempt to control complex social orders as if they are simple, the results are often disastrous. The great political experiments in central control of the twentieth century—several of which involve farming—attest to the wisdom of this observation and to the folly of ignoring it. Instead of control, Hayek sees the role of economic theory and practice—as with the theory and practice of all complex orders—as a matter of "cultivation" rather than "control" (2014, 210).

Hayek seems to think the problem of pretense is limited to the imposition of control over *social* orders. Why do we believe stark costs only come from attempts to control complex *social* orders rather than complex orders that can impact human beings in other ways? As Mark Pennington (2005) argues, we have analogous reasons to prefer market-like approaches to environmental policy. Just as we cannot control the complex market order because it is impossible to ascertain all the relevant facts, it is similarly impossible to control, protect, or manage the environmental order by central command . . . or, in contemporary parlance, through bureaucracy, policy, democratically elected officials, or deliberative bodies.

Pennington's interlocutors are "Green" political theorists and communitarians of various stripes. Many of their objections cite the selfishness of market actors and the complexity of the environment as reasons to prefer deliberative bodies to market-like processes. Pennington addresses these objections in exactly the way Hayek's comments above suggest: the complexity of the issue is exactly why we should prefer market approaches to centrally managed or command approaches. "Experience suggests that governments are not in the best position to pick industrial winners, so we have little reason to believe that they can select an appropriate development path, sustainable or otherwise" (Pennington 2005, 54). Just as we should not expect governments to succeed in centrally planning the economy, we cannot expect them to succeed in centrally protecting the environment.

In Pennington's view, the market is a better vehicle than deliberative democratic policy-making—for all the reasons specified above. However, I am less interested in arguing for or against markets than I am in suggesting that Hayek-sympathetic scholars should consider the ways in which Berry-style small farming draws on reasons familiar to the environmental debate and which undercut support for large-scale industrialized farming. In contrast with much of the literature on environmentalism, Berry (and therefore this chapter) does not rely primarily on arguments about externalities—at least not of the standard kind.[5]

I turn now to the thought of Wendell Berry to draw parallels with Hayek and develop a critique of industrialized agriculture *as planning* that impedes the functioning of spontaneous, ecological orders.

The Great Economy and Small Farm Conservation

Author, farmer, and theologian Wendell Berry occupies a unique place in this chapter. Because he is a successful essayist and novelist, his ideas are widely known and engaged, influencing scholars like Patrick Deneen (e.g., 2007, 2018, 14) and celebrities like Nick Offerman (2021). While Berry is no fan of capitalism, he is also no fan of the state, of bureaucratic or political overreach, nor of the hubris or *pretense* of those who exercise power beyond what they know. Berry sees the world as God's well-ordered house, or "Great Economy." While the ordering of that house may be known to God, it cannot be known by any one human being: the order of creation is too complex and locally variegated to come under the extensive control of a "big" farmer (nor any other human system).

This leads Berry to critique industrialized agriculture as hubristic or, to use Hayek's term, pretentious. As an alternative, Berry counsels several institutions that preserve and generate *knowledge* to a greater degree than comparatively large-scale farming operations. This knowledge helps produce healthier soil, better crops, and economically stable farms. In other words, the epistemic institutionalism of Berry parallels that of Hayek: a complex order is better served by institutions that make better use of knowledge and by institutions that do not disrupt those complex, spontaneous orders upon which we depend. For Hayek, this means not disrupting the market order. For Berry, the overall ecology—and specific sections of it like topsoil—are the orders that we must not disrupt. In this section, I focus on elements that bring Hayek and Berry together.

Berry reflects on God's ordered creation in several works. However, a collection of his essays, *Art of the Commonplace* (2003), is exceptionally well-suited to this discussion. There, Berry explicates the principles of the Great *Oikonomia* of God and the "little economies" of human beings. The Great Economy includes all of creation; nothing is left out; even the fall of a single sparrow is significant. Further, the Great Economy is (or ought to be thought of) as permanent. It is something to preserve and steward, rather than a set of resources to extract.

Some Christians resist this move, since many believe that the return of Jesus Christ will be accompanied by a "new Heavens and new Earth." Why worry about how we treat the earth we have if we will have a new one soon? In Berry's view, and in the view of many theologians, we know neither the day nor the hour of this return, and so we should treat earth as if it is the only one we will ever have. This also includes Berry's understanding of matter: we cannot create more earth; we can only treat what we already have well in the hopes that it will sustain us.

Crucially for this argument, Berry sees the Great Economy as ordered and interconnected, *but never completely knowable or effectively manipulable* by human beings. While God may have all the relevant information to intervene in nature to guide its path in grand ways, human beings are constrained (or ought to be constrained) to much more limited, localized interaction.

Analogizing directly: for Hayek, the economist cannot hope to plan an economy because he simply cannot ascertain all the relevant facts. Further, the market process enables the generation of emergent, coded information in prices that, without the market process, would not exist. In the same way, Berry sees the farmer (or any human being) as unable to scale their plans and master nature because she cannot ascertain all the relevant facts of ecology. Further, God has arranged the Great Economy so that planning over it will fare worse than working within—cultivating—the emergent, complex order of the extant ecology: pathways of farming practices are better than roads, to use a Hayekian analogy (Hayek 2010, 104).

While humans cannot know and manipulate the complete order, they may live in greater or lesser accordance with it (Berry 2003, 219–222). Berry does not think we can leave nature completely alone—we are part of nature, in his view. We can do better or worse in relation to that Great Economy.

The concept of hubris in Berry's work is nearly identical to pretense in Hayek's. For Berry, hubris is the attempt to transcend limitation and extend one's will to control more and more through grand action and planning (2003, 220). Further, hubris is often accompanied by a tendency toward abstraction and extraction (2003, 231 and 301–302). Abstraction smooths away the realities of nature to make extensive scale and planning conceptually possible. If we acknowledge the concrete realities of the Great Economy, we will be less likely to act without limits. Alternatively, abstracting away from concrete facts makes grand action possible.

Further, since hubris is a rejection of limitation, the mentality of extraction often accompanies it. If I conceive of myself as without limit, there is no reason to treat Earth as if it will go on forever or that it is connected in ways that I do not understand; I may farm the soil harder and harder until I cannot make anything grow without the assistance of petrochemical fertilizer whose seepage upsets my own drinking water and the costs of which may outstrip the gains of the farm. To quote Berry:

> Any little economy [i.e., human order] that sees itself as unlimited is obviously self-blinded. It does not see its real relation of dependence and obligation to the Great Economy; in fact, it does not see that there is a Great Economy. Instead, it calls the Great Economy "raw material" or "natural resources" or "nature" and proceeds with the business of putting it "under control." (2003, 231)

And,

> The earth may answer our pinches and pokes "only with spring" as e.e. cummings said, but if we pinch and poke too much, she can answer also

> with flood or drought, with catastrophic soil erosion, with plague and famine. Many occurrences that we call "acts of God" or "accidents of nature" are simply forthright natural responses to human provocations. (2003, 232)

Berry and Hayek share a full account of pretense/hubris: Just as Hayek saw economic and political disaster when human beings tried to plan the complex activity of economic cooperation, Berry theorized ecological disaster when human beings tried to control the complex ecological order. While neither Berry nor Hayek begin with externalities, it is clear that efforts to control complex systems, even if they result in gains for the controller, may result in disaster for people who depend on a well-cultivated complex order.

As Dan Shahar points out (2017), these ecological disasters may be limited to particular places; they need not result in an overall climate disaster. So, ecological destruction may come out in the black after cost-benefit analysis. Granted, perhaps there is a way to justify hubris in the broader economic picture. However, there is reason for concern on the agricultural topic of topsoil. As Berry and scientists point out, topsoil is an emergent, complex system. We rely upon it to cultivate crops, but our subsidized farming practices increasingly deplete the soil (Jang et al. 2021; Thaler et al. 2021). And, as a recent study shows, the financial costs of this practice are rising as well—losses incurred by the use of petrochemical fertilizer are not guaranteed to lag behind gains (Jang et al. 2021).

This implies it may eventually become necessary for governments to *further* subsidize large farms—one interference with the complex ecological order may lead to more interferences in the economic order. Indeed, the replacement of small farms by the largest players has been accompanied by enormous subsidies for farmers. These subsidies are regressive; the largest, wealthiest farms typically receive the most and cultivate a narrow range of crops (Lincicome 2020). This trend shows little sign of stopping as the number of small commercial farms continues to drop while large, industrialized farms produce a larger proportion of the agricultural output (Hoppe et al. 2010). Some estimates indicate that due to topsoil erosion, the world's topsoil will be destroyed in around sixty years (Pimentel 2006). That is hardly an outcome limited to a particular place.

While these claims are controversial, they bear an eerie similarity to Hayek's warning: interferences in the spontaneous order may work for a time but are subject to harmful, even catastrophic corrections, demanding increasingly dramatic interventions that further upset the complex order. Large-scale, industrialized farming may work for a time. However, if it continues to deplete topsoil, there will be harmful, perhaps catastrophic, consequences for future (or merely younger) generations. However, Berry's argument is not simply negative; there is more than a critique of industrialized, large-scale agriculture here.

Continuing the analogy to Hayek, Berry's work suggests that the small farm is preferable to the large, industrialized farm because small farmers can *ascertain and create better forms of knowledge*, which leads to better outcomes. This is epistemic institutionalism in a new frame. Rather than using property, exchange, and competition as ways to enable the market order to emerge and function properly, the farmer must learn how to interact with the complex, emergent order of her surrounding ecology in ways that do not destroy it. Indeed, the small farmer may simply use the same practices as industrialized agriculture and fail in the same ways; farming well and farming small are not synonymous because the small farm can be extractive and abstractly planned. The right remedy to hubris is humility and the rejection of extractive and abstract practices. Fittingly, humility comes from the Latin "*humus*" meaning "ground." The remedy for pretense is to return in humility to the soil.[6]

Beyond the attitude of humility as a remedy to hubris, Berry discusses several principles for land use, including farming (2003, 195–204). First, Berry states that to care for the land, one must be intimately familiar with it, knowledgeable in methods of care, strongly motivated, and be able to afford to care for the land. Further, Berry claims that neither principle nor money will be sufficient to motivate a person to care for the land. This rejects a simple profit-motive approach *and* an altruistic approach to motivation. Indeed, at least for now, large farms that contribute to topsoil erosion are often the most profitable (Hoppe et al. 2010). Altruistically, "doing the right thing" will wear out if it prevents us from (literally) putting food on the table. True, an owner may want to sell their land for a good price and so will have self-interested reasons to protect the topsoil; a large amount of capital and cultivated land do not (necessarily) make farmers shortsighted. However, this mistakenly assumes that a higher price could not be obtained by selling to a condominium developer; not all profitable uses of land depend on healthy soil. Even if self-interest mitigates some of these pressures, self-interest is distorted by regressive subsidies. Regressive subsidies press on the scales in favor of techniques that deplete soil health, making it rational to do so. This is especially true because soil depletion takes time—more than a generation.

Instead of either mere economic self-interest or naive altruism, Berry suggests that one can be motivated to care for the land if their interest in caring for it is "direct, dependable, and permanent" (2003, 195). What could make this the case? Berry's answer is rather inconvenient for our times:

> They will be motivated to care for the land if they can reasonably expect to live on it as long as they live. They will be more strongly motivated if they can reasonably expect that their children and grandchildren will live on it

> as long as they live. In other words, there must be a mutuality of belonging; they must feel that the land belongs to them, that they belong to it, and that this belonging is a settled and unthreatened fact. (2003, 195–196)

This suggests secure property rights, which fits nicely with many liberal theorists, including Hayek. However, most people do not often live on the same plot of land their entire lives, let alone intend for their descendants to live there as well. I set this aside for now, as the cases below may provide useful illustrations.

Last, Berry spells out the meaning of belonging to a place in the concept of land ownership. Here, I must quote Berry, as the place of property is important.

> It is well understood that ownership is an incentive to care. But there is a limit to how much land can be owned before an owner is unable to take proper care of it. The need for attention increases with the intensity of use. But the quality of attention decreases as acreage increases. (2003, 196)

First, notice that Berry endorses the importance of ownership as an incentive to care. Hence, there is a distinction between "being paid to care" and having a stake in the land. The farmer-cum-entrepreneur makes better decisions than the farmer-cum-wage laborer.

Second, Berry introduces an ingenious alteration of Locke's (1980) approach to property limitations. Rather than being limited by taking only enough so that it does not spoil or by how much land one can "improve," Berry's understanding of the complex Great Economy spells out the "enough and as good" condition in a new way. Because of the complexity of creation and the attention and knowledge it requires to interact well with that order, the more intense one's use of the land is, the more limited it must be in scope. If a billionaire wishes to buy a swath of wilderness merely to walk in it and hunt on occasion, this is similar to the impact that a farmer will have by cultivating a few acres through traditional methods. However, if a farmer wishes to clear hundreds or thousands of acres to cultivate a single variety of corn, using a variety of machines and petrochemical fertilizers to do so, this intensity of use goes beyond natural limitations, beyond knowledge and care. Such practices will be unlikely to leave the land in good enough condition for the next generation; they will not leave "enough and as good" for those who come after. Such use is hubristic because it treats a complex order as simply manipulable and, in doing so, disrupts the spontaneously ordered system of topsoil upon which we rely.

The complex order with which the farmer engages is not the market. Instead, the farmer must learn how to interact with the Great Economy. So, *within* the farm, competition is not the rule of the day. As Allen and Lueck (2002) point out, owners *could* contract out each phase of the farming process, hiring one farmer to prepare the soil, another to plant, another to tend, another to harvest, and so on. But, following the analogy, the issue is not specialization by farming task; it is knowledge of farming practice as it uniquely relates to specific species, climes, topography, and soil preservation. It would likely be too costly and time-consuming to educate each contracted farmer on the local eccentricities of ecology.

Summing up, Berry's epistemic institutionalism is driven by the relationship between the complex order of the Great Economy and the farmer's need for knowledge of particular facts that enable her to interact with and benefit from that order without upsetting it. One internally complex and emergent element of that order, topsoil, is especially important for farmers. Further, Berry argues that the size of the farmer's endeavor is determined by a combination of their knowledge and the intensity with which they intend to act in the Great Economy. Rightly calibrating the scale of the small farm depends on how knowledgeable the farmer is and the assumption that they do not accept methods that destroy the underlying order upon which they rely. Part of these commitments is an acceptance of the extended time horizon implied by intergenerational care for the land.

Hence, industrialized agriculture as a set of institutions fails in comparison to small, traditional farms by Berry's lights because they cannot hope to know all the relevant facts to farm at that scale. As Berry puts it, "[j]ust the changing shape or topography of the land makes for differences of the most formidable kind. Abstractions never cross these boundaries without either ceasing to be abstractions or doing damage" (2003, 303). So, large-scale, intensive farming will necessarily do damage because it cannot hope to (or does not attempt) transform abstractions of farming into applications of farming at the micro-level. Further, intensive, large farms are extractive—they gain greater profits at the cost of upsetting and depleting the underlying complex order of topsoil.

Why do we see so much large-scale farming? If it does not make good use of local knowledge, wouldn't such farms shrink over time? First, the feedback loop is weak in the crucial case of topsoil: industrial methods deplete topsoil over time, not all at once. Second, regressive farm subsidies have a distorting effect.

Combining Berry and Hayek allows us to provide two additional arguments against regressive farm subsidies—likely their closest point of agreement.[7] Regressive subsidies distort the chain of knowledge from the small farmer to the market by artificially expanding the size of the farm. Regressive subsidies also *incentivize* externalities rather than working to internalize costs.

First, large farms that employ local knowledge-destroying techniques receive subsidies. According to Berry's argument on complexity, farming at this scale entails a loss of knowledge in application: the greater the scale and intensity of farming, the less the farmer is able to understand and make productive use of the complex local ecology. This destroyed knowledge is both environmentally and economically salient. Without subsidies, farmers must turn a profit based on their knowledge, planting different crops and cultivating the land according to the local optimal approach. *With* subsidies, farmers can forego some of that knowledge to produce subsidized crops, especially the big five: corn, soybeans, wheat, rice, and cotton (Lincicome 2020). Hence, without subsidies, we would likely *not* see the massive monocrop agriculture that taxpayers currently support. Without subsidies, farmers would likely choose to cultivate crops that are better suited to their particular context and would lack artificial incentives to monocrop. Removing regressive subsidies would therefore shrink the size of the farm and diversify its produce.

Second, because industrialized agriculture depletes topsoil health, leading to the use of expensive fertilizer and eventual "dead soil," subsidizing such farms actually *incentivizes* negative externalities. While there are familiar negative spillover effects from the use of fertilizer (e.g., harmful algae blooms), the relevant point is the intertemporal negative externality of depleted topsoil. By subsidizing industrialized agriculture, we make gains in the present by significantly discounting the future. Hayek and Berry both argue against interferences with complex order because they lead to catastrophic corrections. Hence, these subsidies are doubly bad: they interfere with the agricultural market, *and* they provide incentives to disrupt the complex order of topsoil, both of which we rely upon and both of which can lead to dramatic, destructive "corrections" in the future.

Taking Berry and Hayek together leads us to phase out regressive subsidies: we should not incentivize industrialized, monocrop agriculture. Removing regressive subsidies would improve the chances of small, traditional farms relative to their large competitors. This is, at least, some indication that the disparate views of Berry and Hayek can be brought together into an actionable policy: one need not reject liberalism to support policies that acknowledge the value of humility before complex phenomena.

Before moving on to Berry's further criticisms of industrialized agriculture, I should look the elephant in the room in the eye: I am not suggesting that industrialized agriculture be tossed away. That would *certainly* (rather than merely probably) lead to catastrophic outcomes. Our food system is extremely reliant on industrialized methods and should not simply be abruptly rejected. Doing so would be hubris of another kind. Instead, the argument above calls for experimentation in the direction of traditional farming and a gradual elimination of regressive subsidies. Before we can discuss ways forward, Berry's more radical criticisms should be understood.

Two Paths Diverge: Membership, Blasphemy, and the Small Farm

For the sake of argument, assume that Berry's epistemic arguments are wrong. Assume there is a way of cultivating monocrop agriculture on a single farm the size of Texas without subsidy and without negative externality.[8] The farm shifts how much land it cultivates according to the price it can obtain on the market. There is, so far as I can see, no Hayekian argument against such a farm. Berry, however, would take issue. While Berry and Hayek walk a similar path on epistemic institutionalism, those paths diverge when they meet Berry's further theological constraints.

While his epistemic arguments on the Great Economy and the advantages of the small farm provide connecting points to Hayek and liberal political economy, Berry's normative commitment to place-based membership and sacral treatment of creation are further, non-liberal reasons for traditional small farms. Hayek's position on economic activities is governed by the price mechanism and subjective preference satisfaction in the market. Related to (and moving beyond) his epistemological defense, Berry draws on what he thinks to be true in theology and human nature to defend a limited scale of farming: Industrialized agriculture is destructive of one's membership in community and is itself blasphemous. The Great Economy informs both critiques.

First, the Great Economy informs our understanding of membership. For Berry, God orders the divine *Oikonomia* in such a way that it is not merely a sum of its parts—the good of a place is not a matter of aggregation. Instead, because each is connected to all (more or less), we are part of a membership "inextricably joined to each other, indebted to each other, receiving significance and worth from each other and from the whole" (2003, 233). Of course, this relationship is constituted between human beings. Hence, farming practices that eliminate or pervert connections between independent human beings in favor of industrialized operations are morally suspect. Techniques that lead to oppression or isolation are to be rejected. The factory farm includes a high degree of cooperation, but much of this is mediated by machinery and organized at scale. As Allen and Lueck (2002) show, smaller farms do tend to coordinate with neighboring farms to a greater degree than larger operations. Berry's focus on small farms and communities is empirically supported.

However, Berry's understanding of membership is more substantial than an impulse to coordinate with what we would typically refer to as neighbors.

Instead, membership is also intertemporal; we are connected to our ancestors and descendants. These relationships are not to be abstracted—they are relationships constituted by concrete particulars. Hence, one's use of traditional practices may be epistemically advantageous if it provides leverage on the complexities of ecology—traditions often encase knowledge. Traditions also enable us to connect to a place, one's grandparents, and one's unborn descendants. When the community comes together for harvest, they do so in membership with their deceased great-grandparents and their unborn grandchildren, as well as with their living neighbors. Gathering for a harvest feast to enjoy the product of one's labors alongside neighbors and being indebted to one's ancestors acknowledges and deepens our membership. Replacing these connections to practices and place with methods that abstract away from the particulars of place and person is therefore morally suspect, in Berry's view. Large-scale industrialized agriculture wipes away these connections. Even if it is better money, it is worse for one's membership in the Great Economy.

If all this was not suspect enough for liberals, Berry's idea of membership extends even further, including the non-human living things and the topography upon which they depend. "One is obliged to 'consider the lilies of the field,' not because they are lilies or because they are exemplary, but because they are fellow members and because, as fellow members, we and the lilies are in certain critical ways alike" (2003, 233). We are all caught up in the Great Economy, not just as fellow humans but as *creatures* of God. We should not reroute the river or clear-cut the forest for the same sort of reasons we should not engage in industrialized agriculture. These practices upset our connection to the full range of neighbors: human, animal, vegetable, living, dead, and yet to come. Here, Berry clearly diverges from Hayek in ways that Deneen suggested at the outset of this chapter. Berry sees human beings as inseparably part of creation, eschewing any simple distinctions between nature and human beings, natural and social phenomena.

Second, industrialized agriculture is unacceptable for Berry because it is blasphemous. There are no unsacred places for Berry, only sacred places and desecrated places (2001). Why is this? All of creation is both a gift of the creator and intimately tied to and dependent upon the creator. Because God is so intimately involved in creation, to treat creation as if it were not a gift of God is to curse God, to "[fling] God's gifts into His face, as if they were of no worth beyond that assigned to them by our destruction of them" (2003, 307). Put another way, something's market price is not necessarily reflective of its value in the Great Economy. Instead, it has value because God created it to be used as a gift. While some farming methods acknowledge, treasure, and respect this gift, others are blasphemous.

What makes farming glorifying to God? Here, we come back around to criteria that relate to the good work of complexity-preserving farming and membership:

> To work without pleasure or affection, to make a product that is not both useful and beautiful, is to dishonor God, nature, the thing that is made, and whomever it is made for. This is blasphemy: to make shoddy work of the work of God. But such blasphemy is not possible when the entire Creation is understood as holy and when the works of God are understood as embodying and thus revealing His spirit. (2003, 312)

So, to treat the land as holy is to make good use of it. The exact meaning of what it means to make good use of something is what connects us back to membership. Berry's membership and blasphemy objections to industrialized agriculture are interwoven:

> The aims of production, profit, efficiency, economic growth, and technological progress imply, as I have said, no social or ecological standards, and in practice they submit to none. But there is another set of aims that does imply a standard, and these aims are freedom (which is pretty much a synonym for personal and local self-sufficiency), pleasure (that is, our gladness to be alive), and longevity or sustainability (by which we signify our wish that human freedom and pleasure may last). The standard implied by all of these aims is health. They depend ultimately and inescapably on the health of nature; the idea that freedom and pleasure can last long in a diseased world is preposterous. (2003, 202)

As Berry argues elsewhere, health *just is* membership (2003, 144–158). Berry argues for small, traditional farming for epistemic reasons that Hayekian liberals can accept or at least entertain. However, his commitment to these methods is bound up in a love of beauty in creation, connection to one's neighbors in the Great Economy, and the flourishing of individuals. The Texas-sized soy farm isn't just destroying useful information; it is ugly, alienating, and blasphemous.

> That is not to suggest that we can live harmlessly, or strictly at our own expense; we depend upon other creatures and survive by their deaths. To live, we must daily break the body and shed the blood of Creation. When we do this knowingly, lovingly, skillfully, reverently, it is a sacrament. When we do it ignorantly, greedily, clumsily, destructively, it is a desecration. In such desecration we condemn ourselves to spiritual and moral loneliness, and others to want. (2003, 304)

All this leads us to one last parallel between Berry and Hayek, one that can help ground a liberal commitment to care for the environment through smaller scale, epistemically bounded approaches. Both Berry and Hayek are concerned that hubris/pretense in farming and politics are connected to deep (i.e., more than epistemic) character faults.

For Berry, when we interact with creation "ignorantly, greedily, clumsily, and destructively" (2003, 304), it is a deep moral and theological wrong—a desecration. A person who acts like this is doomed to "moral and spiritual loneliness" (2003, 304). They are alienated from themselves, from their neighbors (broadly conceived), and sin blasphemously against God. No well-informed person wants the moral, spiritual, and practical wrongs described here. Putting it harshly, the large-scale agriculturalist feeds many people, but at a steep moral cost.

Hayek's "Why the Worst Get on Top" presents a similar account of character and planning in *The Road to Serfdom* (1944). In Hayek's estimation, the political actor who can organize and carry out an economic plan for society is, by necessity, unscrupulous. To carry out any great plan, they must be willing to cut across a complex fabric of relationships, figuratively and literally destroying life in the process. The political actor who works on the pretense of knowledge is not merely wrong; they are wicked. James Scott (1998) picked out this similarity, noting the complexity of social and ecological orders and the willingness of planners to cut across both disastrous and (Berry would say) desecrating effects.

Beyond the epistemic features of large-scale agriculture, liberals should consider the moral dangers of character inherent in such planning. This is not to draw an equivalence where there is none: taking a human life and clearing a field for monocropping are far from morally equivalent. Instead, the point is that liberals should care about the disposition required to engage in complexity-destroying activity. It is not enough to say such planning is merely *epistemically* flawed. It is also the work of an agent who sees themselves as masters of nature or commanders of human beings; neither is a suitable liberal attitude. Though not equivalent, both deserve harsh liberal criticism. Liberals should cultivate humility in the face of complex phenomena, whether economic or ecological.

Conclusion: Implications and Exploring Possibilities

Critics believe liberalism is inadequate to the task of environmentalism or "creation care" because it separates human beings from nature, thereby placing them over and superior to it. By bringing Berry and Hayek into conversation, we can reject this claim. While Berry does see humans as part of the Great

Economy, I have not relied on that element of his work when drawing comparisons to Hayek. (In fact, I suspect Berry would greatly dislike the comparison.) What *is* sufficient to reject the impulse toward manipulation is the identification of complex orders and the moral, practical, and personal response of humility, accompanied by the exploration of comparatively better epistemic institutions. Contrary to the critics, Hayekians can read Berry and endorse much of its epistemic components, albeit for theologically unladen reasons. Humility is the essential thing, and this is something Berry *and* Hayek value with respect to complex orders. Liberals can encounter and cultivate nature without seeking to "command" or "plan" it. In fact, as the last section showed, there are both epistemic and moral reasons to look at large-scale, industrialized agriculture.

Accordingly, this chapter provides those who find Hayek's arguments on market order compelling pro tanto reasons to prefer small, traditional farms. Of course, the parallels between Berry and Hayek can be swamped by other concerns, such as the current reliance on large-scale farming and its success along several important dimensions. However, so far as the analogy holds, as I have argued, Austrian-leaning scholars should prefer experimentation with farming arrangements that make use of Berry-style institutions on the grounds that they may be epistemically superior to large-scale farms. If there is more knowledge of traditional practices, there are potential gains to be made in the market. That is to say, we "should" experiment because we can learn more and *earn* more through alternative methods. Berry says as much, even though he rejects pure profit-seeking.

Further, as both Hayek and Berry argue, the attitude of the planner is hubristic and pretentious in both the epistemic and moral senses. Liberals should take an interest in farming approaches that acknowledge the limits of complexity because they are reflective of humility, a worthwhile moral value for liberalism. At the very least, Berry and Hayek provide us reason to reject regressive farm subsidies. If liberals are not prepared to prefer Berry-style farming, we can at least agree that the economic scales should not be prejudiced against them through intervention in the market.

The theological component of Berry's work also suggests that many religious communities will see value in this approach. Indeed, many do and have various "commitments to place" as a result (LeVasseur 2017). Tradition, contrary to what Deneen-style critics of liberalism may contend, may play an important epistemic role in farming *under Hayekian lights*. Some liberals have implicitly or explicitly endorsed the role of tradition (e.g., Hayek 2013; Gaus 2021). Unfortunately, that point seems to have been lost on critics of liberalism. Perhaps this is because liberals seem reluctant to try or endorse these methods. Again, while commitments to place and tradition may be contrary to the liberal ethos, they are not impossible within a liberal order, nor do they contradict liberal principles.

Where does this leave us? Consider the reality of industrialized agriculture alongside the trend of farming in the United States (Hoppe et al. 2010). On one hand, the number of small commercial farms decreases as competition from large commercial farms drives them out. While large farms benefit from various returns to scale, it is unclear whether these gains are sustainable considering topsoil loss (Jang et al. 2021). Further, as Allen and Lueck (2002, 201–202) point out, various factors, including weather and seasonal growth, mean that some large-scale farming is economically irrational. Add to this that the number of *non-commercial* small farms has climbed over the past decade, now accounting for more than half of all farms (Hoppe et al. 2010).

While non-commercial farms are *much* smaller and *much* less productive than large commercial farms, the point is not where we are now but where we might go. These trends indicate an opportunity for experimentation with traditional farming practices and learning among consumers. Perhaps surprisingly, two of Berry's (2003, 203–204) practical suggestions for reform are the growth of local economies about farming and the increased knowledge of consumers around traditional agriculture. Indeed, Deneen's (2018, 41) "more local forms of self-government by choice" seems an emerging possibility among non-commercial farms.

Market forces may shift toward traditional farming, even if large-scale farming remains a significant part of the food system. The case of craft beer is instructive. A generation ago, independent breweries producing "craft beer" were not the norm. Because of clever entrepreneurship, shifting consumer demand, lower equipment, and lower advertising costs, the number of craft breweries rose dramatically between 2006 and 2016 (Thompson, 2018).[9]

If consumers want a locally grown product cultivated through traditional or regenerative methods, there are avenues to explore. This is particularly true for community-supported agriculture (CSA). Within driving distance of my home in Durham, NC, (at least) two farms offer CSA options, which allow consumers to pay upfront for a weekly share of produce throughout the growing season. Coon Rock Farm (n.d.) and Elysian Fields Farm each offer distinct products and supply several local restaurants to the acclaim of a James Beard award-winning chef (Elysian Fields Farm, n.d.). In the case of Elysian Fields, the farm is neither an inherited, ancestral plot nor is it obvious that it will remain in the family for generations—perhaps the methods that Berry prefers are possible without the sort of intergenerational motivations he prescribes.

For Little Way Farm, which supplies individual consumers as well as a local retailer and restaurant, these practices are carried out in the context of a community committed to a "life of prayer, simplicity, and voluntary poverty alongside the poor" (Little Way Farm, n.d.). The goal of community within a liberal, market society is not hopeless. There is a deep epistemic coherence between

Berry and Hayek, coherence that makes experimentation with the traditional small farm alongside like-minded others worth trying under liberal lights. Some reasons for farming in this way go beyond the liberal frame and are non-liberal or illiberal in some important sense. However, this does not mean people who want to practice a different life have no place in liberal society; in fact, they may play a vibrant role in the local economy and the health of the soil.

Notes

1. The title is a pun on Abraham Singer's *The Form of the Firm* (2018). Unfortunately, *The Nature of the Farm* is already taken by Allen and Lueck (2002).
2. Many thanks to the editors of this volume, the other contributors (especially Abigail Staysa and Edgar Cook), Nora Hanigan, Matthew Young, and Jeff Spinner-Halev for their excellent comments.
3. As others have discussed, Deneen's work has significant historical and argumentative flaws. His view is used here to discuss and bridge a gap between illiberal critics and Hayekian thinking on the environment. Importantly, Deneen's views have intensified since the publication of *Why Liberalism Failed* (2018).
4. I am not committed to such a separation. Even so, as I discuss in the introduction, it is argumentatively useful to bracket that position in the process of drawing parallels between Hayek and Berry. I introduce other aspects of Berry's thought which are less complementary to Hayek's position.
5. Berry's arguments may be redescribed as concerns over intertemporal externalities. There are also elements of the standard externality debate, but the main component of Berry's view alongside Hayek, complexity, is not primarily about externalities but about making better use of knowledge within the farm.
6. I thank Andrew Borror for this apt etymological note.
7. Berry does advocate for government support for small farms. But the removal of regressive subsidies is a move in the right direction for both Hayekians and Berry.
8. I thank Peter Boettke for this hypothetical.
9. Thanks to Erwin Dekker for this example.

References

Allen, Douglas, and Dean Lueck. 2002. *The Nature of the Farm: Contracts, Risk, and Organization in Agriculture.* Cambridge, MA: The MIT Press.

Berry, Wendell. 2001. "How to be a Poet." *Poetry*, January.

———. 2003. *The Art of the Commonplace: The Agrarian Essays of Wendell Berry.* Edited by Norman Wirzba. Berkeley, CA: Counterpoint.

Boettke, Peter. 2018. *F. A. Hayek: Economics, Political Economy, and Social Philosophy.* London: Palgrave Macmillan.

Coon Rock Farm. n.d. "About Us." Farm Website. Retrieved June 13, 2022. https://www.coonrockfarm.com/aboutus.asp.

Deneen, Patrick. 2007. "My Afternoon with Mr. Berry." Personal blog. Accessed May 10, 2022. http://patrickdeneen.blogspot.com/2007/05/my-afternoon-with-mr-berry.html.

———. 2018. *Why Liberalism Failed.* New Haven, CT: Yale University Press.

Gaus, Gerald. 2021. *The Open Society and Its Complexities.* New York, NY: Oxford UP.

Hayek, Friedrich A. 1944. *The Collected Works of F. A. Hayek, Volume II: The Road to Serfdom.* Edited by Bruce Caldwell. Chicago, IL: University of Chicago Press, reprinted 2007.

———. 1945. "The Use of Knowledge in Society." *American Economic Review* 35 (4): 519–530.

———. 2010. *The Collected Works of F. A. Hayek, Volume 13: Studies on the Abuse and Decline of Reason: Texts and Documents.* Edited by Bruce Caldwell. Chicago, IL: The University of Chicago Press.

———. 2013. *Law, Legislation, and Liberty.* New York, NY: Routledge.

———. 2014. *The Collected Works of F. A. Hayek, Volume 15: The Market and Other Orders.* Edited by Bruce Caldwell. Chicago, IL: The University of Chicago Press.

Hoppe, Robert A., James M. MacDonald, and Penni Korb. 2010. "Small Farms in the United States: Persistence Under Pressure." Economic Information Bulletin No. (EIB-63). *Economic Research Service U.S. Department of Agriculture.*

Jang, W. S., J. C. Neff, Y. Im, L. Doro, and J. E. Herrick. 2021. "The Hidden Costs of Land Degradation in US Maize Agriculture." *Earth's Future* 9: e2020EF001641.

Klein, E. 2021, September 10. "Are We More Polarized or Just Weirder? The Economist Tyler Cowen Discusses Political Division, G.D.P. Growth and Classical Music." In *The Ezra Klein Show*. New York Times. https://www.nytimes.com/2021/09/10/opinion/ezra-klein-podcast-tyler-cowen.html.

LeVasseur, Todd. 2017. *Religious Agrarianism and the Return to Place: From Values to Practice in Sustainable Agriculture.* Albany, NY: State University of New York Press.

Lincicome, Scott. 2020. "Examining America's Farm Subsidy Problem." *Cato Institute.* https://www.cato.org/commentary/examining-americas-farm-subsidy-problem.

Little Way Farm. n.d. "About Us." Farm website. Accessed June 13, 2022. https://littlewayfarmsilercity.com/community.

Locke, John. 1980. *Second Treatise of Government.* Edited by C. B. Macpherson. Indianapolis, IN: Hackett.

Milbank, John, and Adrian Pabst. 2016. *The Politics of Virtue: Post-Liberalism and the Human Future.* New York, NY: Rowman and Littlefield.

Offerman, Nick. 2021. *Where the Deer and the Antelope Play*. Random House.

Pennington, Mark. 2005. "Liberty, Markets, and Environmental Values: A Hayekian Defense of Free-Market Environmentalism." *The Independent Review* 10 (1): 39–57.

Pimentel, David. 2006. "Soil Erosion: A Food and Environmental Threat." *Environment, Development and Sustainability* 8: 119–137.

Scott, James C. 1998. *Seeing Like a State: How Certain Schemes to Improve the Human Condition Have Failed*. New Haven, CT: Yale University Press.

Shahar, Dan. 2017. "Hayek's Legacy for Environmental Political Economy." In *Interdisciplinary Studies of the Market Order: New Applications of Market Process Theory*, edited by Peter J. Boettke, Christopher J. Coyne, and Virgil Henry Storr, 87–110. New York, NY: Rowman and Littlefield.

Singer, Abraham. 2018. *The Form of the Firm: A Normative Political Theory of the Corporation*. New York, NY: Oxford University Press.

Thaler, Evan A., Isaac J. Larsen, and Qian Yu. 2021. "The Extent of Soil Loss Across the US Corn Belt." *Proceedings of the National Academy of Sciences* 118 (8): e1922375118.

Thompson, Derek. 2018. "Craft Beer Is the Strangest, Happiest Economic Story in America." *The Atlantic*. Accessed June 13, 2022. https://www.theatlantic.com/business/archive/2018/01/craft-beer-industry/550850/.

5

Friedrich Hayek on Freedom and the Rule of Law in *The Constitution of Liberty*

Abigail Staysa

THIS CHAPTER ANALYZES FRIEDRICH HAYEK'S defense of freedom and his political ideal of the rule of law in *The Constitution of Liberty* with a view to clarifying the differences between Hayek's political-philosophical project and classical political philosophy. One of Hayek's more thoughtful and critical graduate students has described Hayek's account of the rule of law in *The Constitution of Liberty* as "the most important contemporary formulation of the principle" (Miller 1979, 182).[1] Of course, Hayek's presentation of the rule of law falls within his broader political and philosophical project that reformulates the classical liberalism of Locke, Hume, and Smith (Miller 1979, 183). According to Hayek, the rule of law is essential to "preserve and enlarge freedom," to use Locke's phrase. It does this by securing a private sphere of freedom and a framework of rights within which individuals can pursue their own plans and interests without the encroachment of other individuals or political authorities. On Hayek's understanding, the primary purpose of government is not to educate human beings or to legislate the activities and conduct to be expected and forbidden of citizens, as in classical political thought, but to delimit and secure a private sphere within which individuals are free to determine their own lives and courses of conduct (Hayek [1960] 2011, 129, 309–310, c.f. Aristotle NE 1.2.1094a26-b6, 2.1.1103b3-5). Much Hayekian scholarship, understandably, focuses on the relationship between freedom and the rule of law (see Hasnas 1995; Zwicki 2003). This chapter focuses on the principles of Hayek's thought for another purpose, namely, for distinguishing and clarifying the differences between Hayek's political philosophical project and classical political philosophy. Hayek makes occasional references to ancient authors throughout *The Constitution of Liberty*. He even suggests that some of his ideas are a reformulation of "old truths" with roots in ancient political thought (Hayek [1960] 2011, 48). This chapter aims to discuss the differences between Hayek and the ancients on the following issues: the meaning of freedom and the rule of law, the ultimate aims of political life, the status of the individual and individuality, the nature and naturalness of law, and the nature and legitimating ground of political authority or coercion.

Hayek's Defense of Freedom

Hayek begins his defense of individual freedom in the first section of *The Constitution of Liberty* by clarifying the definition of freedom at the center of his project. According to Hayek, freedom, or the politically relevant definition of freedom, is the condition of an absence of coercion. Freedom is "the state in which a man is not subject to coercion by the arbitrary will of another or others" (Hayek [1960] 2011, 58). What is essential for freedom is not that one has a wide array of choices available, the ability to attain what one wants, or even the ability to act in accordance with one's considered deliberation rather than one's passions. Rather, what matters is that a person can "follow his own plans and intentions" and direct himself "toward ends for which he has been persistently striving" rather than merely performing "necessities created by others in order to make him do what they want" (Hayek [1960] 2011, 61). In brief, freedom consists in being free from manipulation or the power of another to shape one's own life path and to pursue one's ends (Hayek [1960] 2011, 60–61).

Hayek distinguishes this conception of freedom from three other definitions that he dismisses. The first notion that he rejects is "political freedom," or the "participation of men in the choice of their government, in the process of legislation, and in the control of administration" (Hayek [1960] 2011, 61–64). Hayek notes that Aristotle embraces this definition in *Politics* when describing the activity of free citizens as ruling and being ruled in turn (*Politics* 6. 3.1317b; Hayek [1960] 2011, 61). Hayek dismisses this definition as the aim of liberal government on the grounds that there may be a tension between collective political freedom and individual freedom; the former may exist where the latter does not. The second and more interesting definition of freedom that Hayek rejects is "inner freedom" or "metaphysical freedom," that is, the capacity to act in accord with one's rational deliberation or lasting conviction as opposed to fleeting impulse (Hayek [1960] 2011, 64). Hayek acknowledges that we may call men who are unable to choose well or are unable to carry out a resolution unfree or enslaved to their passions, but this is a distinct problem from being under the coercion of another. The third definition of freedom that Hayek distinguishes and rejects is the strength or ability to do whatever one pleases or desires (Hayek [1960] 2011, 65). Hayek emphasizes that freedom is not the power to do anything one wants but consists of not having one's environment and circumstances controlled by another such that one is made to serve another's ends rather than one's own (Hayek [1960] 2011, 71).

The obvious question that arises is why Hayek rejects three robust definitions of freedom in favor of a minimalist definition, one that he himself describes as a "negative" notion. As Hayek says, freedom understood as the absence of coercion "does not mean all good things or the absence of all evils." In fact, it may even mean "freedom to starve" or "make costly mistakes" (Hayek [1960] 2011, 68–69). As such, it does not necessarily guarantee positive outcomes but "becomes positive only through what we make of it" (Hayek [1960] 2011, 70). If freedom, defined as noncoercion, sometimes leads to undesirable outcomes, why does Hayek endorse it over other forms that preclude negative results?

Further, as Hayek acknowledges, a defense of freedom as non-coercion is, paradoxically, reliant on the use of coercion; coercion is needed to secure and preserve the conditions for freedom. As Hayek notes, "coercion cannot be altogether avoided because the only way to protect it [freedom] is by the threat of coercion" (Hayek [1960] 2011, 71). Liberal political thought attempts to deal with this problem by granting a "monopoly of coercion" to the state and then limiting the state's application of coercion and force to only those circumstances in which it is absolutely necessary for preserving freedom (Hayek [1960] 2011, 72). According to that argument, the state is justified in holding a monopoly on coercion because it delimits and protects "known private spheres," wherein individuals are free to determine their own conduct within the bounds of clearly defined rules. By aiming to preserve a private sphere of freedom, the liberal state authorizes as broad a range of human activities and behaviors as possible. It does not legislate the activities and conduct that are expected and forbidden of citizens, as in classical political thought, but promises to secure a private sphere within which individuals are free to discover for themselves how they will shape their individual lives. Hayek, interestingly, does not argue that the state's monopoly on coercion is justified by the consent of the people or through a social contract but rather by the state's limited use of coercion to protect freedom and individuality.

Hayek's defense of freedom as non-coercion is grounded in an account of the nature and limits of human knowledge. The purpose of Chapter Two of *The Constitution of Liberty* is to establish that no single human being possesses the comprehensive knowledge that would be needed to govern or instruct individuals in matters of individual choice. As Hayek says, "the case for individual freedom rests chiefly on the recognition of the inevitable ignorance of all of us concerning a great many of the factors on which the achievement of our ends and welfare depends" (Hayek [1960] 2011, 80). What is "essential" is that each individual is able to act on "his particular knowledge, always unique, at least in so far as it refers to some particular circumstances and that he be able to use his individual skills . . . for his own individual purpose" (Hayek [1960] 2011, 80). Hayek is in agreement with the classical tradition that knowledge of particular circumstances is essential for political judgment and action (consider, for example, Aristotle NE 2.2.1103b34-1104a10). But he departs from that tradition by elevating individuality and individual purpose. Hayek argues that individuals benefit from a state that limits coercion and protects a private sphere for individual action and choice because the purposes and choices of individuals cannot be determined at the level of generality or abstraction.

There is a connection between Hayek and Edmund Burke on this point. Leo Strauss describes the fundamental difference between Burke and the classical tradition of political philosophy in the final paragraph of *Natural Right and History* as follows:

> Burke disagreed with the classics in regard to the genesis of the sound social order because he disagreed with them in regard to the character of the sound social order. As he saw it, the sound social or political order must not be "formed upon a regular plan or with any unity of design" because such "systematical" proceedings, such "presumption in the wisdom of human contrivances," would be incompatible with the highest possible degree of "personal liberty"; the state must pursue "the greatest variety of ends" and must as little as possible "sacrifice any one of them to another, or to the whole." It must be concerned with "individuality" or have the highest possible regard for "individual feeling and individual interest." It is for this reason that the genesis of the sound social order must not be a process guided by reflection but must come as close as possible to a natural, imperceptible process: the natural is the individual, and the universal is a creature of the understanding. Naturalness and free flowering of individuality are the same. Hence the free development of the individuals in their individuality, far from leading to chaos, is productive of the best order, an order which is not only compatible with "some irregularity in the whole mass" but requires it. . . . The quarrel between the ancients and the moderns concerns eventually, and perhaps even from the beginning, the status of "individuality." Burke himself was still too deeply imbued with the spirit of "sound antiquity" to allow the concern with individuality to overpower the concern with virtue. (Strauss 1953, 322–323)

If the status of individuality distinguishes ancient and modern political thought, then Hayek falls squarely in the modern camp. Neither Plato nor Aristotle argued that the purpose of government is to encourage a diversity of ends for the development of individuality or that each individual is an equally competent judge of the circumstances or even of what is good for himself. The ancients reject the notion that the human good is subjective or individually determined and argue, by contrast, that correct judgment about what is good and bad in the circumstances is difficult and requires virtue and an experienced eye in such matters (Aristotle NE 6.11.1143b13-14). In other words, for the ancients, there is a human good that is objective, that accords with our nature, and that is discoverable by reason—or more precisely, the reason of the best man, understood as he who has acquired the characteristics of virtue and has experience in judging the circumstances and actions of life. Hayek begins Chapter Two with a reference to the "Socratic maxim" that "the recognition of our ignorance is the beginning of wisdom," but his conclusion entails a fundamental departure from the teaching of ancient political philosophy (cf. Hayek [1960] 2011, 73).

Hayek's political project and his defense of freedom must, therefore, be understood as a fundamental departure from the classical tradition, despite Hayek's numerous references to ancient authors and his occasional suggestion that his ideal has ancient roots. For example, consider the epigraph to the Introduction of *The Constitution of Liberty*, an epigraph that includes several selective inclusions and omissions from Pericles' famous speech, "The Funeral Oration," in Thucydides' *History of the Peloponnesian War*.

> What was the road by which we reached our position, what the form of government under which our greatness grew, what the national habits out of which it sprang? . . . If we look to the laws, they afford equal justice to all in their private differences . . . The freedom which we enjoy in our government extends also to our ordinary life . . . But all this ease in our private relations does not make us lawless as citizens. Against this fear is our chief safeguard, teaching us to obey the magistrates and the laws, particularly such as regard the protection of the injured, whether they are actually on the statute book, or belong to that code which, although unwritten, yet cannot be broken without acknowledged disgrace. (Thucydides, II.36–38)

In the paragraph following the quotation from Thucydides, Hayek notes that it is necessary to make "old truths" palatable to successive generations. As he says, "if old truths are to retain their hold on men's minds, they must be restated in the language and concepts of successive generations" (Hayek [1960] 2011, 48). What old truths does Hayek purport to translate into modern language? Does he mean to suggest that his defense of individual liberty and the rule of law is a modern restatement of the principles of classical Athens that, according to Pericles, made the Athenians great? Hayek tells us, quoting Pericles' speech as reported by Thucydides, that the Athenians "afford equal justice to all in their private differences," that their public freedom extends to private life, and that while the city enjoys "ease in private relations," it commands lawful obedience in matters of public or common concern. These passages, in other words, might be taken to imply a kinship between the portrayal of classical Athens, on the one hand, and the principles of Hayek's own project, on the other. But does Hayek's abbreviated version of the speech accurately capture Pericles' portrayal and praise of democratic Athens, as Thucydides reports it? One must compare Hayek's shortened selections from the speech with the full text of the passage in question. Hayek's omissions are included in brackets.

> What was the road by which we reached our position, what the form of government under which our greatness grew, what the national habits out of which it sprang? [We enjoy a form of government that does not emulate the institutions of our neighbors; indeed, we ourselves are more often the model for others than their imitators. Democracy is the name we give to it, since we manage our affairs in the interests of the many not the few.] If we look to the laws, they afford equal justice to all in their private differences [but in terms of public distinction preferment for office is determined on merit, not by rank but by personal worth; moreover, poverty is no bar to anyone who has it in them to benefit the city in some way, however lowly their status.] The freedom which we enjoy in our government extends also to our ordinary life [where we show no animosity at our neighbors' choice of pleasures, nor cast aspersions that may hurt even if they do not harm.] But all this ease in our private relations does not make us lawless as citizens. Against this fear is our chief safeguard, teaching us to obey the magistrates and the laws, particularly such as regard the protection of the injured, whether they are actually on the statute book, or belong to that code which, although unwritten, yet cannot be broken without acknowledged disgrace. (Thucydides, II.36–38; bracketed text from Jeremy Mynott's translation)

I draw attention to three aspects of the full passage that distinguish the classical position from Hayek's. First, Pericles refers to Athens as a democracy because the democratic principle (equality) is reflected in the regime's concern for the welfare of many over the few, but Pericles also acknowledges the presence of the aristocratic principle (virtue) in the regime's preference for distributing political offices on the basis of merit or worth. The city's combination and accommodation of both democratic and aristocratic principles (equality *and* virtue) make it something of a mixed regime and point to an important aspect of Athenian greatness that Hayek does not mention. In Hayek's later discussion of the rule of law, he argues that no formal criterion of justice beyond "generality and equality" is said to be an essential feature of his political ideal (Hayek [1960] 2011, 318). This means that in matters of distributive justice, or the allocation of political honors and goods on the basis of a notion of merit, the government ought to avoid distributing goods (economic and political) to particular individuals altogether. Instead, it ought to lay down laws that are "general and abstract" in character and equally applied to all citizens. As a result, Hayek denies the aristocratic principle any place in the political architecture that he recommends. His reasons for this go back to his thesis that human beings are constitutionally unable to possess the comprehensive knowledge needed for the central direction of shared resources or political offices according to one common plan (Miller 1979, 187). Hence, whereas the ancients accommodated both the democratic and the aristocratic views of the requirements of justice in the form of a mixed regime, Hayek does not. Rather, he strives to eschew any decision about matters of distributive justice altogether.

The second aspect separating Hayek from the classical tradition is the public-spirited character of the latter. Pericles praises the Athenian regime as democratic on the grounds that poverty does not preclude one from benefiting the city, presumably by sacrificing one's life in battle for one's country.[2] Hayek's omission of this sentence reflects his general prioritization of the freedom and self-interest of the individual over a concern with the freedom of the city as a whole.

Thirdly, Hayek quotes Pericles' statement that the Athenians are tolerant of the "choice of pleasures" that others pursue in private and that, despite that tolerance in private, the Athenians are nevertheless "severely law-abiding" in public. One might interpret this passage to mean that the laws of Athens leave the Athenians free to live as they please, so long as they obey the law in public matters. But this reading is undercut by the important difference between the ancient and modern conceptions of law. Whereas the modern tradition understands law to be strictly prohibitive, the ancients understood law to have the character of command, requiring citizens to perform certain actions and practices. Hence, when Pericles praises the Athenians for being fiercely law-abiding in public, he does not simply mean that they refrain from doing what they ought not, but means that they act and do what the law commands of them, some of which may strike the modern reader as an intrusion into private matters. Let me provide just one example. Solon instituted a law in Ancient Athens according to which it is illegal during times of civil discord to remain neutral in the conflict since remaining neutral reflects a preference for one's safety and comfort over the good of the political community (on this particular law, see Leão and Rhodes 2015, 59–61). Under such a law, doing the lawful thing may require the sacrifice of one's life for the city, a command that is likely to strike the modern reader as an intrusion into private life.

We can then see that Pericles' portrayal and praise of Athens may not necessarily depict a city dedicated to the protection of a private sphere and to the freedom of the individual from coercion. The distance between classical political philosophy and Hayek comes to the fore in at least three key issues: the status of virtue's claim to merit political honors, the public-spirited character of classical political life, and the nature of law. In the introduction following the epigraph, Hayek notes that the central purpose of *The Constitution of Liberty* is to clarify and defend the value of freedom at a time at which that fundamental principle has fallen into disrepute and has lost its hold on the minds and hearts of men. It remains an open question, it seems to me, as to whether Hayek can successfully rekindle the love of individual freedom and the "spirit of individual initiative" that he so wishes to reawaken until he recognizes and addresses the fundamental differences between ancient and modern political philosophy and the set of considerations to which the former points.

Hayek's Political Ideal of the Rule of Law

Hayek underscores the irresponsible character of "idealism" and "perfectionism" across his various works. He rebukes intellectuals for their "exclusive concern with the creation of 'better worlds'" and warns that "it has been perfectionism of one kind or another that has often destroyed whatever degree of decency societies have achieved" (Hayek [1960] 2011, 48, 54). Liberalism is "as remote from perfectionism as it is from the hurry and impatience of the passionate reformer," whose indignation "blinds him" to the potential harms inherent in his plans (Hayek [1960] 2011, 54). Hayek endorses liberalism as a politics that, far from being a politics based on perfectionist hopes, is "a modest and even humble creed" that is "based on a low opinion of man's wisdom and capacities" and aware that "even the best society will not satisfy all our desires" (Hayek [1960] 2011, 54). Given his general criticism of idealism, it is perhaps a surprise that he should label the rule of law, one of the fundamental principles of his political project, an "ideal."

By "ideal," I follow Eugene Miller in understanding Hayek to mean that the rule of law stands above and serves as a standard by which to judge the actual laws that exist in societies (Miller 2010, 64). Indeed, there is a live set of scholarly debates in contemporary analytic philosophy about the relation of Hayek's political thought to "ideal theory" and "non-ideal theory." If by "ideal theory" scholars mean a form of political theorizing that is based on idealized assumptions about the goodness of human nature and that strives for an "ideal" societal structure that is perfectly just, this is clearly not what Hayek is after.[3] Hayek does not introduce an "ideal" in the expectation that he can guide society to perfect justice. Eugene Miller argues, correctly in my estimation, that Hayek introduces the "ideal" of the rule of law for two purposes: "it shows that liberty is something of high value" since the purpose of the rule of law is to preserve a private sphere of individual freedom, and it enables him "to appeal to something above existing or possible arrangements that offers a criterion by which to judge them" (Miller 2010, 34–35). In brief, the rule of law is intended to be a general standard for all societies in existence. But what precisely is this ideal? And from where does it come? Analyzing the nature and origins of the ideal of the rule of law presents an opportunity to reflect on further differences that mark the two perspectives.

Before presenting the precise aspects of his "ideal," Hayek dedicates three chapters to the question of the origins of the rule of law. In addressing both its conceptual and its institutional development, he argues, in alignment with his broader theory of social evolution, that the rule of law is not the result of central planning or legislation but of an evolutionary process whereby emerging beliefs and norms enable men to discover the principles of human freedom. According to Hayek, social and political order emerges spontaneously, and the values, traditional practices, and habits of a society do too. Just as social order comes into being through an unplanned and organic process that produces patterns of behaviors and norms, so too, apparently, does the recognition of the conception of the rule of law as a political ideal. This process makes possible both the discovery of the ideal as well as our ability to judge the actual bodies of laws and norms that always approach but never fully embody it.[4]

While both the ideal and the actual laws and institutions come to be through this process, the "ideal" somehow transcends all actual particular laws through its being universal: the "ideal" of the rule of law provides a standard to which all extant constitutions can conform and thereby protect individual freedom (Miller 2010, 103). Hayek calls the ideal of the rule of law "a meta-legal doctrine": "the rule of law is . . . not a rule of the law, but a rule concerning what the law ought to be, a meta-legal doctrine or a political ideal" (Hayek [1960] 2011, 311). In being a meta-legal or trans-political standard, the rule of law, surprisingly, resembles the older notion of natural law or natural right, which acted as a guide and limit on human and political action (Miller 2010, 105). Although the rule of law resembles the older notion of natural law in this regard, it contrasts with the older notion by being neutral with respect to the ends of human action (Miller 2010, 104). Here is another departure from classical political philosophy: the task of the lawmaker is not to order the entire lives of citizens or to guide them toward certain ends but to set up the conditions wherein individuals are free from coercion to discover and pursue their own ends.

Eugene Miller has observed that Hayek is here "dealing with the problem of transcendence" and that his account departs from three prior ways with which the problem had previously been dealt (Miller 2010, 104). Of those three, the most important for our purpose is his departure from the natural law or higher law tradition. According to that older tradition, the natural law is understood to be a timeless standard discoverable by human reason through reflection on the nature of reality (Miller 2010, 104). Hayek's ideal resembles the older notion of natural law in functioning as a guide and limit on action, but Hayek denies natural law or natural right proper because he denies the existence of a natural order with constant principles that are intelligible to the human mind and that can serve as a standard for human action (Miller 2010, 64). Hayek thus rejects the classical notion of natural law or natural right, as well as the very foundation of ancient rationalism as such: the existence of a nature whose principles are intelligible to the human mind (Miller 1976, 383–393). As Miller puts it, "the idea of a constant nature with moral meaning is ruled out by [Hayek's] absorption of reason into civilization or his understanding of being as process" (Miller 2010, 104). If Hayek's ideal is not grounded in the classical notion of nature or the classical tradition of natural law or natural right, then in what sense, if at all, is it supported by reality and not a mere and arbitrary construct?[5]

In grappling with the problem of the transcendental status of the ideal of the rule of law, Hayek rejects post-Hegelian German historicism, on the one hand, and Max Weber's theory of "ideal types," on the other (Miller 2010, 104–105). He rejects the former on the grounds that it eventually leads to "radical relativism," on the one hand, by positing separate ideals for separate epochs rather than one universal ideal for civilization, and to "constructivism," on the other, by rejecting "all rules that have not been deliberately designed to achieve a specific purpose" (Hayek [1960] 2011, 345). The third position that Hayek rejects is Max Weber's position, according to which "the social scientist is confronted with boundless facts of experience, from which he must select those that will give focus to his research . . . by constructing 'ideal types,' which are very different from ideals of a moral or aesthetic character" (Miller 2010, 105). Hayek rejects this position because he does not accept the position that

> ideals lack a foundation, that there is no rational basis for judging one to be superior to another, and that the decision among them is ultimately an arbitrary one, based on an act of faith or sheer will—like choosing between God and the Devil. (Miller 2010, 105)

While Hayek says that the ideal and the actual laws come into being through an evolutionary process, he supplies no final account of how his ideal becomes a universal standard for civilization. He says that the ideal became effective in the West on account of the fact that it was an ideal that came to be believed by a people: "like most of the governing ideas of any age, it was held not because its rationale was fully understood, but rather because the success of the groups and civilizations who had held it had brought it [the Rule of Law] to dominance" (Hayek 1955). The ideal becomes recognized and believed through a process of social evolution, but Hayek supplies no account for how it becomes a *rationally* affirmed standard for all nations.

After discussing the problem of the origins of his political ideal, Hayek lists the "essential factors which together make up the rule of law." In going through each aspect of the rule of law, what is most striking is the formality of its features. In a word, the rule of law is concerned with limiting political authority or coercion, dividing political powers through constitutional mechanisms, and establishing legal neutrality or indifference toward citizens of various classes or groups. Hayek's political project marks a break with classical political philosophy in this respect too: Hayek's rule of law concerns such matters as the institutionalized division of powers, and it has relatively little to say about the actual content or character of the political community that those institutions and structures are in place to preserve.

The first aspect of the rule of law is that the government's powers, including the legislative power, must never be used "to coerce an individual except in order to enforce a known rule" (Hayek [1960] 2011, 309–310). This aspect of the rule of law follows directly from Hayek's discussion of freedom: its purpose is to protect "the free sphere of the individual," which "includes all action that is not explicitly prohibited by a general law" (Hayek [1960] 2011, 129). By supposing that human beings are free to do what the law does not forbid, Hayek follows the political tradition of John Locke. In his Second Treatise, Locke notes that

> freedom of men under government is to have a standing rule to live by, common to every one of that society and made by the legislative power erected in it, a liberty to follow my own will in all things where the rule prescribes not, and not to be subject to the inconstant, uncertain, unknown, arbitrary will of another man. (Locke 1960, §22)

Hayek notes that Aristotle endorses a different principle—that the law forbids what it does not expressly command—a conception that he calls "socialist" and "detrimental" to the rule of law. It is then strange that Hayek names

Aristotle as a thinker who adopts the "socialist" principle and yet simultaneously refers to Aristotle as an early expounder of the rule of law (see Miller 1979, 183; Hayek [1960] 2011, 352).[6]

The second element of Hayek's notion of the rule of law is that the laws must be known and certain (Hayek [1960] 2011, 315). Hayek shares this principle with John Locke, who underscores the necessity for laws to be promulgated and clearly understood by the people who are subject to them (Locke 1960, §137). The third element of the rule of law is equality before the law. This means not only that the laws must apply equally to all, including both the authors of the law and those who must obey them, but also that the law would not "make different provisions for different classes" of citizens (Hayek [1960] 2011, 316–317). In this context, Hayek highlights that *no formal criterion* of justice beyond "generality and equality" is said to be an essential feature of the rule of law.

> It is sometimes said that, in addition to being general and equal, the rule of law must also be just. But though there can be no doubt that, in order to be effective, it must be accepted as just by most people, it is doubtful whether we possess any other formal criteria of justice than generality and equality. (Hayek [1960] 2011, 318)

This has an important implication for matters of distributive justice, or the allocation of political honors or goods on the basis of a notion of merit or just distribution. According to Hayek, the government should abstain from distributing goods and honors to particular individuals. Instead, it ought to defend laws that are "general and abstract" in character and equally applied to all citizens. Distributive justice is, according to Hayek, to be avoided because human beings are constitutionally unable to possess the comprehensive knowledge needed for the central direction of the resources of shared resources toward one common plan (Miller 1979, 187).[7]

The separation of powers—specifically, the separation of legislative and judicial powers—is a fourth element of Hayek's conception of the rule of law. The "laying down of new general rules" and "their application to particular cases" must be "performed by different persons or bodies" (Hayek [1960] 2011, 319). In describing the judiciary's function, he notes that someone must decide in particular cases whether coercion by the government is to be used.

> Rules must not be made with particular cases in mind, nor must particular cases be decided in the light of anything but the general rule—though this rule may not yet have been explicitly formulated and therefore have to be discovered. This requires independent judges who are not

> concerned with any temporary ends of government. The main point is that the two functions must be performed separately by two coordinated bodies before it can be determined whether coercion is to be used in a particular case. (Hayek [1960] 2011, 319)

It is the function of an independent judiciary to adjudicate and decide whether particular governmental acts of coercion are justified. Hayek's fifth element of the rule of law entails that proper limits be set for executive or administrative discretion. The final element of the rule of law is a limitation on the emergency powers of government. The purpose of these final three aspects is to limit the possibility of coercion or the abuse of power. In sum, the rule of law limits coercion and requires that laws be known and certain, and equally applied to all. It must also secure an independent judiciary, use legislative and judicial regulations to check the executive power, and limit the government's emergency powers. The rule of law is thus highly generalized and abstract and says little about the activities of the citizens who constitute and are constituted by the political order. Unlike the classical tradition, Hayek's rule of law does not address the education of citizens to virtue but focuses almost exclusively on the problem of coercion and the division of political power.

I conclude this chapter with a final word about Hayek's doctrine of the rule of law as it relates to the treatment of law by the ancient political philosophers. Hayek names Aristotle in particular as an early expounder of the ideal of the rule of law (Hayek [1960] 2011, 241–242). In support of this claim, he quotes a selection of lines from Aristotle's *Politics* and *Rhetoric*. It seems to me that his selective inclusions and omissions of Aristotle, just as in the Thucydidean case, do not capture the spirit or message of the original text. Hayek cites these passages as proof that Aristotle was an early proponent of the rule of law, but he passes over much of the subtlety and complexity of Aristotle's account. I quote Hayek at length:

> In the *Politics* he [Aristotle] stresses that "it is more proper that the law should govern than any one of the citizens," that the persons holding supreme power "should be appointed to be only guardians and the servants of the law," and that "he who would place the supreme power in mind, would place it in God and the laws." He condemns the kind of government in which "the people govern and not the law" and in which "everything is determined by a majority vote and not by a law." Such a government is to him not that of a free state, "for, where government is not in the laws, then there is no free state, for the law ought to be supreme over all things." A government that "centers all power in the votes of the people cannot, properly speaking, be a democracy: for their decrees cannot be general in their extent." If we add to this the following

> passage in the *Rhetoric*, we have indeed a fairly complete statement of the ideal of government by law: "It is of great moment that well-drawn laws should themselves define all the points they possibly can, and leave as few as possible to the decision of the judges, [for] the decision of the lawgiver is not particular but prospective and general, whereas members of the assembly and the jury find it their duty to decide on definite cases brought before them." (Hayek [1960] 2011, 241–242)

Let us take a closer look at the passages that Hayek cites in the context in which they occur. In a discussion of permanent monarchy in Book 3 of the *Politics*, Aristotle raises the question of whether it would be better for the best man to rule as a king or whether the best laws ought to rule. In 3.16.1287a1-1287b35, Aristotle argues that the law ought to rule, because in a political community of roughly equal men, it is just for each to rule and to be ruled in turn. By sharing in rule, citizens serve as "law-guardians" and "servants of the laws." Thus, if one man were to rule, others would be unjustly deprived of the great good of sharing in rule (Politics 3.16.1287a17-20). Hayek's third substantive reference to Aristotle refers to Aristotle's discussion of the advantage of the rule of law on the grounds that law is not subject to distortion by the passions in the same manner that human beings are. As Aristotle says,

> he who asks law to rule, therefore, seems to be asking God and intellect alone to rule, while one who asks man adds the beast. Desire is a thing of this sort, and spiritedness perverts rulers and the best men. Hence law is intellect without appetite. (Politics 3.16.1287a30-32)

However, Aristotle continues, "while these arguments hold in some cases, in others perhaps they do not" (Politics 3.17.1287b35-37). Having acknowledged that "it is evident that among similar and equal persons it is neither advantageous nor just for one person to have authority over all matters," Aristotle then proceeds to affirm that where one man far surpasses all others with respect to virtue or excellence, it would be just for him to have ultimate authority in all matters and to set up a permanent kingship (Politics 3.17.1288a29, see also Miller 1979, 205–206).

In other words, in the best regime, it would be just for the wise and good man to rule indefinitely rather than the law! Aristotle does not then uphold the rule of law as an absolute, as Hayek himself does. Aristotle affirms that, in the best case, the rule of the best man would be better and more just. Now, Aristotle's endorsement of permanent kingship is accompanied by a recognition of the fact that the existence of a man of such outstanding virtue and wisdom is exceedingly rare. As Miller has emphasized, Aristotle was fully aware that actual politics will usually present a choice between the rule of the vicious or the rule of the law (Miller 1979, 206). Consequently, Aristotle comes to an endorsement of the law in his discussion of the best *possible* regime, the politeia, or mixed regime.[8] Despite this agreement, a comparison of the reasons that bring Aristotle and Hayek to their endorsements of the law reveals a deeper and more fundamental disagreement over their political principles. This chapter began by observing that Hayek's purpose in *The Constitution of Liberty* was to defend the principles of freedom and the rule that had fallen into increasing disregard and oblivion. The purpose of this essay has been to demonstrate why a defense of those principles requires a more rigorous encounter and confrontation with classical political philosophy.

Notes

1. Eugene Miller was a student of Friedrich Hayek in the Committee on Social Thought at the University of Chicago, where he wrote a dissertation on David Hume under Hayek's supervision in the 1960s. Miller's other dissertation committee members were Leo Strauss and Joseph Cropsey. In the introduction to Miller's essay "Hayek's Critique of Reason" (1976), Miller says the following about his teacher: "Hayek knew that intellectual freedom is likely to produce instead a diversity of ideas" and, as a result, "he continued to offer his full help and encouragement when my inquiries led me to question some fundamental principles of his thought. He sought not to cultivate disciples but to challenge his students to face difficult issues with the same integrity and manliness that marks his own thought" (Miller 1976, 383).

2. This interpretation of the passage is justified by the fact that a central purpose of Pericles's speech is to remind the citizens of Athens why their regime is worth defending and to inspire their continued efforts in the war.

3. For a general overview of the literature, see Gerald Gaus' *Tyranny of the Ideal: Justice in a Diverse Society*. Gerald Gaus, Chandran Kukathas, and John Gray are three scholars who have developed Hayek's thought in "anti-ideal" directions (modus vivendi, non-ideal theory).

4. Eugene Miller notes that "It must be emphasized that in embracing the idea of evolution, Hayek has in mind social or cultural evolution as anticipated in the teachings of eighteenth-century thinkers, particularly the Scots, and not physical evolution as taught later by Charles Darwin and others. What is crucial to cultural evolution is not the selection and transmission of physical characteristics, but rather the selection and transmission of values or rules of conduct. Cultural evolution takes place through a process of 'winnowing and sifting,' and where it will lead is unknowable and thus unpredictable. Certainly, it does not exhibit an intelligible law. Its tendency, however, is to produce orders or structures that reflect 'the differential advantages gained by

groups from practices adopted for some unknown and perhaps purely accidental reasons' (1979: 155; cf. 153–9, 196–200). Hayek returns to spontaneous order at the very end of Chapter 10, where he draws a parallel between natural and social order. Often in the physical world we must 'rely on the spontaneous adjustments of individual elements to produce a physical order.' . . . Hayek reasons that spontaneous forces can likewise produce human society when individuals act in accordance with general rules or laws. Lawmakers can promote social order by establishing the conditions for it, but cannot do so by trying to arrange individuals in an orderly way. Thus the lawmaker's task 'is not to set up a particular order but merely to create conditions in which an orderly arrangement can establish and ever renew itself' (161). Hayek draws support here from Michael Polanyi, who speaks of 'the spontaneous formation of a "polycentric order."' Polanyi explains that such order 'is achieved among human beings by allowing them to interact with each other on their own initiative – subject only to the laws which uniformly apply to all of them.' Their individual efforts are coordinated 'by exercising their individual initiative;' and 'this self-coordination justifies this liberty on public grounds' (160)" (Miller 2010, 61–62).

5. I quote Eugene Miller at length on Hayek's rejection of post-Hegelian German Historicism, on one hand, and Max Weber's theory of "ideal types," on the other (Miller 2010, 104–105): "Historicism was "a school that claimed to recognize necessary laws of historical development and to be able to derive from such insight knowledge of what institutions were appropriate to the existing situation" (Hayek 2011, 345). As Eugene Miller notes, this school of thought "assumed that the mind, by transcending limitations of time and place, can 'explicitly recognize how our present views are determined by circumstances and use this knowledge to remake our institutions in a manner appropriate to our time.' Hayek objects to historicism on two grounds: it leads to an 'extreme relativism,' inasmuch as it posits a separate ideal for each epoch and not a universal ideal for civilization; and it is 'constructivist,' since it rejects 'all rules that cannot be rationally justified or have not been deliberately designed to achieve a specific purpose' (235–236). A third alternative was laid out by Max Weber. Weber rejected the historicist claim that there are discoverable laws of history, holding instead that the social scientist is confronted with boundless facts of experience, from which he must select those that will give focus to his research. This selection is achieved by constructing 'ideal types,' which are very different from ideals of a moral or aesthetic character. Ideal types, such as 'capitalism,' are indispensable to social science. While they are designed to study people's values, they rigorously avoid any value judgements of their own or any claim as to what ought to be. Moral and aesthetic ideals have no place in social science, since they have no rational or empirical basis whatever. A scholar may decide to become the advocate for an ideal, but in doing so he leaves science behind and enters the ceaseless conflict that 'rages between different gods.' Weber's 'war of the gods' is his characterization of the conflict between ideals. The choice among them is ultimately a matter of faith or the individual's subjective decision (Weber, 2004: 17–31; Weber, 1949: 17–19, 22–6, 50–59, 89–101). Hayek greatly admired Weber, especially for denying that history exhibits discoverable laws and for advocating methodological individualism in social inquiry. He could not, however, accept Weber's conclusion, with its deep Nietzschean

overtones, that ideals lack a foundation, that there is no rational basis for judging one to be superior to another, and that the decision among them is ultimately an arbitrary one, based on an act of faith or sheer will – like choosing between God and the Devil. To be sure, the political philosopher, by Hayek's reckoning, must not be 'afraid of deciding between conflicting values.' He recognizes 'that he must choose which he should accept and which reject' (114–15). Nevertheless, Hayek looks for some foundation for this choice and refuses to see it as only a matter of faith or subjective will." (Eugene Miller 2010, 104–105).

6. Aristotle claims in the *Nicomachean Ethics* that "what the law does not command, it forbids" (1138a7). He illustrates his point by way of the example of suicide. The law does not command suicide and so forbids it, imposing a penalty of dishonor on the person who kills himself (1138a12–14).

7. For Hayek's fuller statements on distributive justice, see p.340-341: "This, however, is precisely what a government bound by the rule of law cannot do. If the government is to determine how particular people ought to be situated, it must be in a position to determine also the direction of individual efforts. We need not repeat here the reasons why, if government treats different people equally, the results will be unequal, or why, if it allows people to make what use they like of the capacities and means at their disposal, the consequences for the individuals will be unpredictable. The restrictions which the rule of law imposes upon government thus preclude all those measures which would be necessary to insure that individuals will be rewarded according to another's conception of merit or desert rather than according to the value that their services have for their fellows or, what amounts to the same thing, it precludes the pursuit of distributive, as opposed to commutative, justice. Distributive justice requires an allocation of all resources by a central authority; it requires that people be told what to do and what ends to serve. Where distributive justice is the goal, the decisions as to what the different individuals must be made to do cannot be derived from general rules but must be made in the light of the particular aims and knowledge of the planning authority. As we have seen before, when the opinion of the community decides what different people shall receive, the same authority must also decide what they shall do. This conflict between the ideal of freedom and the desire to "correct" the distribution of incomes so as to make it more "just" is usually not clearly recognized. But those who pursue distributive justice will in practice find themselves obstructed at every move by the rule of law."

8. For an illuminating discussion of these points, one to which I am greatly indebted, see Eugene Miller's essay "Prudence and the Rule of Law" in the American Journal of Jurisprudence (1979).

References

Aristotle. 1984. *The Politics*. Translated by Carnes Lord. Chicago, IL: University of Chicago Press.

———. 2012. *Nicomachean Ethics*. Translated by Susan Collins and Robert Bartlett. Chicago, IL: University of Chicago Press.

Hasnas, John. 1995. "The Myth of the Rule of Law." *Wisconsin Law Review* 1995: 199–223.

Hayek, Friedrich A. 1955. *The Political Ideal of the Rule of Law*. Cairo: National Bank of Egypt.

———. 2011. *The Constitution of Liberty*. Edited by Ronald Hamowy. The Collected Works edition. Chicago, IL: University of Chicago Press.

Leão, Delfim F., and P. J. Rhodes. 2015. *The Laws of Solon: A New Edition with Introduction, Translation, and Commentary*. London: I.B. Tauris.

Locke, John. 1960. *Two Treatises of Government*. Edited by Peter Laslett. Cambridge: Cambridge University Press.

———. 1976. "Hayek's Critique of Reason." *Modern Age* 20 (4): 383–394.

———. 1979. "Prudence and the Rule of Law." *American Journal of Jurisprudence* 24 (1): 181–206.

———. 2010. *Hayek's the Constitution of Liberty: An Account of Its Argument*. London: Institute of Economic Affairs.

Strauss, Leo. 1953. *Natural Right and History*. Chicago, IL: University of Chicago Press.

Thucydides. 2013. *History of the Peloponnesian War*. Translated by Jeremy Mynott. Cambridge: Cambridge University Press.

Zwicki, Todd. 2003. "The Rule of Law, Freedom, and Prosperity." *Supreme Court Economic Review* 10: 1–26.

6

Imperfect Laws and Liberties

The English Common Law in Medieval Ireland

Craig Lyons

In a survey of the medieval European legal tradition, Hayek observed that: "The only country that succeeded in preserving the tradition of the Middle Ages and built on the medieval 'liberties' the modern conception of liberty under the law was England" (Hayek 2021, 112). This line, which appeared in the first volume of his *Law, Legislation, and Liberty*, situated his analysis of the emergence of England's common law in a narrative that stretched back to seventeenth-century struggles between the Crown and Parliament. Hayek's narrative presents the emergence of England's medieval legal system as a popular check on royal power (Hamowy 2003, 260). Scholarly trends since Hayek's writing have tended to emphasize the top-down development and imposition of the king's justice, which would eventually become the common law of the realm (Hamowy 2003, 257), as well as the variety of competing jurisdictions that comprised the broader medieval English legal system (e.g., Berman 1983, 17). Nevertheless, interest remains in exploring the role of medieval English law in the development and promotion of liberty (e.g., Brennan and Schmidtz 2010, 60–85), while Hayek's legal theory continues to inspire investigations into medieval legal evolution (e.g., Ogus 1989; Mahoney 2001; Beaulier et al. 2005). According to this theory, laws that emerge through a process of discovery and are revealed through the unarticulated norms of human action are preferable to laws created through legislation by an individual or group. In Hayek's view, the "deeply entrenched tradition of the common law," which was "not conceived as the product of anyone's will but rather as a barrier to all power," was particularly well-suited to development by discovery (Hayek 2021, 113). This chapter will turn to a specific episode in the early development of that legal system that adds complexity to a Hayekian understanding of the common law's medieval development, one in which English administrators transplanted that legal system into the colonial environment of Ireland and artificially restrained its ability to adapt to its new environment. Under such conditions, even a legal system that, in Hayek's view, was well-suited to the promotion of liberty could act instead as a constraint on liberty.

After a brief introduction to the historical setting of medieval Ireland, the chapter will first offer an overview of Hayek's legal theory and its position in subsequent investigations of medieval legal history, particularly for those interested in understanding the role of this period in the development of institutions conducive to the promotion of liberty and the rule of law. As Beaulier et al. have emphasized, Hayek's conception of a "pure" rule of law requires that rules, such as those codified in a legal system, must be general, non-arbitrary, and equally applied (Beaulier et al. 2015, 215). While Hayek viewed the English common law as a system conducive to this type of development, we shall see that the same legal system, transported to and imposed in a colonial environment, acted as a constraint upon liberty and the principles of Hayek's rule of law. The second section will then consider the specific historical context of the common law in Ireland, where that legal system inhibited liberties for the Irish while securing them for the English. In this colonial transplant of one people's legal system to lands already containing another, "English law and liberty" gradually became an institutional barrier to cooperation and development in Ireland. Over time, English administrators began to use the common law to "corral" the English in and around their walled towns and to deprive the surrounding Irish of legal protection for their property (Frame 2005, 144). Attempts to develop workable compromises at the local level emerged in response to the hardening institutional barriers that hindered access to the common law for a large part of the island's inhabitants. In response, efforts to prevent such accommodations emanated from the English Crown and from the Irish Parliament in the form of statutes and administrative decisions. The third section, "Coroners and Defamation," will turn to two specific case studies to explore local responses to an artificially rigid legal system. In medieval Ireland, we can see the limits of the common law as a liberty-promoting institution when there is no opportunity to incorporate local feedback.

The imposition of England's common law, which was itself in the early stages of its development in the late twelfth century, onto the frontier environment of post-Conquest Ireland presents us with a medieval example of a colonial legal system kept artificially rigid by administrative anxieties over identity and control. Top-down attempts to prevent the English common law from doing precisely what Hayek thought it did best, evolving in response to and incorporating social norms, ultimately resulted in that legal system becoming the foundation for a "colonial judiciary" (Brand 1995). It is a familiar story of state power expanding into supposedly ungoverned regions with the goal of establishing the rule of law, of imposing an institutional "blueprint," and of neglecting or overruling local feedback to those institutions (for this issue in a broader contemporary context, see Murtazashvili 2018; for the role of institutional "blueprints" in medieval European conquests, see Bartlett 1993, 309–310). When English soldiers of fortune launched the first waves of conquest in Ireland in 1169, followed in 1171 by the arrival of King Henry II, it was partly under the justification of bringing the rule of law to the supposedly lawless Irish. Pope Adrian IV had granted his blessing in 1155 for Henry to "enter this island of Ireland, to make that people obedient to the laws" in the papal bull Laudabiliter, according to Henry's chief apologist (Giraldus [1189] 1978, 144–145). Henry's son John formally extended the "laws and customs of the English" to Ireland, but this applied primarily to those who could claim to be English by language, custom, or, eventually and increasingly, by blood and descent (for this trend in medieval Europe more broadly, see Bartlett 1993, 197–220). With some exceptions, the Irish themselves faced barriers to accessing the king's court and thus, crucially, to legal defense of their rights and property from intrusion or seizure by English settlers. The native Irish *Brehon* legal system remained in place in Irish-controlled or border regions, but where the English held the power to enforce their law access to their courts was crucial.

The tensions caused by the hardening of institutional barriers around English law in Ireland ultimately produced conflicts on both large and small scales. The exclusion of the Irish from the king's court, which administered the common law, benefited the English landholding class immensely while their expansion throughout the island had momentum (Hand 1967, 187–213). As the English expansion slowed toward the end of the thirteenth century, though, the English settlers who had inevitably mixed with Irish communities and families found ways to overcome cultural, linguistic, and legal barriers. They gradually adopted the Irish language, dress, and hairstyles, which became a source of frustration and anxiety for English administrators in an environment where such outward indicators of ethnic identity could determine one's legal identity. We can see this tension play out in the records of the king's court in Ireland, where the cross-cultural compromises that the realities of life in a fluid frontier environment produced met with top-down efforts to ensure that the English common law operated in Ireland as it did in England. The final section of this chapter will explore two examples of this type of conflict in those court proceedings, as accusations of Irish identity became a strategy in legal proceedings and a source of institutional corruption among coroners. Frustration and anxiety over local challenges to administratively legible ethnic and legal identities grew over the fourteenth century and boiled over in a series of acts known as the Statutes of Kilkenny, which the Irish Parliament passed in 1366. The statutes were an expression of concern among the English landholding elite in Ireland that English expansion in Ireland had not only stalled but was reversing. They represented an ultimately doomed effort to prevent English settlers in Ireland from becoming "degenerate" by adopting the language, customs, and dress of their Irish neighbors and relatives (Duffy 1997). The "corral" of English institutional barriers eventually became territorial borders, defining English enclaves, most notable the Pale of Dublin.

Hayek's Legal History and Theory

Hayek's understanding of the English common law as a legal system conducive to the promotion of liberty acts as historical support for his broader legal theory, making challenges to his stylized history relevant to his theory. This first section will address those challenges and establish the Hayekian perspective with which we will move into the case of medieval Ireland. Hayek initially set his legal theory in a historical narrative of institutional development toward the promotion of liberty, in which the common law of medieval England played a prominent role. His economic and political theories have tended to overshadow his legal theories, which can lead to misinterpretation by those who engage with them separately from the rest of Hayek's research program. As Beaulier et al. have demonstrated, though, Hayek's legal theory is an integral part of his overall corpus and one of the foundational sources of his own intellectual development (Beaulier et al. 2005, 210). Coordination, they emphasize, was the central concern of Hayek's overall project, including his legal theory (Beaulier et al. 2005, 213). The institutional environments in which humans interact help to shape or direct their activities, which can either facilitate or distort the coordination process. Laws and legal systems are an important part of that institutional environment and can have a major impact on the ability of individuals to predictably cooperate with each other. Hayek emphasized this in his three-volume series *Law, Liberty, and Legislation* (the single-volume 2021 edition is used in the chapter), in which he set out the conditions for a "pure 'rule of law'" that enables efficient coordination among imperfect agents operating in the market: rules must be general, nonarbitrary, and equally applied to all individuals. Given a predictable set of rules, whether customary or set out in a legal code, "individuals can learn to adapt their behavior in order to better coordinate their activities with those of others" (Hayek 2021, 215). In Hayek's view, laws that emerge through discovery rather than through legislation imposed from above achieve this end more efficiently. Laws that emerge from below, at the communal level, are thus more likely to provide the individual with liberty to effectively adapt their behavior and coordination (Hayek 2011, 232–260; 2021, 114–116).

The most dedicated challenge to Hayek's view of legal history concerning the common law has come from Ronald Hamowy, the most recent editor of Hayek's *The Constitution of Liberty.* This challenge, I will argue, is better viewed as a complication of Hayek's legal history rather than, as Hamowy asserts, a refutation. Hayek situated his legal theory in a historical narrative that viewed the common law of England, as it developed in the Middle Ages, as a system that emerged through discovery rather than legislation. Parliament was, in this view, a "law-finding body" before it became a "law-creating" one toward the end of the later Middle Ages (Hayek 2011, 236). Hamowy noted: "The common law that Hayek holds in such esteem is the common law as understood by the medieval lawyers and legal theorists, when its legal rules reflected custom and precedent and where statute and deliberate design played no, or at best a minimal, role" (2003, 246). This common law developed, like all ancient and medieval law, "through the gradual articulation of prevailing conceptions of justice rather than by legislation" (Hayek 2021, 110). The discovery of laws occurred at the communal level when a case before a court did not have a satisfactory solution among previously discovered laws. These laws were "embedded in the disparate and unarticulated rules under which Englishmen operated in dealing with each other" (Hamowy 2003, 246) and did not ultimately emerge through the legislation of any individual or court. Insofar as kings promulgated laws or jurists such as Bracton compiled them, they were confirming as laws those rules discovered over the centuries at the communal level. England was unique in "preserving the tradition of the Middle Ages" through the institution of the common law, Hayek argued, and this served as a foundation for the modern British conception of liberty under the law (Hayek 2021, 112).

Hayek's historical narrative of English legal history derives from a liberal tradition that owes much to the early modern conflicts between the English Parliament and the Tudor and Stuart monarchs. This tradition, which jurists such as Edward Coke championed at the turn of the seventeenth century, located the rights of the people in the common law, which it set in opposition to the power of the Crown. Coke and his liberal successors traced these rights back to the Anglo-Saxon period, which followed the Norman Conquest of 1066, a period that became an idealized antiquity in the English historical imagination. This narrative, termed the "Saxon myth" in some analyses (Colbourn 1998, 237–243), had a long lifespan in British and American views of medieval English history; it endured well into the nineteenth century. The notion that the common law was a medieval fount of liberty, if not quite as ancient or Saxon as once believed, remained prominent into the middle of the twentieth century, and Hayek was familiar with that scholarship (Hayek 2011, 234–236, especially the footnotes). Hamowy has set out many of the problems that subsequent scholarship has unearthed concerning this narrative. In particular, he notes, what came to be known as the common law of the realm was ultimately that body of laws that was enforced by the king through his courts. The king's courts in turn operated alongside and, at times, in conflict with a constellation of other courts: manor courts, ecclesiastical courts, municipal courts, and so on. Over time, the king's courts and the "common law" they enforced became more popular with plaintiffs because they offered them a more efficient and definitive resolution than other courts. As more disputes went directly to the king's courts, the jurisdiction of those courts expanded into areas previously handled by other courts, and the king's law became increasingly "common" to the realm (Hamowy 2003, 427).

Hamowy set the role of the English monarch in spreading and enforcing the emerging "common" law of the realm through the king's courts in opposition to Hayek's view of a legal system discovering laws at the local level, as though one excludes the other. What this new perspective does, though, is complicate rather than refute Hayek's understanding of the common law as a "law-finding" system. Hamowy noted that Hayek was most interested in tracing an institutional evolution toward a liberty-promoting rule of law, which he saw in the English common law (Hamowy 2003, 246). He was thinking about the "unformulated web of rules" that governed society in medieval England and entered the legal system through innumerable individual court cases and their resulting decisions. What subsequent scholarship has done is to expand our awareness of the various avenues for such action in the court systems operating in medieval England. As Hamowy points out, the imposition and shaping of legal institutions from the top down often met resistance from existing local institutions and traditions, leading to institutional tensions and conflicts. The eventual dominance of the king's courts was, in part, a solution to a coordination problem in the medieval English legal system. As demand grew for a quicker "final" judgement than might be had from the myriad competing courts from which any decision might be appealed, royal writs emerged to funnel legal disputes (and fees) into the king's courts along determined paths. The king's courts and the laws they enforced eventually emerged from that "constellation" of competing courts as the guarantors of the common law of the realm. Our greater understanding of that constellation of courts emerging, vanishing, colliding, or merging over the centuries of medieval English history now presents us with a more complex picture than Hayek's admittedly brief survey allowed. What this does, though, is reposition Hayek's legal theory and the institutional analysis integral to it at all of the points of that constellation where a coordination problem, a tension between discovery and legislation, did indeed play out. This may have played out in different ways than Hayek imagined and moves the analysis into the category of "hard cases" in spontaneous order studies (Boettke 2014, 244; Leeson 2010). The institutional analysis moves to the jurisdictional conflicts that emerge in the records of county, episcopal, or municipal court records.

The complication of the view held by Hayek and others of the common law as an expression of popular sovereignty in opposition to royal power adds new dimensions to studies that seek to understand the role of medieval legal evolution in the development of liberty-promoting institutions. In Hamowy's analysis, the presence of royal influence in the development in the creation of the common law seems enough to label it a state project and to deny its spontaneity, which, he notes, is key to Hayek's legal theory (Hamowy 2003, 246). Hamowy emphasizes the growing reach of the king's justice and of the courts that enforced it, but leaves aside the question of how those laws emerged in the first place. The multiplication of avenues for jurisdictional conflict in the evolution of the medieval English legal system is itself just one of many areas where our historical understanding of that evolution has become more complex. The role of literacy in the promotion of state authority in medieval England (e.g., Clanchy 1985, 2013), the impact of Roman and Canon law upon English law (e.g., McSweeney 2019), and local impulses toward localized governance on the Continent (e.g., Møller and Doucette 2022) are further examples of this trend. The remainder of this chapter will focus on another aspect of in the imposition of that legal system in Ireland following the English conquest of that island. This offers a counterexample to the narrative of the English common law as a liberty-promoting institution, presenting us instead with the same legal system acting as a constraint on liberty in a colonial environment. Efforts to halt the evolution of that system in response to local circumstances by English administrators and landholders produced tensions that boiled over in court proceedings at the local level and resulted in a gradual loss of control over Irish-controlled regions on a larger scale.

The Common Law in Ireland

As Henry II and his successors established English administrative rule in Ireland, they brought to the island what Bartlett has termed a "codifiable blueprint," a package of laws and institutions set within a "documentary framework" (Bartlett 1993, 309–310). This "blueprint" allowed the English to "export" their administrative institutions across the Irish Sea relatively quickly. When King John extended the "laws and customs of the English" (*leges et consuetudines Anglicanas*) to the Lordship of Ireland in 1210, he was importing a system that was itself in the early stages of development in

England. In this new cultural environment, though, access to these laws and customs came to depend on one's linguistic, ethnic, and eventually racial identity (Bartlett 1993, 170; Frame 2018, 529). Part of the justification for the English conquest had been the extension of the rule of law to a supposedly lawless people on the periphery of Christendom, but in 1210, the conquest was still fully underway as English landholders spread deeper into the island. This produced a medieval example of what Lauren Benton has called the "legal logic" of colonial wars of conquest (Benton 2018, 427), characteristic of the early modern and modern periods. So long as the Irish remained "lawless," in this case meaning that their customary laws did not fully conform with the standards of Canon law emanating from the Continent, continued conquest was justified. As in England at the beginning of the thirteenth century, local disputes were still more likely to pass through manorial, municipal, or ecclesiastical courts, to which the Irish had access. By the end of the thirteenth century, though, the English conquest had begun to stall, the king's court was becoming a more popular recourse in legal disputes in both England and Ireland, and a century of cultural and familial mixing along the frontiers of English control began to challenge the institutional barriers that governed access to the king's courts and the laws and liberties of the English.

As those sources of tension grew and seeped into the king's courts, surviving records for which begin in 1295, so too did anxiety over identity among the English administrators and landholders who comprised the Parliament of Ireland. The king's justiciar in Ireland, his personal representative, oversaw both the Irish Parliament and the administration of the king's justice, the common law of the realm, in Ireland. From the first Irish Parliament for which records survive, that of 1297, the English common law became an institutional tool for the erection of barriers around a colonial English society, acting to "corral" the English and distinguish them from the native Irish (Frame 2005, 144–149). By the middle of the fourteenth century, those anxieties frequently dominated parliamentary statutes, as the "middle nation" of the English in Ireland sought to preserve its English identity (Lydon 2019). This concern with identity is another recurring feature of colonial environments throughout history, and we can see processes that James C. Scott observed in modern upland Southeast Asia at work in English-controlled Ireland (Scott 2009, especially Chapter 7). Contemporary English writers, most notably Gerald of Wales, engaged in a project of ethnogenesis in which they sought to create a barbaric and lawless ethnic identity for the Irish, much as later colonial regimes would do in an effort to define those on the edges of the state (e.g., Scott 2009, 284). For Gerald of Wales, as for twentieth-century colonial administrators, hills, bogs, and forests were the dwelling places of lawless barbarians like the Irish, and treachery, sloth, and sexual depravity were their distinguishing traits. These were already established tropes of barbarity on the edges of Christian civilization when Gerald turned his attention to the Irish and would remain so into modernity (Bartlett 1982, 85–105). This type of rhetoric, which Gerald applied to the Irish in the twelfth century, found its way into the official language of the Irish Parliament by the end of the thirteenth. The extension of the rule of law to the Irish, the ostensible justification for English rule over their fellow Christian Irish neighbors, was largely abandoned in favor of using law to define English identity.

The Irish Parliament of 1297 provides an example of this trend toward using law as an expression of and safeguard for English society, using its enactments as "a declaration of identity through law" (Smith 1997, 65):

> Englishmen also, as if degenerate in modern times, attire themselves in Irish garments and having their heads half shaven, grow and extend the hairs from the back of the head and call them *culan*, conforming themselves to the Irish as well in garb as in countenance, whereby it frequently happens that some Englishmen reputed as Irishmen are slain, although the killing of Englishmen and of Irishmen requires different modes of punishment. (Berry 1907, 211)

The boundaries of legal identity set out by the Irish Parliament and in the king's courts were more porous and flexible in practice, though. As was often the case in such frontier environments on the "edge" of the state, "state" and "nonstate" processes existed in dialectic and even symbiotic relationships (for Ireland, Frame 2013, 115; more broadly, Protevi 2019, 38). Gerald and his contemporaries, both English and Continental, had attacked the Irish primarily through their perceived lawlessness, which the papal bull *Laudabiliter* confirmed in charging Henry II to "make that people obedient to the laws" (*ad subdendum illum populum legibus*) (Giraldus [1189] 1978, 144–145). The charge of lawlessness was just one of Gerald's attacks upon the Irish, but it proved to be one of the most enduring, influencing debates over Irish self-governance into the twentieth century. The incomplete nature of England's military conquests in Ireland resulted in the prolongation of that narrative as a "legal logic" justifying a perpetual state of war. The lawlessness of the Irish justified the English conquest, and so long as the conquest remained incomplete, the Irish remained partially lawless, at least by the standards of English law.

The English view of Irish law as unnatural and invalid thus continued after the Conquest, with Edward I declaring in 1277 that the customary Irish laws were "detestable to God, and so contrary to all law that they ought not to be deemed laws" (Hand 1967, 187–213). At the heart of this charge were discrepancies between the native Irish *Brehon* laws and the canon laws of the Church, particularly concerning marriage. The degree of conformity with the procedures and standards of canon law, resurgent throughout Europe at the time Gerald wrote, had become something of a litmus test for the validity of secular or customary legal systems, such as that of the Irish. Gerald made it clear that the customs of the Irish, which he did not consider laws, violated the laws of God and nature. "No wonder if among an adulterous and incestuous people," Gerald claimed in his *Topographia*, "a nation out of the pale of the laws, nature herself should be foully corrupted" (Giraldus [1188] 1978, 82). Gerald regaled his audience with examples of the supposed frequency of physical deformity among the Irish, which was another emerging trope of the non-European in twelfth-century literature (Heng 2018, 40). This, Gerald claimed, was the judgment of God, who allowed nature to produce such deformities "contrary to her own laws" as punishment for those who lived in defiance of His laws (Giraldus [1188] 1978, 82). This hostile attitude toward the laws of the Irish, combined with the refusal to extend English law to the Irish beyond individual grants, resulted in an institutional conflict acknowledged by the Irish Parliament in 1366:

> whereas diversity of government and different laws in the same land cause difference in allegiance, and disputes among the people; it is agreed and established . . . that no Englishman be governed in the termination of their disputes by March law nor Brehon law, which reasonably ought not to be called law, being a bad custom; but they shall be governed, as right is, by the common law of the land, as liege subjects of our lord the king. (Berry 1907, 435)

Such proclamations by the Irish Parliament may not have had much effect beyond the walled towns and hinterlands, which were under direct English control, but in such regions, the institutional barriers separating much of the population from the English common law could have dramatic consequences for individuals and communities. Two such examples will be explored in the next section. England was by no means unique in facing a conflict between two competing legal traditions split along lines of language or ethnicity. This was characteristic of much of medieval Iberia, for example. What was unique and surprising is that the general trend in such cases in the early and high Middle Ages was toward accommodation, with a dualistic or pluralistic legal system operating under one sovereign. "Recognizing their jural autonomy was one way of trying to reconcile the conquered to their lot" (Bartlett 1993, 208). The refusal of the English to either acknowledge the Irish legal system or allow the Irish access to the English common law was an exception. The tension between local customary law on the one hand and a developing *ius commune* tied heavily to canon law on the other was also not unique to Ireland, though the English monarchs were perhaps already beginning to diverge from their Continental peers in the manner of their imposition of a "common" law upon the realm (e.g., Herzog 2018, 93–115; Bartlett 1993, 42–44; Winroth 2012, 338–353). The way in which the English imposed that common law in Ireland provides us with an example of the legal system that, in Hayek's view, was most conducive to the promotion of individual liberty, acting in such a way as to constrain liberty for a large part of the island's population. As the parliamentary statute quoted above indicates, English settlers who could not deal with their Irish kinsmen and neighbors under English law were liable to turn to other options: the *Brehon* law of the Irish or the March law, a tradition of cross-cultural dispute resolution that emerged along the borders of English and Irish territories. In maintaining and reinforcing an artificial institutional rigidity to the common law in Ireland, English administrators deprived the English common law of precisely the feature that Hayek felt was its best: its ability to incorporate and encode social norms.

Coroners and Defamation

The most contentious issue resulting from the institutional barriers blocking the Irish from the laws of the English was the fact that, under English law, it was not a felony for an Englishman to kill an Irishman (Hand 1966). Concerns over manipulation or bribery by jurors and officials in efforts to falsify the details concerning the legal identity of murder victims demonstrate the anxieties that arose from this, and efforts to clarify the ethnic identity of murder victims could occur years after the event took place. This can be seen in several cases relating to coroners suspected of falsifying the ethnic identity of murder victims to secure a lighter penalty for the accused. Coroners were responsible, at the county or borough level, for keeping records of inquests held into all sudden deaths, particularly violent ones (Hunnisett 1961, 9–36). In February of 1307, the coroner of Limerick, Robert de Trym, was charged with having falsely classified a man slain in the city named Maurice as *hibernicus* (Irish) in order to protect the accused killer, Walter de Loung. The coroner argued in his defense that he had understood Maurice to be an Irishman "by public fame in the city" and on the testimony of the last priest to hear Maurice's confession, to whom Maurice had allegedly admitted his Irish identity. The jurors found upon investigation "that Maurice was regarded as an Englishman," born in County Tipperary, "and as such was accustomed to plead and be impleaded within the liberty." They found that Robert had falsely declared Maurice an Irishman "by his simplicity and ignorance" rather than to protect the killer and had him replaced as coroner. Walter de Loung, the killer, had since sold his goods and fled. "Therefore let him be exigented and outlawed" (Mills 1905, 517). The role of "public fame" cited in this case helps to explain the anxiety expressed in Parliamentary statutes over Englishmen adopting Irish manners and customs: in the absence of written records, a jury was likely to determine an individual's legal identity by precisely such outward indicators.

On January 4, 1313, in Drogheda, to the north of Dublin, the coroners and jurors of an earlier trial concerning the slaying of one Adam Rauth were charged with falsely declaring Adam an Irishman in order to spare the accused murderers the penalty of felony. The jurors testified that, at the time of their arrival in Drogheda to serve as jurors, "Adam who was killed was commonly held among the commons of the town to be an Irishman and . . . was had for an Irishman to the day of his slaying" (Mills 1905, 168). The jurors determined that Adam was in fact English but that the original jurors had genuinely held Adam to be Irish, "and it was for this cause that they made the said oath, and not for any other falseness or collusion." The two killers of Adam, having fled Drogheda at word of the Justiciar's impending arrival to reexamine the case, were declared "of ill fame." "Let them therefore be put in exigent and outlawed and their chattels confiscated for flight" (Mills 1905, 168). In a fragmentary portion of the surviving text, the coroners of Drogheda were fined for failing to update the identity of the deceased once they learned that Adam was English. It was a regular feature of English law, insofar as such cases occurred, for new discoveries concerning an individual's legal status to be assiduously recorded (Hand 1966, 94). Lives, livelihoods, and property could be at stake for generations. In Ireland, a colonial frontier environment in which legal identities and jurisdictions were constantly being negotiated, there were implications beyond freedom and unfreedom. One could be Irish and free, but freedom did not necessarily give an Irishman the benefit of English law. It could be purchased from the king or bestowed as a favor upon an individual or a lineage. The fact the coroners were fined for failing to keep the legal identity of the deceased updated hints at the importance to the English administration of keeping track of this distinction, as does the emphasis, found in many such cases, that the deceased was held to be Irish or English *to the day* of the incident in question.

For Englishmen residing on the borders of English-controlled territory or those who found more compelling or immediate ties to their Irish kin and neighbors than to the English community, or who simply did not have the property and standing for it to matter, the stakes of losing access to English courts over the perception of Irish identity might be low. For others, the prospects of losing recognition of one's English identity and thus the right to defend one's property in the king's court could be catastrophic. For this reason, charges of defamation over accusations of Irish identity reached the king's court in Ireland earlier than defamation cases in England. Such cases were generally a matter for ecclesiastical courts and remained so in England for at least a century (Baker 2019, 67). False accusations of villeinage, or unfree status, are found among the early cases of slander in English law (Hand 1966, 94), but in the colonial context of Ireland, such accusations were heavily intertwined with anxiety over identity. An ecclesiastical court could restore one's reputation through public penance in standard cases of defamation, but in cases of accusations of Irish identity, access to the king's court was at stake. Publicly labelling another Englishman as Irish was grounds for legal action and justified the hearing of defamation cases before the Justiciar on multiple occasions. This was an example of the type of responsiveness to local conditions that Hayek saw in the common law, and indeed, it foreshadowed subsequent developments in England. In Ireland, it was a response to the needs of local English communities, which the king's court could permit because it helped to maintain the institutional barriers keeping the Irish out of the same court.

In Dublin, 1308, one Simon de Cromhal brought a plea of trespass against Hugh Dunnyng and Geoffrey Wollebeterre, alleging that they had "maliciously charged Simon with being an Irishman and so defamed him throughout the barony of Dyvelek and the adjacent parts" (Mills 1905, 102). Simon brought the initial pleas in February, and the jurors found "that Simon is an Englishman of the surname of Cromhals, and his father was named Adam de Cromhal and dwelt at Atherde and was regarded as an Englishman all his life, and that Simon is not an Irishman" (Mills 1905, 41). Simon complained that Geoffrey and Hugh had instigated this slanderous rumor because Simon had "interfered" in Hugh's attempt to marry "a certain woman," whom Simon himself subsequently married. Simon was awarded damages of 40*s*. from each man. Geoffrey paid his fine, but Hugh did not appear when summoned and was hunted down by the sheriff. He was finally caught, charged, and fined in July of that year. This same Simon had also brought a plea of defamation before an ecclesiastical court, where such a case more properly belonged. He was "charged with presenting a plea in court Christian against Hugh for the said defamation," setting up a potential clash of jurisdictions after Hugh also obtained from the king's court a writ of restraint against the proceedings of the court Christian, effectively hedging his bets. Defamation was generally viewed as a spiritual matter, in which the purgation of the guilty party's soul, made visible through acts of penance, was the appropriate solution (Baker 2019, 467–470). This was one area of the law where even the crown and parliament were content to leave the jurisdiction of "courts Christian" relatively unchallenged. In 1295, a case of defamation originating in Ireland appeared before Parliament in England. At issue was the matter of jurisdiction, and even though the defendant was accused of slandering King Edward I himself, the case was dismissed due to errors in procedure, beginning with the determination that "it is not used in this realm that pleas of defamation should be pleaded in the king's court" (Veeder 1903, 556). In Ireland, though, the charge of Irish identity carried the potential for serious harm to the "slandered" party in the potential loss of the right to English law. This also threatened the institutional barriers established around the common law: if it was not easy to determine an individual's ethnic identity, it was not easy to include them as English or exclude them as Irish.

Such pleas continued to appear before the king's court in Ireland, framed as pleas of trespass and, in the surviving records at least, always concerning accusations of Irish identity. On May 30, 1295, in Limerick, William the merchant brought a complaint against Ricard de Wodeford, "that he defamed him and called him an *hibernicus* (Irish)." Ricard acknowledged this but claimed that he had made peace with William, which William denied. The jury determined that Ricard had not satisfactorily made peace, "Therefore it is adjudged that Ricard be committed to prison for trespass" (Mills 1905, 18). A similar case was heard in Dublin in May 1302. "Alan, son of Walter, and Cristiana, his wife," were charged with having defamed William Grane "by calling him *hibernicus*" and did not deny it. William was awarded damages "to be assessed" (Mills 1905, 18). These early examples of cases of defamation heard before the king's court in Ireland generally do not appear in analyses of the development of the law of defamation in the common law (e.g., Veeder 1903; Lovell 1962, 1051–1072). If they provide an example of the common law attempting to evolve in response to circumstances in Ireland, though, they are also an example of the English reinforcing barriers to their legal system. The common law continued to act as a constraint on the liberty of the Irish and, thus, upon coordination and development in Ireland as a whole.

Conclusion

By the end of Ireland's medieval period, its administrators concluded that depriving the Irish of access to the English legal system and leaving them with their own laws had been a mistake. Sir John Davies, who was appointed Attorney General for Ireland after the 1603 conclusion of the Nine Years War, the last substantial effort of Ireland's Gaelic lords to retain their autonomy, set out this conclusion in his 1612 *Discoverie of the True Causes Why Ireland Was Never Entirely Subdued.* Poring over the records of England's four centuries of administration in Ireland, Davies noted that the chief obstacle to the "perfect" conquest of Ireland had been that "the Crown of England did not from the beginning give Laws to the Irishry" (Davies [1612] 1751, 44). This, he quickly clarified, was the fault of the English landholders in Ireland and not the Crown.

> This then I note as the great defect of the civil Policy of this Kingdom, in that for the space of Three Hundred and Fifty Years at least . . . the English Laws were not communicated to the Irish, nor the Benefit and Protection thereof allow'd unto them, though they earnestly desir'd and sought the same. (Davies [1612] 1751, 52)

This institutional barrier, Davies noted, denied the Irish the ability to "converse or commerce" with their English neighbors. His opinion of the native Irish legal system was no more positive than that of Gerald nearly four centuries earlier. The lack of capital punishment for murder led to an anarchic free-for-all, he argued, while the traditional Irish methods of property inheritance prevented the Irish from improving their lands or settlements. "For, who would plant or improve, or build upon that Land, which a Stranger, whom he knew not, should possess after his Death?" (Davies [1612] 1751, 75). Davies' proposed remedy was one that would bring its own set of problems to the colonial ventures of early modernity: the conqueror ought to completely replace the legal systems of a conquered people (Davies [1612] 1751, 117).

The establishment of the common law in medieval Ireland presents us with an interesting episode of legal evolution precisely because that evolutionary process was artificially disrupted by colonial anxieties over identity. Administrative authority in Ireland blocked the very benefit that Hayek saw in the common law of England: its ability to incorporate and encode social norms. In a further twist, the same impulses toward a shared Christian rule of law in twelfth-century Europe, of which the English common law was a unique part, had also brought with them animosity toward "lawless" peoples on Europe's peripheries, which supported England's conquest and administration. Irish language and ethnicity became barriers to the very rule of law that Gerald had claimed the English were bringing to the Irish for their benefit. So long as the English conquest held its momentum, this state of affairs was advantageous to the great English landholders in Ireland. In Davies' analysis, they "might oppress, spoil, and kill" the Irish without consequence, and "the Irish inhabiting the Lands fully conquered and reduced, being in a Condition of Slaves and Villains, did render a greater Profit and Revenue, than if they had been made the King's free Subjects" (Davies [1612] 1751, 63–64). Local efforts to overcome this barrier, such as the Englishmen turning to the Irish *Brehon* laws to resolve disputes with their Irish neighbors and kinsmen, met with vigorous resistance from the English administration in Ireland.

The same administrators also halted workable solutions from entering the codified legal system operating in English-controlled Ireland, aside from those that reinforced the very barriers causing tension. The lack of a substantial penalty for murder had been, in the view of both Gerald and Davies, one of the greatest failings of the Irish *Brehon* laws. Yet, this was also one of the most glaring deficiencies of the liberty-constraining institution that the English common law became in Ireland. The lack of meaningful punishment for the killing of an Irishman by an Englishman created tensions within communities, which, by 1295, motivated the Irish Parliament to demand that Englishmen avoid Irish hairstyles, precisely so that the coroners could determine whether or not their potential murder was a felony. The corruption it encouraged among

Ireland's coroners is just one example of the ways in which the legislated institutional barriers around this legal system compromised the rule of law at the local level. In the manner of its imposition in Ireland, the English common law violated the crucial aspects of Hayek's pure rule of law: it was not generally applied to the people of Ireland; it was arbitrary in the treatment allowed to the Irish people, their lives, and their property; and it was certainly not applied equally. English administrators in Ireland sought both to prevent the common law from adapting to local circumstances and to prevent the English from using alternative legal systems, such as the Irish *Brehon* laws. As those administrators in Ireland shifted the focus of institutional barriers in Ireland from language or ethnicity to "blood" and descent, English law became one of the key factors behind medieval Ireland's development into a colony "in the modern sense" (Bartlett 1993, 309). The case of the imposition of English law in Ireland is an example of a medieval European legal system, the common law of England, which, in a Hayekian view, was a significant step in institutional evolution toward a rule of law conducive to the promotion of liberty, acting in the opposite direction. The English Crown and its administrators in Ireland imposed the common law upon a colonial environment, constructed rigid institutional barriers around it, and artificially maintained those barriers in the face of mounting tension at the local and regional levels. It was a preview of the tensions that early modern colonial legal regimes would create (Benton 2004, 1–30) and presents us with an early example of a legal system that Hayek saw as evolving toward the promotion of liberty acting as an externally imposed and artificially rigid institution as a constraint on liberty.

References

Baker, John H. 2019. *An Introduction to English Legal History* (5th ed.). Oxford: Oxford University Press.

Bartlett, Robert. 1982. *Gerald of Wales, 1146–1223*. Oxford: Clarendon Press.

———. 1993. *The Making of Europe: Conquest, Colonization, and Cultural Change, 950–1350*. Princeton, NJ: Princeton University Press.

Beaulier, Scott A., Peter J. Boettke, and Christopher J. Coyne. 2005. "Knowledge, Economics, and Coordination: Understanding Hayek's Legal Theory." *New York University Journal of Law & Liberty* 1: 209–224.

Benton, Lauren A. 2004. *Law and Colonial Cultures: Legal Regimes in World History, 1400–1900*. Cambridge: Cambridge University Press.

———. 2018. "The Legal Logic of Wars of Conquest: Truces and Betrayal in the Early Modern World." *Duke Journal of Comparative and International Law* 28 (3): 425–448.

Berman, Harold J. 1983. *Law and Revolution: The Formation of the Western Legal Tradition*. Cambridge, MA: Harvard University Press.

Berry, Henry F., ed. 1907. *Statutes and Ordinances, and Acts of the Parliament of Ireland: King John to Henry V.* Dublin: Alexander Thom & Co.

Boettke, Peter J. 2014. "Entrepreneurship, and the Entrepreneurial Market Process: Israel M. Kirzner and the Two Levels of Analysis in Spontaneous Order Studies." *The Review of Austrian Economics* 27 (3): 233–247.

Brand, Paul. 1995. "The Birth and Early Development of a Colonial Judiciary: The Judges of the Lordship of Ireland, 1210–1377." In *Explorations in Law and History: Irish Legal History Society Discourses, 1988–1994*, edited by W. N. Osborough, 1–48. Blackrock: Irish Academic Press.

Brennan, Jason, and David Schmidtz. 2010. *A Brief History of Liberty*. Hoboken, NJ: Wiley-Blackwell.

Clanchy, Michael T. 2013. *From Memory to Written Record: England 1066–1307* (3rd ed.). Chichester: Wiley-Blackwell.

———. 1985. "Literacy, Law, and the Power of the State." *Publications de l'École Française de Rome* 82 (1): 25–34.

Colbourn, Trevor. 1998. *The Lamp of Experience: Whig History and the Intellectual Origins of the American Revolution*. Indianapolis, IN: Liberty Fund.

Davies, Rees. 1989. "Frontier Arrangements in Fragmented Societies: Ireland and Wales." In *Medieval Frontier Societies*, edited by Robert Bartlett, and Angus MacKay, 76–100. Oxford: Clarendon Press.

Davies, Sir John. [1612] 1751. *Historical Relations; or, a Discovery of the True Causes Why Ireland Was Never Entirely Subdued, nor Brought under Obedience of the Crown of England, Until the Beginning of the Reign of King James the First. Making of the Modern World* (3rd ed.). Dublin: Matt. Williamson.

Duffy, Seán. 1997. "The Problem of Degeneracy." In *Law and Disorder in Thirteenth-Century Ireland: The Dublin Parliament of 1297*, edited by James F. Lydon, 87–106. Dublin: Four Courts Press.

Frame, Robin. 2005. "Exporting State and Nation: Being English in Medieval Ireland." In *Power and the Nation in European History*, edited by Len Scales, and Oliver Zimmer. Cambridge: Cambridge University Press.

———. 2013. "Ireland after 1169: Barriers to Acculturation on an 'English' Edge." In *Norman Expansion: Connections, Continuities and Contrasts*, edited by K. J. Stringer, and Andrew Jotischky. Farnham: Ashgate Publishing Limited.

———. 2018. "Contexts, Divisions and Units: Perspectives from the Later Middle Ages." In *The Cambridge History of Ireland: Volume I, 600–1550*, edited by Brendan Smith, 523–549. Cambridge: Cambridge University Press.

Giraldus Cambrensis. [1189] 1978. *Expugnatio hibernica: The Conquest of Ireland.* Edited by A. B. Scott, and F. X. Martin. Dublin: Royal Irish Academy.

Hamowy, Ronald. 2003. "F. A. Hayek and the Common Law." *Cato Journal* 23 (2): 241–264.

Hand, G. J. 1966. "The Status of the Native Irish in the Lordship of Ireland, 1272–1331." *The Irish Jurist* 1 (1): 93–115.

———. 1967. *English Law in Ireland, 1290–1324*. Cambridge: Cambridge University Press.

Hayek, Friedrich A. 2011. *The Constitution of Liberty: The Definitive Edition*. Edited by Ronald Hamowy. Chicago, IL: University of Chicago Press.

———. 2021 *Law, Legislation, and Liberty*. Edited by Jeremy Shearmur. The Collected Works of F. A. Hayek. Chicago, IL: University of Chicago Press.

Heng, Geraldine. 2018. *Invention of Race in the European Middle Ages*. Cambridge: Cambridge University Press.

Herzog, Tamar. 2018. *A Short History of European Law: The Last Two and a Half Millennia*. Cambridge, MA: Harvard University Press.

Hunnisett, R. F. 1961. *The Medieval Coroner*. Cambridge: Cambridge University Press.

Leeson, Peter T. 2010. "Anarchy Unbound: How Much Order Can Spontaneous Order Create?" In *Handbook on Contemporary Austrian Economics*, edited by Peter J. Boettke, Chapter 10. Cheltenham: Edward Elgar.

Lovell, Colin. 1962. "The 'Reception' of Defamation by the Common Law." *Vanderbilt Law Review* 15 (4): 1051–1071.

Lydon, James. 2019. "The Middle Nation." In *Government, War and Society in Medieval Ireland: Essays by Edmund Curtis, A. J. Otway-Ruthven and James Lydon*, edited by Peter Crooks, 332–352. Dublin: Four Courts Press.

Mahoney, Paul G. 2001. "The Common Law and Economic Growth: Hayek Might Be Right." *The Journal of Legal Studies* 30 (2): 503–525.

McSweeney, Thomas J. 2019. *Priests of the Law: Roman Law and the Making of the Common Law's First Professionals*. Oxford: Oxford University Press.

Mills, James, ed. 1905. *Calendar of the Justiciary Rolls; or, Proceedings in the Court of the Justiciar of Ireland, Preserved in the Public Record Office of Ireland. XXIII to XXXI Years of Edward I*. Dublin: Alexander Thom & Co.

Møller, Jørgen, and Jonathan Stavnskær Doucette. 2022. *The Catholic Church and European State Formation, AD 1000–1500*. Oxford: Oxford University Press.

Murtazashvili, Jennifer. 2018. "A Tired Cliché: Why We Should Stop Worrying About Ungoverned Spaces and Embrace Self-Governance." *Journal of International Affairs* 71 (2): 11–29.

Ogus, A. I. 1989. "Law and Spontaneous Order: Hayek's Contribution to Legal Theory." *Journal of Law and Society* 16 (4): 393–409.

Protevi, John. 2019. *Edges of the State*. Minneapolis, MN: University of Minnesota Press.

Scott, James C. 2009. *The Art of Not Being Governed: An Anarchist History of Upland Southeast Asia*. New Haven, CT: Yale University Press.

Smith, Brendan. 1997. "Keeping the Peace." In *Law and Disorder in Thirteenth-Century Ireland: The Dublin Parliament of 1297*, edited by James F. Lydon, 57–62. Dublin: Four Courts Press.

Veeder, Van Vechten. 1903. "The History and Theory of the Law of Defamation. I." *Columbia Law Review* 3 (8): 546–573.

Winroth, Anders. 2012. "The Legal Revolution of the Twelfth Century." In *European Transformations: The Long Twelfth Century*, edited by Thomas F. X. Noble, and John H. Van Engen, 338–353. Notre Dame, IN: University of Notre Dame Press.

7

Microenterprise Development in the Caribbean

Entrepreneurial Opportunity, Cultural Context, and Emergent Orders

Kayleigh Thompson

Microenterprise development has captured the interests of development scholars, economic practitioners, and governments internationally since the 1980s (Chamlee-Wright 2005). Advocates of microenterprise promote policies and programs as a "cure-all" for poverty and un/underemployment, and an avenue for women's empowerment and self-sufficiency in developing regions (Johnson and Kidder 1999; Karides 2005, 2010). However, postcolonial and feminist scholars argue that these "bottom-up" programs share similarities to top-down development strategies by imposing mechanistic and Western methods of entrepreneurialism and business training and disregarding the cultural, economic, and historical conditions of diverse postcolonial regions and communities. This chapter analyzes these debates and critiques leveled against microfinance and argues that simply stimulating entrepreneurship does not necessarily create a successful outcome in all contexts. This has been demonstrated in the Caribbean region, where the lack of appreciation for cultural and historical context has hindered the success of microenterprise.

This chapter also draws on Austrian cultural dimensions of markets and entrepreneurship to emphasize the importance of studying cultural considerations and economic practice with qualitative methods, paying attention to the subjective perspectives of economic actors, and thinking of culture as an interpretive lens. Austrian criticisms about top-down development initiatives are integral to this analysis of microenterprise, which is widely recognized as a bottom-up development approach. Austrian scholarship and feminist scholarship share converging concerns of top-down development, namely that it imposes individualistic, one-size-fits-all development frameworks onto local contexts affected by complex sociocultural, political, and historical circumstances. This chapter argues that microenterprise programs and policies are similar to top-down development approaches, as they also fall into the knowledge problem since they are implemented by planners and experts who believe they have the necessary knowledge to fix development problems.

Both feminist economists and Austrian scholars also share similar epistemological and methodological insights into bottom-up, self-help grassroots initiatives. This chapter contrasts examples of microenterprise programs and policies with examples of emergent orders found in the Caribbean and argues that emergent orders are beneficial and generally more successful when compared to microenterprise development because they open space for agency, they are attentive to local contexts, and they involve entrepreneurial opportunities that serve both community well-being and economic production. This chapter proposes that beneficial emergent orders can be interpreted as market processes that encompass the lived experiences of local knowledge and are both attendant to the economically productive and socially reproductive sustainability of individuals and communities. Therefore, microenterprise programs and policies are largely ineffective in many global contexts since they do not attend to the local cultural contexts and knowledge systems and narrowly focus on the income generation process.

The first section analyzes cultural dimensions of markets and entrepreneurship in Austrian scholarship. It briefly explains why foreign aid and top-down economic development often fail. The second section provides an overview of feminist economic frameworks, comparing them to Austrian scholarship. Gendered perspectives are often not considered in Austrian theories. However, feminists investigate frameworks such as gender relations, which are critical aspects of culture as they shape the lived experiences of families and the wider community. The third section provides an overview of microenterprise development, focusing on research in the Caribbean context. This section considers the gendered inequalities perpetuated by microenterprise programs and argues that microenterprise development strategies often overlook the social, political, and cultural contexts and, therefore, cannot adequately solve the problems they set out to address. While Austrian economic scholarship complements postcolonial and feminist critiques of microfinance development programs and policies, it also offers new pathways of debate regarding the cultural dimensions of microenterprise. The final section investigates the concept of emergent orders from the Austrian tradition and argues that the idea helps depict the strengths of grassroots entrepreneurial initiatives versus microenterprise development programs and policies. This section considers two broader case studies: Life Yard, a community-led initiative in Kingston, Jamaica, and Rotating Savings and Credit Associations (ROSCA) found throughout the Caribbean region. The chapter concludes with the implications of this research and suggestions for future research.

Literature Review

Austrian Cultural Dimensions of Markets and Entrepreneurship

According to Dalton (1968) and Purcell (2000), Karl Polanyi argued the importance of considering economic practice embedded in cultural institutions as early as the 1940s. His argument that economic practice both shapes and is shaped by cultural institutions is also consistent with contemporary debates in Austrian economic theory and practice, which argue that to understand the economic phenomenon better, researchers must study the cultural contexts of any given society (Lavoie and Chamlee-Wright 2000; Storr and John 2020). According to Lavoie (1991), neoclassical market theory often focuses on hypothetical scenarios involving isolated characters removed from broader society, which leads to an understanding of the economy as "static" and "fully mechanistic." Instead, he suggests that markets are "open-ended genuinely creative and evolutionary processes, rather than mechanisms that focus on a predetermined end state" (Lavoie 1991, 43). Furthermore, in some non-Austrian economic literature, aspects of culture are studied as separate, single causal factors on their own rather than an overarching framework of meaning that guides our everyday experience (Chamlee-Wright and Lavoie 2000, 14; Storr 2013, 16). As Storr (2013, 31) suggests, culture is not a tool or capital or an informal institution separate from market activity, but rather a framework, or a lens, that allows us to make sense of the world, our interactions, and our economic options.

According to Storr and John (2020), the Austrian approach to studying culture differs from other non-Austrian efforts. They outline three key approaches that Austrian economic theory applies to the study of culture. Firstly, the Austrian approach focuses on culture as meaning rather than culture as norms and attitudes. Austrian economic theory engages with the meaning that economic actors attach to their own experiences and the interpretations and meanings they apply to make sense of their actions (Hayek 1952; Mises 1949; Storr and John 2020). This type of analysis goes beyond the researcher's observation and interpretation of participant's actions and decisions from an outsider's perspective (Storr and John 2020, 27). This approach allows the researcher to get at a closer interpretation of their participant's actions "that are closer to the subjects' true motives in economic decision-making" (Storr and John 2020, 29). Lavoie and Chamlee-Wright (2000) also argue for the importance of studying cultural contexts when examining economic decision-making and enterprise. They argue that "cultural studies can explicitly show how limited the narrower instrumental sense of self-interestedness is and demonstrates by solid ethnographic work the complex interconnectedness and interdependence of individuals in society" (Lavoie and Chamlee-Wright 2000, 41). Non-western economies are complex and "have well-established roots in the history and culture of their respective indigenous societies" (Lavoie and Chamlee-Wright 2000, 48). Research that investigates such markets should examine their cultural and historical underpinnings, which ultimately influence "the various moral and social factors, the beliefs and values that drive the interactions of entrepreneurs, workers and consumers" (Storr and John 2020, 29).

Secondly, the Austrian approach emphasizes culture as an interpretive lens rather than as a tool that can be applied at will when needed. In the worst cases, understanding culture as capital has led to economists passing value judgments about the strengths or weaknesses of a given culture (Storr and John 2020, 39). As Storr and John (2020, 30) argue, "culture equates to shared patterns of meaning that make life navigable" and it's the "lens through which they interpret and make sense of their actions, opportunities, and environment." Drawing on Clifford Geertz (1973), Storr and John (2020) illuminate the key features of his concept of culture, which helps to emphasize culture as an interpretive lens rather than a tool. According to Geertz (1973), "culture represents a complex totality of meanings, such that culture is not irreducible to one or another particular belief or value" (Storr and John 2020, 30). Geertz also argues that "the set of beliefs and values that comprise a cultural system constitute a stock of knowledge that has evolved over time, and that knowledge is continuously evolving" (Storr and John 2020, 30). These "stocks of knowledge" are both adopted by each person through their community interactions, and, in turn, they are cultivated through ongoing processes of meaning-making. This perspective is significant as it demonstrates the dynamic nature of culture, which is not static but constantly shifting. According to Lavoie (1991), culture shapes our interpretive frameworks, and "as people's interpretative frameworks change, or as they attempt to change them, they begin to discover and act on different opportunities. In turn, their markets begin to look different" (Storr and John 2020,10). If markets and economic activities are grounded within and informed by shifting and dynamic cultural contexts, theoretical economic frameworks should not remain stagnant either.

Finally, the Austrian approach to cultural analysis of markets insists that cultural analysis be a qualitative exercise rather than quantitative (Storr and John 2020, 4). Storr and John (2020) emphasize that issues can arise from drawing on quantitative approaches to the study culture. For instance, they can't tell us much about why or how culture matters. They also tend to assume that cultures are homogenous, which disregards the meaningful variations within a cultural context (Storr and John 2020, 36). Storr and John (2020, 36) argue that this is significant because a culture can have dualities of meaning or "countervailing values that exist and that moderate the tendencies described." Considering Storr's (2004) research in the Bahamas, this is detailed through the duality of an "enterprising spirit" and "a cunning spirit." An enterprising spirit is a belief that "success through hard work is possible even in the face of extreme obstacles." In contrast, a cunning spirit contains the belief that actors can get ahead by taking all opportunities, even those that take advantage of others (2004, 36). In this sense, quantitative approaches that attempt to isolate specific cultural factors "prevents them from recognizing the complex trade-offs people make and the context-dependent solutions they arrive at and lead us to make unfortunate and unfair comparisons between different groups of people and environments" (Storr 2004, 38). This can also lead to the pitfall of painting cultures as static by focusing on the "steadfast qualities of groups of people" (Storr 2004, 38). Qualitative research reveals the nuances and complexities of everyday experiences and actions, as detailed by Storr's research in the Bahamas.

Chamlee-Wright (2010) also details the importance of applying qualitative methods in her research on post-disaster Hurricane Katrina community recovery efforts. According to Chamlee-Wright (2010, 24), qualitative research was significant in this context, as her participants possessed local knowledge about how and why recovery processes were failing, which was an understanding that she and her research team lacked from an outsider's perspective. Furthermore, qualitative research was necessary based on the responses she gathered through open-ended interviewing. Before their interviews, they anticipated that participants would cite the physical challenges of repairs as their biggest challenge post-Hurricane Katrina. However, she learned that the most significant challenges her participants faced were related to the uncertainty of dealing with various bureaucracies (Storr and John 2020, 41). Had she approached her research using quantitative measures, she may have missed these insights due to the intangible way bureaucratic uncertainties manifested in the research participants lives (Chamlee-Wright 2010, 33). With the open-ended nature of interviews, participants guide the discussion in directions that matter most to them. This method contrasts with quantitative methods such as survey research, in which the questions are created beforehand, which requires a lot of introspection from the researcher and closes off the possibilities of nuance in participant responses (as well as thoughtful interjections and connections they might make in open-ended interviews) (Chamlee-Wright 2010, 40). The example from Chamlee-Wright's (2010) research details the importance of qualitative methods for getting at participants' personal assessments of their lived experience.

Austrian scholars such as Boettke (1998) argue that institutional stickiness is only possible if development policies and programs account for a community's cultural beliefs and practices (Boettke 1998). Without factoring in the complex history and culture, top-down development models risk imposing culturally incompatible rules and development paradigms that do not fit in that context (Boettke 1998). As discussed later in the chapter, this has also been the case with microfinance development in the Caribbean region. The following section looks at some key Austrian criticisms of top-down approaches to development, especially those of international foreign aid and government development programs. It argues that these methods often fail because they ignore the necessary knowledge of local contexts.

Foreign Aid and Top-down Development

Foreign aid and government development programs have proposed solutions for economic development, and according to William Easterly (2005, 2007), these attempts often fail. Research on the structural adjustment programs (SAPs) following the national debt crisis and the rise in oil prices in 1978–1979 has echoed these findings. The policies were meant to provide relief in Asia, Africa, Latin America, and the Caribbean, yet they exacerbated problems (Bolles 1996, 108). According to Austrian economic theory, the failure of government and development agencies to achieve economic development and growth can be attributed to the fact that they tend to equate economic development with neoclassical economic growth theory while ignoring institutional infrastructure and focusing on measures of development (Boettke 1994). Furthermore, they tend to think of poverty as a technical problem with simple solutions, and development workers often lack the necessary knowledge of local contexts (Hall-Blanco 2016, 176). According to Boettke (1994, 9), to understand economic development, "what is needed is not more elaborate formal models of growth or better techniques for measurement, but more detailed historical studies of the pattern of development across countries and periods."

According to Austrian economic theory, one critical issue with top-down development programs is that the people who work in development act as "planners" who have the necessary knowledge to implement effective policies (Hall-Blanco 2016, 175). According to Easterly, a "planner" thinks they know the answers to the problem at hand, whereas a "searcher" admits that they don't have all the answers and understand "that poverty is a complicated triangle of political, social, historical, institutional and technological factors" (Easterly 2006, 6). He suggests that many economists and development experts are planners. The general assumption within development planning is that "enlightened experts can design reforms and other programs to 'fix' development problems" (Hall-Blanco 2016, 177). While experts may have a general understanding of what conditions are necessary for economic development, they don't have the proper mechanisms to acquire the necessary knowledge they lack to create effective top-down development policies and programs (Hall-Blanco 2016, 177). Hayek (1948, 80) argues that an individual or group of planners can't have the precise information required to construct a rational economic order through central planning. The information needed for effective economic calculation is dispersed among many individual actors. It can only be brought together through the mechanisms of entrepreneurial discovery and the competitive process of the market (Hall-Blanco 2016, 177; Hayek 1948).

Another issue that impacts the effectiveness of economic development programs and agencies is that the agents involved face perverse incentives that lead to suboptimal development outcomes (Hall-Blanco 2016, 175). For instance, instead of competing in the marketplace for profit, bureaucracies compete with other agencies for government resources:

> This dynamic implies that bureaucracies will engage in intense rent-seeking behavior in an effort to increase their budgets and expand their personnel. The logic is straightforward. If an agency demonstrates to the larger government that some of its programmes are successful, it can then claim it would be able to achieve still greater results with more resources. Even if an agency cannot produce any positive reports, it can still use such data to solicit greater government support. Failure can easily be blamed, not on poor planning or execution or fundamental issues of knowledge and competence, but on lack of resources. (Hall-Blanco 2016, 179)

This rent-seeking behavior in development agencies has further implications for the allocation of resources, as they follow a predetermined set of rules rather than profit and loss signals (Mises 1944, 50). Without these signals, making meaningful changes within bureaucracy is very difficult. Moreover, agents tend to cater to bureaucratic superiors rather than clients' needs in development projects (Hall-Blanco 2016, 179). Hall-Blanco (2016, 179) argues that those in the best positions to say what is needed (those receiving the aid) often go unheard, and development resources are usually "allocated not to those who most need them or can best use them, but to those with a comparative advantage in rent-seeking."

Easterly highlights the failings of international funding bodies such as the World Bank and the IMF throughout his scholarship, which have failed to bring about economic progress and, in some cases, have worsened conditions.

One crucial pitfall of top-down development echoed throughout Austrian scholarship on the cultural dimensions of markets is that development agencies ignore the institutional structures in which development programs are implemented (Boettke 1994). Planners who cannot know and interpret all the necessary information attempt to impose relatively simple plans on dynamic and complex societies (Hall-Blanco 2016, 181). For instance, Boettke et al. (2008) argue that cultural context and history matter for economic development. They suggest that some countries have institutions and practices that resist change, even when the change is wanted and desirable. Governments and international organizations will often impose rigorous programs and policies based on program outlines that worked in other contexts and circumstances with the hope of forcing people out of their previous ways of living (Boettke et al. 2008, 332). But these externally imposed institutional frameworks often fail because they don't reflect the "metis" of the local community. The metis refers to a group's social stock of knowledge. It's a particular way of seeing and interpreting the world (Boettke et al. 2008, 338; Storr and John 2020, 43). It can also be considered "the glue that gives institutions their stickiness" because institutions have a higher likelihood of adoption when they align with a group's metis (Boettke et al. 2008, 338; Storr and John 2020, 43). According to Chamlee-Wright (1997, 24), "not only does culture provide the 'glue' which enables social institutions to stick, it is the context in which individuals make sense of the world around them." Her research considers the failings of formal interventions made by the government and international organizations that tried to stimulate entrepreneurship through credit schemes. This case study demonstrates how cultural contexts dictate the rules governing credit and institutional stickiness and is discussed further in the following sections.

Feminist economists and Austrians share similar methodological and epistemological criticisms of neoclassical economic theory and top-down development. For instance, they both tend to attribute the failings of economic development and government development policies to an emphasis on neoclassical economic theory and the exclusion of institutional infrastructure. However, Austrians specifically argue that the knowledge problems plague development planning, such as the assumption that planners have the necessary knowledge to design programs that fix development problems through central planning. Another criticism unique to Austrian economics (but valuable to feminist epistemologies) is the potential for perverse incentives within economic development programs. For example, rather than catering to the needs of those receiving aid, agencies often compete for government resources.

Both feminist and Austrian scholars argue that development agencies often ignore institutional structures and the cultural dimensions of markets by overlooking critical cultural phenomena and historical contexts. As mentioned previously, the Austrian tradition argues that "institutional stickiness" is unlikely if cultural dimensions are overlooked. In this regard, feminist economists and Austrians share common ground. They both focus on the subjective perceptions of economic actors and argue that top-down development tends to disregard sociocultural, political, and historical contexts. The main difference between feminist and Austrian frameworks is that feminists consider gender relations and argue that the neoclassical economic theories on which economic development is based are either male-centered or based on a non-gendered "human" point of view (and removed from border cultural contexts). From a feminist economic framework, an analysis of gender relations can add meaningful cultural contexts often missing from neoclassical economic theory and top-down development initiatives. These criticisms will be discussed further concerning the failings of microenterprise development in the Caribbean in the final section of this chapter and the potential of bottom-up grassroots initiatives and emergent orders. The following section discusses some similarities between feminist and Austrian frameworks and argues for the importance of a gendered perspective within cultural analyses of microenterprise development in the Caribbean region.

A Feminist Framework and Entrepreneurship in the Caribbean

Feminist frameworks contribute a gendered perspective to the study of microenterprises grounded in the subjective perceptions of individuals and communities and engrained within local sociocultural, political, and historical contexts. According to Steven Horwitz (1995), feminist economists and Austrians share epistemological and methodological insights, especially in terms of their focus on the subjective perceptions of economic actors and their criticisms of top-down development models and neoclassical theory. Feminists argue that mainstream neoclassical theory is gendered, both in its approach to what constitutes "acceptable scientific economics" and in terms of the subjects that their models are based on, which are either male-centered or representative of a non-gendered "human" point of view (Bolles 1996, 109; Horwitz 2016, 262). In many cases, mainstream economics has ignored women's work in the household by not including it in GDP statistics, even though this work contributes to the reproduction of labor and the production process, remaining inattentive to local cultural contexts (Bolles 1996; Horwitz 1995, 264).

Both Austrians and feminists focus on the interconnections of human actors and the way they are embedded in historical, cultural, and social contexts to make sense of their experiences (Day 1995; Macdonald 1995). The

Austrian view understands this interconnectedness in terms of the knowledge problem, in which each person has incomplete knowledge. Through communication, human beings learn from one another by sharing their dispersed and contextual knowledge through market interactions. Whereas Austrian scholars do not tend to include gender in their analysis, their attention to the cultural dimensions of markets and entrepreneurship benefits from feminist frameworks that consider gender relations since they are critical aspects of culture that shape the lived experiences of families and the wider community. For instance, Browne (2001) argues that female entrepreneurship in the Caribbean is patterned according to a society's particular configuration of gendered institutions and ideologies. For example, the social histories of plantations and slave labor are distinct throughout the region and, therefore, have shaped differences in the intensities and specific forms of patriarchal institutions and ideologies throughout the region (Browne 2001, 326). The differences in patriarchal institutions and ideologies have resulted in disparities in the incidence of female entrepreneurship and local patterns of gender roles. Browne (2001, 326) argues that "the barriers to women achieving equal status are the result of specific forces, not monolithic constructs. These specific forces are associated with assumptions about male breadwinners and female homemakers and can be located at the domestic level, in the workplace, and state policy."

Peter Wilson's (1973) foundational cultural paradigm of reputation and respectability shows how gendered assumptions can have pervasive implications for how men and women are viewed in workplaces, state policy, and even development paradigms. His scholarship distinguishes two separate value systems attributed to men and women in the Caribbean, divided based on European versus traditional African values. According to Wilson (1973, 7), it also represents a clear division between gendered values and experiences based on the structure of social life as reflected in their everyday lives. Respectability is based on sexual modesty, household manners, and adherence to the values and social mores of the church (Wilson 1973, 102). Wilson (1973, 227) sees all domestic and kinship activity as the province of females, to which men are primarily peripheral (1973, 135). Conversely, men secure their identity from external values based on recognition from friends and political and economic matters.

Christine Barrow (1986) and Carla Freeman (2000) argue that Wilson's mutually exclusive duality fixes women to the household and emphasizes a western male breadwinner/dependent family ideal, which has never corresponded with the reality of the Afro-Caribbean family. Suggesting that women are more "naturally" propelled to the domestic domain and men to the public overshadows women's economic contributions to the family and the household (Barrow 1986, 166). However, these perceptions have skewed (and continue to skew) women's experiences in the Caribbean. For instance, their presumed status within the household might imply that their earnings are not primary sources of household economic support (Freeman 2000, 104). Freeman's ethnographic research in the context of Barbados reveals that the value systems are not isolated but rather a fluid dialectic within contemporary creolized Caribbean culture. This is clear in terms of how her participants engaged in the realm of reputation. Women in the informatics sector demonstrate self-sacrifice, ingenuity, and hard work, piecing together a living to support themselves and their families (Freeman 2000, 111). However, the feminine ideal of domesticity, morality, and respectability displayed through Wilson's cultural paradigm represents the tendency to naturalize women's status as homemakers, secondary labor force participants, and economically dependent on men (Green 1994, 165). Essentially, they are positioned as noneconomic agents, which explains the disregard for women's labor in measurements of GDP. Drawing on Storr's (2004) cultural duality of the "enterprising spirit" and the "cunning spirit" mentioned in the previous section, qualitative research on subjective experience that considers sociocultural, political, and historical contexts offers a more complex picture of the experiences of individuals. Feminist critiques of Wilson's paradigm also problematize top-down development and theoretical frameworks that attempt to oversimplify human experiences.

These gendered assumptions, expectations, and ideologies can also affect development policies and practices. Feminist scholars argue that development programs and policies such as SAPs and NAFTA are based on androcentric thinking (Bolles 1996). Furthermore, female entrepreneurs are underrepresented at the high end of the labor market, where economic growth is located (Browne 2001, 108). Barriteau (2001) argues that the Caribbean state draws on assumptions about women's economic activities in constructing economic programs and has little understanding of women's engagement with the formal economy or their actual output/experience as entrepreneurs. This state policy planning tends to overlook gender roles in the local context, and this inattention leads to development policies that replicate gender biases (Barriteau 2001, 122). For instance, women in business are more averse to taking risks because they are often in charge of raising children and taking care of elderly family members. Compared to men, they are less likely to risk using their capital gains or borrowing from family and friends for entrepreneurial interests. They are also less likely to take out business loans to start or grow businesses.

Furthermore, they are more likely to put earnings from business ventures into family and household expenses. For these reasons, the women in Barriteau's (2001, 143) research complained that their ventures received less support and resources than men's because they did not fit a male entrepreneurial pattern. Women combining work and family roles often experience taken-for-granted complications in establishing work-life balance, which is often neglected in entrepreneurial policy formation (Esnard 2016, 108). Very little research within developing regions like the Caribbean investigates the complexities related to the experiences and practices of navigating the combined roles of work and family for vulnerable subgroups like single mothers (Esnard 2016, 108). This reflects the assumed autonomy and rationality of female entrepreneurs, who, in the context of the Caribbean, are not the self-interested economic actors portrayed in neoclassical economic theory and top-down development policy (Barriteau 2001, 147). Their business success and interests are interconnected with families, households, extended networks, and broader community dynamics.

Feminist frameworks contribute a gendered perspective to the study of microenterprise grounded in the subjective experiences of individuals and communities and engrained within local sociocultural, political, and historical contexts. Female entrepreneurship is shaped by the gendered institutions and ideologies in place, and this is demonstrated based on the way particular colonial histories have shaped social institutions throughout the region. Peter Wilson's paradigm demonstrates the implications of cultural paradigms based on gendered theories that create assumptions and expectations regarding the roles of men and women. These ideologies have implications for development policies and practices as well. For example, planners and experts of microfinance programs, similar to those of foreign aid and structural adjustment program, lack knowledge of local community contexts. As a result, programs are administered by agents who rely on gendered and racial stereotypes in the administration of credit loans. This will be discussed further in the following section.

A Critical Assessment of Microenterprise Development in the Caribbean

Microenterprise development is an international movement consisting of many forms of entrepreneurial support, such as microcredit, loan provision, business skills training, administrative support, technical assistance, and savings skills (Karides 2005; Karides 2010; Prentice 2017). These programs target self-employed individuals and businesses with less than ten employees that function within the informal sector, such as "small production units, street vendors, and transportation services engaged in undocumented and unregulated economic activity" (Johnson and Kidder 1999; Karides 2010, 193). Microfinance became popularized in the 1970s by the Bangladeshi economist Dr. Muhammed Yunnus for his Grameen Bank microfinance model, which envisioned rapid and affordable poverty reduction through small loans to low-income individuals (Bateman 2010). Hossein (2016, 149) describes it as a "reinvention of bankers-to-the-poor," and a movement to make business finance more inclusive. Advocates of microenterprise initiatives claim that microfinance can facilitate the end of poverty by creating jobs, increasing incomes for the most economically vulnerable populations by encouraging "bottom-up" economic and social development, and impacting women's empowerment (Bateman 2010, 1). However, scholarship on microenterprise development has questioned whether microenterprise is successful in reducing poverty and to what extent it proliferates top-down power structures (Bateman 2010; Karides 2010; Prentice 2017). Research has also considered whether these programs cultivate the financial self-sufficiency and social empowerment (especially that of women) they propose (Esnard-Flavius and Aziz 2011; French 2008; Karides 2005; Moodie 2013; Prentice 2017; Strier 2010).

Microenterprise in the Caribbean is mainly state-driven, supported by government resources and the assistance of the World Bank, International Labour Organization, and UNDP (Karides 2010; Prentice 2017, 212). Scholars have raised concerns over these government-led microcredit programs and their viability in the Caribbean for various reasons, including the small size of Caribbean countries and lack of infrastructure, and the heavy reliance on government funding and international intervention (Esnard-Flavius and Aziz 2011, 98; Karides 2010). Government support of microenterprise in the Caribbean is largely the result of the debt crisis and the failure of other development strategies promoted by SAPs to adequately address poverty and unemployment (Karides 2005; Prentice 2017). In Trinidad, microenterprise development has been implemented as a key strategy to alleviate poverty and unemployment and encourage economic growth. For instance, the Government of Trinidad and Tobago, in a 1997 policy document entitled "Creating a Nation of Entrepreneurs," emphasized the need to offer new avenues for economic opportunity to manage under/unemployment for its citizens, considering dwindling opportunities in agriculture and factory work (Prentice 2017, 203). The largest microfinance agency in Trinidad is a state-run program by the National Enterprise Development Company (NEDCO), which provides "trainings, funds, advice and marketing support for entrepreneurs looking to start or develop a small business or microenterprise" (Prentice 2017, 212). Karides (2010) argues that microenterprise in Trinidad can be considered a form of social assistance that combines informal self-employment with government transfers.

Hossein (2016) argues that the failure of state-run microfinance programs in the Caribbean is primarily due to issues with political patronage in the region. She notes that NEDCO has a high loan default rate due to "its political affiliation and the perception that these loans are entitlements and not to be repaid" (2016, 152). She notes similar trends in Jamaica, where government-assisted MFIs have negatively affected microenterprise initiatives. For instance,

> In the late 1980s, Jamaica's state-owned banks—such as Workers Savings and Loans Bank, Solidarity, and the ASSIST program—made loans to the entrepreneurial poor; however, these programs, used by politicians to reward party loyalists, were disbanded because none of the "loans" were ever repaid. (Hossein 2016, 152)

Despite these failings, there are still two state-run microfinance programs in Jamaica: the Micro Investment Party (PNO) and the Self Start Fund (SSF) by former PM Edward Seaga of the JLP, which both rely on subsidies (Hossein 2016, 152). The JLP Government also contributed USD 1.7 million to its state agency, the Jamaican Business Development Corporation (JBDC), in 2009 to support microenterprise initiatives (Hossein 2016, 161). This demonstrates that state-led microenterprise development has been an ongoing trend in the Caribbean region since the early 1980s. This complicates the conception of microenterprise development initiatives as "bottom-up" approaches.

Microenterprise is an international movement endorsed by a number of "experts," such as government officials and practitioners from private financial institutions and international development agencies, who promote it as a solution to Third World poverty and a women's empowerment strategy (Karides 2005, 30). However, studies have considered the gender dynamics of microenterprise development, considering that these programs often target women, and women apply to these programs more often than men (Cagatay 1998; Esnard-Flavius and Aziz 201, 98; Hoque and Itohara 2009; Karides 2005, 30; Mayoux 2001; Rahman 1999). Some research highlights the positive impact that microenterprise programs have on the social empowerment of marginalized women, as they offer opportunities for self-employment that can be balanced with household responsibilities (Cagatay 1998). However, other constraining factors within the social and political backdrop have impacted women's success rates in these programs. For instance, Hoque and Itohara (2009) point to the marginal social empowerment of women in Bangladesh based on other constraining elements of familial ties, resources, and the institutional characteristics of microenterprises. While microfinance programs did contribute in some ways to women's empowerment in Cameroon, the women in these studies faced other issues. For instance, their income was affected by issues of gender segregation in markets of "unequal 'vertical linkages,' institutional discrimination, and gender-based intra-household relations" (Esnard-Flavius and Aziz 2011, 98; Mayoux

2001). Goetz and Sen Gupta's (1996) paper in Bangladesh also share similar findings. Their research demonstrates that women often lose control of their microloans to male partners, yet they retain the responsibility of repaying the loans (Bateman 2010, 43–44). In this sense, scholars have raised concerns about microenterprise development because the policies and programs often claim to increase female empowerment and self-sufficiency. However, numerous studies have demonstrated the disregard for the local cultural contexts of gendered responsibility and experience.

Marina Karides' (2005) research provides a gendered critique of microenterprise development in the Caribbean. She argues that microenterprise programs and lenders reinforce gender stereotypes while using the language of empowerment. For instance, women are more often provided loans due to stereotypes that women are more likely to repay them due to their responsibilities to the household and childcare (Karides 2005, 36). The assumption is that "small-scale food processing, handicraft, and textile activities allow women to balance family and childcare responsibilities with economic necessity" (Karides 2005, 47). However, these programs are accused of creating an increase in exploited workers who earn little and become burdened by debt, as well as their increased responsibilities, juggling household obligations and income-earning obligations (Karides 2005, 36). For instance, as Prentice (2017) argues, microenterprise programs often train women for skills that can be carried out in the home alongside household duties, such as sewing. However, this usually leaves women in worse financial circumstances due to the inconsistency of oversaturated markets compared to formal employment (Chamlee-Wright 2005; Ehlers and Main 1998). It also makes women more available for household labor, increasing their work burdens. This disproportionately affects women, who are more often targeted by these programs, which serves to deepen their gender subordination as their responsibilities towards labor and economic survival increase.

Karides (2005) also argues that microenterprise lenders lack a deeper understanding of the borrower's level of business knowledge, informed by their everyday experiences and community networks. The legacy of Caribbean women's self-employment is not appreciated and does not inform microenterprise programs (Karides 2005, 40). In many cases, the programs require participants to complete training programs that largely disregard the experience that women entrepreneurs bring with them. Karides' (2005, 47) interviews with government official program providers also reveal that they fall back on stereotypes and assumptions about African-Caribbean women. For instance, they harbor doubts that the women have the expertise and experience necessary to grow their businesses; they believe that they engage in habits of misspending (spending the loans and earnings of households and families rather than putting them back into the business); and they hold irregular business habits. Karides (2005, 47) argues that these assumptions are misguided and don't consider the savvy business tactics that entrepreneurs learn through years of practical experience, business interactions within extended networks and families, and the casual mentoring and assistance gained from other entrepreneurs.

Hossein's (2013) research on microfinance in Jamaica, Guyana, and Haiti is based on 491 individual interviews and focus group discussions, revealing that microfinance's promised economic and social empowerment has not been reflected in the grounded experiences of the recipients involved. According to Hossein (2013, 52):

> In the Caribbean region, where there is a colonial legacy, the historically rooted cultural politics of local-based elites have permeated the processes in micro-banking programs. As a result, microfinance is misused as a tool to reinforce exclusion practices of large segments of the very people it was designed to help. In culturally diverse settings such as the Caribbean region, there is evidence to suggest that race-, class-, and gender bias by individual managers affects the lending decisions to economically active clients.

The way that gender identity in relation to class and race affected the allocation of financial services was primarily through the stereotyping of recipients by middle-class educated loan agents, who would apply their own class bias to reject segments of the poor who are most different from them (Hossein 2013, 52). For instance, her interviews and focus groups in Jamaica revealed a pervasive anti-male bias that reinforces the exclusion of poor males from the Kingston slums because female lenders viewed them as underperformers at school and defined them as lazy (Hossein 2013, 52). The use of name-calling to explain exclusion through moneylending "exposes the hierarchical class legacy from the colonial period that continues to frame social relations in Jamaica" (Hossein 2013, 59). Her interviews revealed that a senior microfinance agent stated, "I prefer to give loans to women. It is young men between 16 and 30 years old in high crime areas who are so violent" (Hossein 2013, 59). These biases are also reflected in assessments of women who are denied access to microfinance loans. Agents exclude certain types of women who do not fit their expectations of middle-class social mores, for instance, women who are known to have children with multiple partners. In these instances, "women were stereotyped by loan officers as promiscuous, labeled as having 'loose morals' or as 'slack,'" and they were believed to pose a potential risk to the program (Hossein 2013, 59). Her research in Guyana revealed that a woman's gender may not be the only identity disadvantaging her but also her race and class position. This was evidenced by the deep-seated racism exhibited by Indo-Guyanese male bankers who discouraged the allocation of loans to Afro-Guyanese women, who are stereotyped as bad businesspeople, to justify the cultural prejudice of the bankers (Hossein 2013, 64). According to Hossein (2013, 65), this racial and class bias is pervasive in Guyana's society more broadly, which has led Afro-Guyanese women to resist social exclusion altogether by creating their own informal banks.

In general, Hossein's (2013, 60) research still points to the privileging of women loan recipients (75 percent of overall recipients) by microfinance officers who are majority women (73 percent). In addition, the research demonstrates an explicit exclusion of male recipients and a privileging of particular female recipients, who match the microfinance officers' preferred social mores. According to Hossein, this gender bias in microfinance programs often creates local conflicts and a "disempowering effect" for women because it leads to domestic disputes with the men in their lives who have been rejected from the same programs (Hossein 2013, 57). This privileging of women recipients also protects and benefits the agents own financial incentives, which are tied to their performance results and work bonuses.

State-led microenterprise programs can further embolden socioeconomic and political inequalities as well. For instance, Hossein's (2016) research investigates the political bias that interferes with accessing microfinance loans in Kingston. Jamaican MFIs provide business loans to marginalized entrepreneurs who reside in areas in downtown Kingston. However, the process of obtaining loans is shrouded in what Hossein refers to as "Big Man" politics, which essentially relates to clientelism, or, in other words, the process of informal or political leaders rewarding poor people financially in exchange for their support and their votes (Hossein 2016, 161). The Don-controlled system places gangsters with power over poor residents in the downtown slums, negatively impacting their access to loans. For instance, some eligible business owners become excluded from microenterprise programs altogether, as they are not involved in politics and thus cannot network at political events. In other cases, business owners self-exclude from the politics of microenterprises due to their perception that becoming involved with Dons is dangerous, choosing instead to hustle on their own or turning to local grassroots alternatives such as ROSCAs. Overall, the Don-controlled microenterprise system in Kingston harms social development and problematizes the assumption that the lending process is inclusive, equitable, and free from partisan bias. Furthermore, this research points to the issue of simply creating access to loans without considering the cultural and political contexts. Access to microenterprise programs may be helpful to some, but many become further marginalized and excluded.

Not only are microenterprise programs flawed for their disregard of local cultural contexts and gendered experiences of the local communities they work with, but they also reproduce and perpetuate global and local power dynamics and inequalities. The top-down delivery of microenterprise programs is based on the interests of funding agencies, "one that adopts a behavioral, deficit-oriented, pathological view of the poor" (O'Connor 2001; Strier 2010, 197). According to postcolonial scholars, these assumptions reveal deep-seated ethnocentric beliefs about the "Third World" as backward and in need of development (Karides 2005; Mohanty 1997; Said 1978). For instance,

> post-colonial critics emphasize that economic development strategies are created based on prefigured conclusions about Third World nations and people. This research attends to the ideological factors informing the implementation of micro-enterprise programs in Trinidad and contributes to the investigation of how value-driven policies shape economic development. (Karides 2005, 31–32)

Furthermore, the framing of the Caribbean region as in need of Western development and "expertise" is rooted in colonialism and development strategies that serve to deepen dependencies between the Global North and the Global South (Yelvington 1993).

Scholars of the Austrian tradition also advocate for entrepreneurialism and market processes and interactions that are free of centralized, top-down planning by development organizations and governments. Therefore, this body of scholarship contains informative insights for critics of microenterprise programs and policies. Echoing the arguments of postcolonial critics, planners outside the context of market processes are not in the best position to plan and administer programs and policies (Boettke and Coyne 2003). For instance, approaches such as microenterprise development cannot account for the formal and informal rules that facilitate market interactions, which provide incentives for people to act on opportunities. Informal rules include "context-specific norms, beliefs, and attitudes that are formed through spontaneous interactions and are culturally based" (Duncan and Coyne 2015, 683). These rules cannot be accounted for within top-down development, as they will have different consequences once applied to other contexts. Moreover, cultural context informs social institutions, including property rights, rules of contract, and rules concerning credit and finance, and development initiatives that are supplanted from one cultural context to another in a mechanistic form are likely to fail (Boettke 2001; Boettke and Coyne 2003; Chamlee-Wright 1997; De Soto 2000; Lavoie and Chamlee-Wright 2000).

The reason top-down methods of governance and economic development emphasized by microenterprise development fail, according to Hayek (1948), is that program practitioners and experts do not possess all the relevant knowledge. Moreover, no one individual or central authority has all the appropriate expertise. It must be discovered through the market process. According to Rachel Mathers (2012, 71), "relevant local knowledge might relate to culture, workforce skills, viable resources, and a variety of other factors important to the process of development and business planning." Her research investigates the issues with state-led development by considering the experiences of Indigenous Americans, arguing that "government cannot perform the rational economic calculation necessary for economic progress because the kind of knowledge required for such a task is dispersed among all individuals producing and consuming in a society rather than being centralized in one omniscient figure" (Mathers 2012, 70).

Emily Chamlee-Wright's (2005) research on microfinance in Zimbabwe further demonstrates the failures of top-down development methods such as microenterprises. Her assessments of the programs help clarify the shortfalls of their application in the Caribbean context as well. She assesses solidarity loans and argues that they offer a poor cultural fit, considering far better options are already practiced in the local context. For instance, entrepreneurs may favor informal cooperative strategies over those initiated through the group lending process. She looks at cooperative arrangements such as ma rounds clubs in contrast to those advanced through microlending programs and argues that the context they emerge from is critical to their success:

> The former stems from embedded cultural practice and correspondingly operates according to a set of well-established, self-perpetuating rules that mesh with the local cultural context. The latter, on the other hand, is perceived as being imposed from outside the local context and the rules of operation are seen as less reliable, and frequently violate cultural norms important to maintain one's status. (Chamlee-Wright 2005, 16)

She also argues that this finance method is inadequate for cultivating entrepreneurial skills such as innovation and market discovery. For instance, she raises issues with the "mechanistic approach to business development, perpetuating problems of market saturation and vulnerability to economic volatility in import and export markets and industries dependent on tourism" (Chamlee-Wright 2005, 6). Loans are often targeted at a narrow range of enterprises, emphasizing the technical aspects of the production process and overlooking the skills that lead to innovation and the discovery of new market opportunities (Chamlee-Wright 2005, 23). Furthermore, once the women complete the training programs, they are often left with little experience with marketing strategies and limited access outside of their immediate neighborhoods and networks. Chamlee-Wright (2005, 6) argues for business training methods that cultivate "creativity, innovation, market discovery, and strategies that anticipate likely changes in the economic environment, rather than a formulaic approach to entrepreneurship."

While microenterprise has been endorsed globally by experts who promote it as the answer to poverty and unemployment and a solution to gender inequity in developing regions, research that focuses on the Caribbean reveals contrasting evidence of its success rates. Focusing on the subjective perceptions of microenterprise participants and loan recipients, the scholarship introduced in this section considers the problems with state-led programs and the comparisons between top-down approaches to development and microenterprise. For instance, gender and racial stereotyping are tied to broader societal assumptions about men and women in the region and serve to exclude certain entrepreneurs over others. Microenterprise agents also lack a deeper understanding of participants' experience and business acumen. Access to microenterprise programs is further complicated by political bias, as recipients are often rewarded loans based on political support. This calls into question the expert claims that microenterprise is the answer to poverty, unemployment, and female empowerment. Considering both postcolonial and Austrian scholarship, economic development strategies adopted by experts and planners outside the cultural contexts of the region are not in the best position to endorse development strategies.

The following section assesses emergent orders and argues that the success of grassroots entrepreneurialism in the Caribbean, such as Life Yard in Jamaica and ROSCAs throughout the Caribbean, is grounded in the immediate needs of communities and individuals, as well as their value and knowledge systems. They are more beneficial and generally more successful when compared with microenterprise development because they open space for agency, are more attentive to local cultural and social contexts, and make way for entrepreneurial activities that serve community well-being and economic production.

Emergent Orders and Grassroots Entrepreneurship

Spontaneous Orders and Life Yard

Spontaneous orders encompass the self-organization of individuals and communities to meet personal and shared ends and to make adjustments "that are in their own particular interests in reaction to their particular circumstances" without the external guiding force of a central planner (Martin and Storr 2008, 73). Spontaneous order is central to the market process; "it's the idea that individuals striving to achieve their own purposes and plans can through the guiding signals and incentives of the price system result in a socially desirable allocation and distribution of resources" (Boettke 2014, 234). Hayek (1948) contends that knowledge is dispersed and emergent within shifting circumstances and contexts and is, in this sense, subconscious and inarticulate. According to Kirzner (1987, 45), "from the independent decisions of many market participants, there emerges a systematic process of learning and coordination." Emergent orders create an environment for a discovery process that cultivates creativity and innovation and anticipates social change in a way that planning cannot (Chamlee-Wright 2005).

Martin and Storr (2008) outline the key characteristics of spontaneous orders as detailed by (Hayek 1973). Firstly, they can be meaningfully described as orders, and the relationship between the parts/elements is important, according to Martin and Storr. For instance, "just as changing the distance or arrangement of the words in a sentence can dramatically alter its meaning, changing the temporal or spatial relationship between the elements that comprise an order can dramatically alter its nature" (Martin and Storr 2008, 75–76). Secondly, they are the result of human action but not of human design. They are comprised of clear social arrangements and patterns coordinated by individuals' actions but are the unintended consequence of these purposeful actions. Thirdly, the elements of the orders follow rules of conduct, and the formal and informal institutions influence the kinds of orders that emerge. Hayek argues that beneficial orders are brought about by individuals engaging in conventional rules, which share a common understanding of what they ought to or ought not to do rather than acting on desires for what they would like to do (Hayek 1973, 45; Martin and Storr 2008, 77). Finally, they are self-reinforcing, in the sense that feedback guides individual actions and decisions as to whether the order will continue.

I propose that beneficial emergent orders can be interpreted as market processes that encompass the lived experiences of local knowledge and are both attendant to the economically productive and socially reproductive sustainability of individuals and communities. This point may represent another potential convergence of Austrian and feminist scholarships that has not yet been recognized. Furthermore, microenterprise programs and policies are largely ineffective in many global contexts since they do not attend to the local cultural contexts and knowledge systems and narrowly focus on the income generation process. Life Yard is a community-based initiative that exemplifies this point.

Life Yard is a Rastafari community-based organization that started in the middle of downtown Kingston amongst some of the garrison communities, an area that has been stigmatized for its poverty, divisive politics, and gang activity (Mullings 2021). The area, in general, has dealt with high levels of gang warfare and very little investment from the state, leading to high unemployment and poor infrastructure (Mullings 2021, 154). Individuals from the local community conceptualized Life Yard with the broad goal of becoming a source of positivity and self-employment. The original creators teamed up with a street art project in 2014 known as Paint Jamaica, whose mission was "simply to challenge negative perceptions of inner-city communities and to restore a sense of neighborhood pride" (Mullings 2021, 155). Paint Jamaica brought in local artists from Jamaica to turn an empty and ruined warehouse on Fleet Street into an area covered in murals and artwork. As the community project evolves, there have been several unintended consequences. It has drawn in community-led income-generating initiatives such as "a sustainable urban farm, a vegan restaurant and juice bar, education workshops for children, and community tourism" (Mullings 2021, 155). Notably, the movement has influenced networking opportunities from organizations around Jamaica. It has ultimately drawn opportunities and commerce to an area previously isolated from surrounding communities in Kingston. Some unintended results have been the influx of tourists into an area that tourists would not have visited. Another unintended result has been the influx of high-profile celebrities into the area. For instance, many local and international dancehall artists have produced music videos in Life Yard to feature the murals, and it's a regular spot for photography. This has created networking opportunities and drawn more attention to the project's goals.

What's most important about this initiative is that it's community-led and oriented toward community building. It's organized by people who reside in the community and who have a clear sense of the day-to-day struggles that community members face. It's also a project designed and directed by young Rastafarians, whose philosophies have espoused ideologies that reject Western epistemes and promote alternative living (Mullings 2021, 155). Finally, this initiative is

> largely driven by the desire of community members to be respected, to educate and look after each other, and to generate capital. These are initiatives aimed at sustaining these communities both economically and socially, in ways that have never been provided by the state without clientelist "strings attached." (Mulling 2021, 155)

This is not to suggest that Life Yard has wholly reversed the un/under-employment of garrison communities or that it has successfully addressed the systemic issues of poverty, political strife, and gang violence. There is no up-to-date research that looks at the impacts of COVID-19 mandates on tourism in Life Yard or the effects of ongoing police presence and gang politics. However, this case study is informative because it demonstrates why emergent orders from the bottom up are more successful overall compared to top-down methods of entrepreneurial cultivation. For instance, in the case of Life Yard, the isolation of the garrison communities from surrounding communities and the Don-structured microenterprise programs discussed in the previous section mean that mechanistic programs that encourage entrepreneurialism through microfinance are not enough. They do not consider the area's social or political contexts, and they are not adequately informed of the changing circumstances or everyday needs and experiences of the individuals seeking out microenterprise opportunities. Community members are attempting to create their own self-sufficient, community-led, income-generating initiative, which runs counter to the available alternative options. It's also self-reinforcing, in the sense that feedback has guided individual actions and decisions as to whether Life Yard will continue to grow—and this is extremely important in terms of Life Yard, where the feedback has caused the idea to grow into avenues that were not originally anticipated.

According to Mullings, "Life Yard blurs distinctions between reproductive and productive work by orienting its commercial efforts towards community building ends" (Mullings 2021, 155). The initiative's success combines the intentions to attend to the community's social well-being and income generation simultaneously. This sets Life Yard apart from the microenterprise programs discussed in the previous section. Value is placed on "activities driven by motives such as care and solidarity, rather than solely profits" (Mullings 2021, 155). When studying the effects of microenterprise, there is a "discrepancy between how the self-employed are imagined, the qualities of their presumed latent 'entrepreneurialism,' and their own economic needs and goals" (Prentice 2015; Verrest 2013, 60). This idea is echoed in other Caribbean feminist research on women entrepreneurs. For instance, Karides' (2005) research on Trinidadian street vendors and Harrison's (1998) research on women in the Jamaican informal economy demonstrate that Caribbean women's entrepreneurialism is shaped by their domestic and childbearing activities. Therefore, their entrepreneurial activities cannot be separated from their reproductive ones; they are interlinked (Prentice 2017).

ROSCAs, Social Solidarity, and Entrepreneurship

According to Hossein's (2019) research, the Social and Solidarity Economy (SSE) "provides a space for people to congregate and socialize when they are shut out by mainstream business and society—and it is a place where they become aware of their exclusion" (2019, 4). Therefore, Mullings (2021) argues that for racialized and Indigenous communities, both the economically productive and socially reproductive go together, which is an understanding that is often lacking in top-down entrepreneurial programs and policies.

This is also clear through research on ROSCAs, which emphasize community-building, solidarity, support, and the intention of income generation. Understood as "unregulated financial systems that provide quick access to savings and credit systems for people, mainly women, who are excluded from formal banking channels" (Ardener and Burman 1996; Hossein 2018, 84; Purcell 2000; Rogaly 1996). There is a long history of their application in the Caribbean, rooted in slavery and colonization (Hossein 2018; Purcell 2000). They counter mainstream bank rules, attend to the needs of women for social interaction and interconnectedness, and provide a space for racialized people who have been shut out from formal programs and institutions to find economic opportunities and support. Most importantly, they place community before commercial profits, which explains their success and deeply rooted history in the Caribbean (Hossein 2018, 82).

Trevor Purcell's (2000) research investigates ROSCAs in Barbados, Jamaica, and Trinidad. ROSCAs are cooperative grassroots development models based on local/indigenous cultural institutions that are a clear example of development based on well-being as opposed to economic growth that focuses solely on material accumulation. ROSCAs have been documented to varying degrees throughout the Caribbean region, including Antigua, the Bahamas, Montserrat, Martinique, Haiti, St. Vincent, Jamaica, Guyana, Barbados, the Dominican Republic, and Trinidad and Tobago (Purcell 2000, 146). These institutions are formed by a core group of participants who agree to make regular contributions to a fund, which is given either partially or fully to each contributor in a cyclical rotation (Ardener 1964, 201). According to Purcell, the membership revolves around an organizer or "banker" who collects and administers the fund. The ROSCAs may be workplace-based or community-based, characterized by "informality, flexibility, and low cost of operations" (Purcell 2000, 147).

According to Purcell (2000, 148), what makes these institutions successful in the Caribbean is that "they are not based on a singular, impersonal homo-economicus rationality, but on a dual rationality of material gain and cultural solidarity." Further, "the cultural solidarity necessary for the institution to function is rooted in the cultural value and trust, which is in turn rooted in pre-established communal/reciprocal relationships—relationships which together constitute social capital." It is the cultural dimension of social capital, which Purcell argues plays a vital role in "mitigating the well-documented socially disintegrative tendencies of imported models of development" (Purcell 2000, 148).

Drawing on qualitative data from his interviews in Jamaica, Trinidad, and Barbados, Purcell explains the motivations for joining ROSCAs. These motivations are not purely economic—there are social reasons that explain why participants opted to join a ROSCA even though they had access to banks. Firstly, they provide ready cash without the obligation to pay tax or interest. For instance, the primary reasons for joining "pardnas" (partner in Jamaican creole) in Jamaica "were the personalized context for raising capital, forced savings, and the absence of government taxation" (Katzin 1959, 439). Participants in Barbados and Trinidad also cited low interest and taxes and compulsory savings, or a desire to save, as key reasons (Purcell 2000, 158). Some of the noneconomic reasons cited were flexibility and "the opportunity ROSCAs afford each participant to negotiate access to the fund depending on his/her specific need" (Purcell 2000, 160). Responses related to flexibility came up at each research site in open-ended interviews. Another motivation is the familiarity and informality of the system compared to perceptions of the bank. For instance, ROSCA members are usually known to each other, which creates an environment of casual closeness where there's more socializing and trust (Purcell 2000, 161). Purcell notes the critical role of culture in the origin of ROSCAs, which supplies the direction for creating these cooperative economic practices over individualistic ones (such as microenterprises) and the reason for their preference.

The Caribbean ROSCAs have their roots in the traditional West African cultural worldview of solidary group identity and reciprocity (Purcell 2000, 152–153). Their cooperative nature is derived from the cultural adaptive strategies of the region, which is reflected in the monistic cosmology outlined by the Kenyan philosopher-theologian John Mbiti over two decades ago (Purcell 2000, 153). In his view, the cosmos is broken down into five categories: God, spirits, people, animals and plants, and inanimate things that form an interconnected whole. These values are reflected in how ROSCA relations are structured, which are based on long-term personal relations held together by trust and reputation, as opposed to the impersonal ties of mutual benefit sanctioned by state laws (Purcell 2000, 154). Relations based on reciprocity of labor, goods, and services have provenance in preindustrial kin groups, forming the backbone of community organization (Purcell 2000, 167). While slavery destroyed the remnants of many of these communities, the diaspora drew on ancestral knowledge and the ethic of reciprocity to survive slavery and peasant communities (Mintz and Price 1992). Trust is essential to the functionality and organization of ROSCAs because they have traditionally functioned outside of state regulations. The key mechanism used to ensure compliance was communal or personal condemnation for noncompliance (Besson 1995, 167; Senior 1991, 146). The viability of this institution is based on interpersonal relations in small groups, and the members are often involved regularly with other aspects of collective life; they may be kin members, church members, or coworkers. Therefore, incurring a bad reputation would affect relations in different ways (Purcell 2000, 167).

As a capitalizing institution, ROSCAs can boost entrepreneurial expansion without the threat to social cohesion and cultural alienation inherent in the growth model of "development" posed through MFIs and traditional top-down approaches to development (Purcell 2000, 154). ROSCAs also provide an alternative option for those who have been rejected from MFIs. An important benefit is that they are both economically productive and socially reproductive due to their rootedness in Caribbean cultural values of trust and reciprocal relationships, which contrast with the individualistic models of microenterprise.

Conclusion

Drawing on the cultural dimensions of markets and entrepreneurship and the failures of top-down economic development influenced by neoclassical theory, this chapter considered critiques of microenterprise development in the Caribbean region. Postcolonial, feminist, and Austrian scholarship demonstrates that microenterprise programs ignore the local sociocultural, political, and historical circumstances of developing regions, often perpetuating gendered and cultural stereotypes and inequalities within their operations and practices. Moreover, these programs and policies often disregard local grassroots initiatives already in place, which are attendant to the cultural practices and values of the communities where they operate. This chapter advances the idea that there remains a "disconnect between a global market logic that defines work as that which advances market wealth creation, and the sense of agency and social accomplishment that local communities derive from work that advances both economic opportunity and a renewed commitment to human respect and dignity" (Mullings 2021, 156). There is a lack of research outlining the problems with microenterprises from the participants' perspective (especially women), and even less research demonstrating the value and benefit of grassroots initiatives in the social economy. Chamlee-Wright (2005, 25) argues that ". . . NGOs, donor agencies, and commercial organizations will be more successful in meeting their goals and those of entrepreneurs if they are prepared to adjust to the local culture rather than expect the culture to adapt to the development strategy." I would also add that a gendered approach needs to go beyond the acknowledgment of microenterprise for women's empowerment to recognize the intersectional and cultural backdrop of women's experiences. Providing income-earning opportunities is important and necessary. However, they do little good for women and local communities if they are not attendant to cultural context, if they are based on neoclassical economic theories, and if they assume a hegemonic experience. This is why alternative orders, such as the two case studies of Life Yard and ROSCAs, tend better to the on-the-ground circumstances, as they are fostered from the bottom-up and based on the current and changing needs of community well-being.

References

Ardener, Shirley. 1964. "The Comparative Study of Rotating Credit Associations." *Journal of the Royal Anthropological Institute of Great Britain and Ireland* 94 (2): 201–229.

Ardener, Shirley, and Sandra Burman. 1996. *Money-Go-Rounds: The Importance of Rotating Savings and Credit Associations for Women.* Oxford: Berg.

Barriteau, Eudine. 2001. "Women, the Economy and the State." In *The Political Economy of Gender in the Twentieth-Century Caribbean*, edited by Timothy M. Shaw et al., 121–150. New York: Palgrave.

Barrow, Christine. 1986. "Finding the Support: A Study of Strategies for Survival." *Social and Economic Studies* 35 (2): 131–176.

Bateman Milford. 2010. *Why Doesn't Microfinance Work? The Destructive Rise of Local Neoliberalism.* London: Zed Books.

Besson, Jean. 1995. "Women's Use of ROSCAs in the Caribbean: Reassessing the Literature." In *Money-Go-Rounds: The Importance of Rotating Savings and Credit Associations for Women*, edited by Shirley Ardener, and Sandra Burman, 26388. Oxford and Washington, DC: BERG.

Boettke, Peter J. 1994. *The Collapse of Development Planning.* New York and London: New York University Press.

———. 1998. "Why Culture Matters: Economics, Politics and the Imprint of History." *Ama-gi: The Journal of the Hayek Society at the London School of Economics* 2 (1): 9–16.

———. 2001. "Why Culture Matters: Economics, Politics, and the Imprint of History." In *Calculation and Coordination: Essays on Socialism and Transitional Political Economy*, 448–265. London: Routledge.

———. 2014. "Entrepreneurship and the Entrepreneurial Market Process: Israel M. Kirzner and the Two Levels of Analysis in Spontaneous Order Studies." *Review of Austrian Economics* 27 (3): 233–247.

Boettke, Peter J., and Christopher J. Coyne. 2003. "Entrepreneurship and Development: Cause or Consequence." In *Advances in Austrian Economics, Volume 6: Austrian Economics and Entrepreneurial Studies*, edited by Roger Koppl, 67–87. New York: Elsevier Science, JAI.

Boettke, Peter J., Christopher J. Coyne, and Peter Leeson. 2008. "Institutional Stickiness and the New Development Economics." *American Journal of Economics and Sociology* 67 (2): 331–358.

Bolles, Lynn A. 1996. "Paying the Piper Twice: Gender and the Process of Globalization." *Caribbean Studies* 29 (1): 106–119.

Browne, Katherine E. 2001. "Female Entrepreneurship in the Caribbean: A Multisite, Pilot Investigation of Gender and Work." *Human Organization* 60 (4): 326–342.

Cagatay, Nilufer. 1998. "Gender and Poverty." Social Development and Poverty Elimination Division, Working Paper 5. United Nations Development Programme.

Chamlee-Wright, Emily. 1997. *The Cultural Foundations of Economic Development: Urban Female Entrepreneurship in Ghana.* London: Routledge.

———. 2005. "Entrepreneurial Response to 'Bottom-up' Development Strategies in Zimbabwe." *The Review of Austrian Economics* 18 (1): 5–28.

———. 2010. *The Cultural and Political Economy of Recovery: Social Learning in a Post-Disaster Environment*. New York: Routledge.

Chamlee-Wright, Emily, and Virgil Storr. 2010. "The Role of Social Entrepreneurship in Post-Katrina Community Recovery." In *The Political Economy of Hurricane Katrina and Community Rebound*, edited by Emily Chamlee-Wright, and Virgil Storr, 87–106. Cheltenham: Edward Elgar.

Dalton, George. 1968. *Primitive, Archaic and Modern Economies: Essays of Karl Polanyi*. Boston, MA: Beacon Press.

Day, Tanis. 1995. "Symposium on Feminist Economics: Introduction." *Canadian Journal of Economics* 28: 139–42.

De Soto, Hernando. 2000. *The Mystery of Capital: Why Capitalism Triumphs in the West and Fails Everywhere Else*. New York: Basic Books.

Duncan, Thomas K., and Christopher J. Coyne. 2015. "The Political Economy of Foreign Intervention." In *Oxford Handbook of Austrian Economics*, edited by Peter J. Boettke, and Christopher J. Coyne, 678–997. Oxford: Oxford University Press.

Easterly, William. 2005. "What Did Structural Adjustment Adjust? The Association of Policies and Growth with Repeated IMF and World Bank Adjustment Loans." *Journal of Development Economics* 76: 1–22.

———. 2006. *The White Man's Burden: Why the West's Efforts to Aid the Rest Have Done So Much Ill and So Little Good*. New York: Penguin Press.

———. 2007. "Was Development Assistance a Mistake?" *The American Economic Review* 97 (2): 328–332.

Ehlers, Tracy Bachrach, and Karen Main. 1998. "Women and the False Promise of Microenterprise Development." *Gender and Society* 12: 424–440.

Esnard, Talia. 2016. "Mothering and Entrepreneurship: Experiences of Single Women in St. Lucia." *Women, Gender, and Families of Color* 4 (1): 108–132.

Esnard-Flavius, Talia, and Zainab Aziz. 2011. "Microcredit, Microenterprises and Social Welfare of the Rural Poor in North-Eastern Trinidad: An Evaluation of 'HOPE'." *Asian Academy of Management Journal* 16 (1): 95–118.

Ffrench, Sean. 2008. "Funding Entrepreneurship Among the Poor in Jamaica." *Social and Economic Studies* 57 (2): 119–148.

Freeman, Carla. 2000. *High Tech and High Heels in the Global Economy: Women, Work and Pink-Collar Identities in the Caribbean*. Durham & London: Duke University Press

Geertz, Clifford. 1973. *The Interpretation of Cultures*. New York: Basic Books.

Green, Cecilia. 1994. "Historical and Contemporary Restructuring and Women in Production in the Caribbean." In *The Caribbean in the Global Political Economy*, edited by Hilbourne A. Watson, 149–172. Kingston: Ian Randle Publishers.

Goetz, Anne Marie, and Rina Sen Gupta. 1996. "Who Takes the Credit? Gender, Power, and Control over Loan Use in Rural Credit Programs in Bangladesh." *World Development* 24 (1): 45–63.

Hall-Blanco, Abigail R. 2016. "Why Development Programmes Fail: William Easterly and the Political Economy of Intervention." *Economic Affairs* 35 (2): 175–183.

Harrison, Faye V. 1998. "Women in Jamaica's Informal Economy: Insights from a Kingston Slum." *Nieuwe West-Indische Gids New West Guide* 62 (3–4): 103–128.

Hayek, Friedrich A. 1948. "The Use of Knowledge in Society." In *Individualism and Economic Order*, 77–91. Chicago, IL: University of Chicago Press.

———. 1952. *The Counter Revolution of Science: Studies on the Abuse of Reason*. Glencoe, IL: The Free Press.

———. 1973. *Law, Legislation and Liberty: Vol. 1, Rules and Order*. Chicago, IL: University of Chicago Press.

Hoque, Mahmuda, and Yoshihto Itohara. 2009. "Women Empowerment through Participation in Micro-Credit Programme: A Case Study of Bangladesh." *Journal of Social Sciences* 5 (3): 244–250.

Horwitz, Steven. 1995. "Feminist Economics: An Austrian Perspective." *Journal of Economic Methodology* 2 (2): 259–279.

Hossein, Caroline Shenaz. 2013. "Using a Black Feminist Framework: A Study Comparing Bias Against Female Entrepreneurs in Caribbean Micro-banking." *Intersectionalities: A Global Journal of Social Work Analysis, Research, Polity, and Practice* 2: 51–70.

———. 2016. "'Big Man' Politics in the Social Economy: A Case Study of Microfinance in Kingston, Jamaica." *Review of Social Economy* 74 (2): 148–171.

———. 2018. *The Black Social Economy in the Americas: Exploring Diverse Community-Based Markets*. New York: Palgrave Macmillan.

———. 2019. "A Black Epistemology for the Social and Solidarity Economy: The Black Social Economy." *The Review of Black Political Economy* 46 (3): 209–229.

Johnson, Susan, and Thalia Kidder. 1999. "Globalization and Gender—Dilemmas for Microfinance Organizations." *Small Enterprise Development* 10: 4–15.

Karides, Marina. 2005. "Whose Solution Is It? Development Ideology and the Work of Micro-Entrepreneurs in Caribbean Context." *International Journal of Sociology and Social Policy* 25 (1/2): 30–62.

———. 2010. "Theorizing the Rise of Microenterprise Development in Caribbean Context." *American Sociological Association* 16 (2): 192–216.

Katzin, Margaret F. 1959. "'Partners': An Informal Savings Institution in Jamaica." *Social and Economic* Studies 8 (4): 437–440.

Kirzner, Israel M. 1987. "Spontaneous Order and the Case for the Free Market Society." In *Ideas on Liberty: Essays in Honor of Paul Poirot*, edited by Robert G. Anderson and Beth A. Hoffman, 45–50. Irvington-on-Hudson, NY: Foundation for Economic Education.

Lavoie, Don. 1991. "The Discovery and Interpretation of Profit Opportunities: Culture and the Kirznerian Entrepreneur." In *The Culture of Entrepreneurship*, edited by B. Berger, 22–51. San Francisco, CA: ICS Press.

Lavoie, Don, and Emily Chamlee-Wright. 2000. *Culture and Enterprise: The Development, Representation, and Morality of Business*. London: Routledge.

Macdonald, Martha. 1995. "Feminist Economics: From Theory to Research." *Canadian Journal of Economics* 28: 159–76.

Mathers, Rachel L. 2012. "The Failure of State-Led Economic Development on American Indian Reservations." *The Independent Review* 17 (1): 65–80.

Martin, Nona P., and Virgil Henry Storr. 2008. "On Perverse Emergent Orders." *Studies in Emergent Order* 1: 73–91.

Mayoux, Linda. 2001. "Tackling the Downside: Social Capital, Women's Empowerment and Micro-finance in Cameroon." *Development and Change* 32: 421–450.

Mintz, Sidney W., and Richard Price. 1992. *The Birth of African American Culture*. Boston: Beacon Press.

Mises, Ludwig von. 1944. *Bureaucracy*. Grove City, PA: Libertarian Press.

———. 1949. *Human Action: A Treatise on Economics*. San Francisco, CA: Fox & Wilkes.

Mohanty, Chandra Talpade. 1997. "Women Workers and Capitalist Scripts: Ideologies of Domination, Common Interests, and the Politics of Solidarity." In *Feminist Genealogies, Colonial Legacies, Democratic Futures,* edited by M. Jacqui Alexander, and Chandra Talpade Mohanty, 3–29. New York: Routledge.

Moodie, Megan. 2013. "Microfinance and the Gender of Risk: The Case of Kiva.org." *Signs Journal of Women in Culture and Society* 38 (2): 279–302.

Mullings, Beverley. 2021. "Caliban, Social Reproduction and Our Future Yet to Come." *Geoforum* 118: 150–158.

O'Connor, Alice. 2001. *Poverty Knowledge: Social Science, Social Policy, and the Poor in Twentieth-Century U.S. History*. Princeton, NJ: Princeton University Press.

Prentice, Rebecca. 2015. *Thiefing a Chance: Factory Work, Illicit Labor, and Neoliberal Subjectivities in Trinidad*. Boulder, CO: University Press of Colorado.

———. 2017. "Microenterprise Development, Industrial Labour and the Seductions of Precarity." *Critique of Anthropology* 37(2): 201–222.

Purcell, Trevor W. 2000. "Local Institutions in Grassroots Development: The Rotating Savings and Credit Association." *Social and Economic Studies* 49 (1): 143–181.

Rahman, Aminur. 1999. *Women and Microcredit in Rural Bangladesh: Anthropological Study of the Rhetoric and Realities of Grameen Bank Lending*. Boulder, CO: Westview.

Rogaly, Ben. 1996. "Microfinance Evangelism, Destitute Women and the Hard Selling of a New Anti-Poverty Formula." *Development in Practice* 6 (2): 100–112.

Said, Edward. 1978. *Orientalism*. New York: Pantheon Books.

Senior, Olive. 1991. *Working Miracles: Women's Lives in the English-Speaking Caribbean*. Bloomington and Indianapolis, IN: Indiana University Press.

Storr, Virgil Henry. 2004. *Enterprising Slaves and Master Pirates: Understanding Economic Life in the Bahamas*. New York, NY: Peter Lang.

———. 2013. *Understanding the Culture of Markets*. New York, NY: Routledge.

Storr, Virgil, and Arielle John. 2020. *Cultural Considerations within Austrian Economics*. Cambridge: Cambridge University Press.

Strier, Roni. 2010. "Women, Poverty, and the Microenterprise: Context and Discourse." *Gender, Work and Organization* 17 (2): 195–218.

Verrest, Hebe. 2013. "Rethinking Microentrepreneurship and Business Development Programs: Vulnerability and Ambition in Low-Income Urban Caribbean Households." *World Development* 47: 58–70.

Wilson, Peter. 1973. *Crab Antics: The Social Anthropology of English-Speaking Negro Societies of the Caribbean*. New Haven, CT: Yale University Press.

Yelvington, Kevin A. 1993. "Introduction." In *Trinidad Ethnicity,* edited by Kevin A. Yelvington, 1–32. Memphis, TN: University of Tennessee Press.

8

A Tale of Two Crimes

An Inquiry into the Normative Evaluation of Illicit Spontaneous Orders

Florian A. Hartjen

THINGS ARE NOT ALWAYS WHAT THEY SEEM

Can illicit orders be beneficial? For the public, crime is a synonym for anarchy and disorder. This instinct results from crime being defined as a punishable infringement of societal rules. It is deemed to be perverse in the very sense of "turned away of what is right or good" (Merriam-Webster.com 2022). In contrast, criminal orders can be an effective form of ordering outside the state and provide genuine institutions even beyond the underworld (Gambetta 1996; Skarbek 2011). They are a subtype of a wide range of orders outside or in the shadow of the law (Richman 2017). They are something conventional economics ignored for a long time, taking it for granted that the state alone provides an effective and costless institutional order (Dixit [2004] 2006, 3). But informal orders can also fail just like states can collapse (Ostrom [1990] 2015). So, under what circumstances can an order that acts in outright opposition to the formal rules of society, such as organized crime or a black market, be beneficial? And to whom? This chapter joins recent literature that aims to uncover the hidden rules of the underworld, providing a more nuanced view of the normative evaluation of illicit orders.

Things are not always what they seem. And it is the curious task of rational choice-based political economy to look behind the curtain of orders by exploring individual decision-making and the rules that guide it. This perspective allows for understanding human behavior and practices that, from the outside, seem outright puzzling (Leeson 2017). Without a doubt, illicit orders often come with many strange or repulsive features. Crime seems ridden with violence, irrationality, chaos, and exploitation. However, there must be something about illicit orders that makes them resilient and keeps them alive, notwithstanding the seemingly unbearable conditions. In fact, many things are not what they seem. Insured victims of kidnappers actually have an almost 100 percent chance of getting released alive (Shortland 2019). Prison gangs can be effective forms of self-governance where authorities fail to effectively deliver and enforce rules (Skarbek 2016). And a reasonable mafia can be the preferable choice (or even the protection against) an extortionist police force (Varese 2001). However, not only can some orders be beneficial to those who are directly involved, organized crime can also limit externalities and be beneficial for society at large (Buchanan 1979).

The fact that so many criminal orders turn out to be based on efficient and effective rules should only surprise at first glance. Most illicit orders are also spontaneous orders arising unintendedly and as a mere consequence of human action. And spontaneous orders, such as the market economy, are generally seen as a good indicator for beneficial outcomes (Hayek [1944] 2007). Yet, this should not indicate that all illicit spontaneous orders produce beneficial outcomes. In the same manner, as criminal orders should not be considered harmful per se, spontaneous orders are no guarantee for beneficial results. "Unlike positive spontaneous orders, perverse emergent orders cannot be said to be socially beneficial. Although these orders are arguably quite common, spontaneous order theorists have not paid much attention to them" (Martin and Storr 2008, 74). However, spontaneous order theorists tend to be biased toward demonstrating the beneficial effects of the invisible hand. Consequently, perverse spontaneous orders are undertheorized.

This chapter will shed further light on the normative evaluation of spontaneous orders. For this purpose, I will examine the illicit markets for migrant smuggling services in the Mediterranean. Migrant smuggling is defined as the illicit transport of human beings across borders and its facilitation (United Nations 2000a). It is a prominent view that smuggling is based on a consensual relation between migrants and their aides (Campana 2019; Sanchez 2014). In contrast, victims of closely related human trafficking (United Nations 2000b) have no agency and are degraded into tradeable objects (Campana and Varese 2016). However, this benevolent view on smuggling and the subsequent distinction between good smuggling and bad trafficking are not unquestioned. Gallagher (2008, 792) calls the differentiation between smuggling and trafficking a "strange legal fiction . . . involving helpless, virtuous victims on the one side and foolish or greedy adventurers, complicit in their own misfortune, on the other." In contrast to the above, Gallagher (2015) sees "markets are the key drivers of illegality and exploitation."

This can be seen as an expression of a multifaceted debate about the true nature of migrant smuggling that tries to uncover the nuances. And, in fact, the now dominant "smuggling as a business" approach is only one out of many (Baird and van Liempt 2015). Meanwhile, the policy stance is not nearly as nuanced as the academic debate is now. The most recent 2021–2025 migrant smuggling action plan of the European Union states that

> smuggling often involves the organized exploitation of migrants, showing little respect for human life in the pursuit of profit. This criminal activity damages both the humanitarian and the migration management objectives of the EU. Therefore, the prevention and fight against migrant smuggling must be at the centre of a strong European migration and asylum system.

This does not come without practical consequences as the EU derives from this assessment the political imperative to shower neighboring regimes with money in their attempt to stop every irregular movement in the Mediterranean (Vogt 2020).

Those who look at migrant smuggling favorably must confront the question of how their view can be reconciled with counterfactual observations. After all, field research also reports that "smuggled migrants may be coerced, punished, tortured, or taken hostage by their smugglers while in transit, defying the demarcation of what would otherwise be considered voluntary in this category" (Baird and van Liempt 2015, 402). And they need to address why their assessment does not convince policymakers and the wider public that smugglers would be just a straw man when trying to improve migrants' situations.

I posit that spontaneous order theory can aid this task. It provides a systematic view of the migrant smuggling markets in the Mediterranean. One that puts evolving rules at the center of attention and how individuals respond to them. This approach allows for disentangling puzzling observations from opposing explanatory models. Hence, I will look at patterns of migrant smuggling practices across the Mediterranean. The underlying theme will be "the tale of the two crimes," good and bad smuggling. Are the markets for migrant smuggling in the Mediterranean just what they seem and what the EU suspects? Or are they, after all, individually beneficial for migrants? Because that is the question of which different strands of research, the public, and policymakers have reached so strikingly different conclusions. The other hotly debated question in the field of migrant smuggling—whether it is socially beneficial—will be omitted. This is not so much a strange puzzle that needs to be solved but rather a consideration of many socioeconomic and cultural factors that are not less interesting but would go far beyond this scope.

For the following analysis, I will be using a wide range of existing fieldwork supplemented by a set of six in-depth expert interviews conducted with individuals with partly significant field experience.[1] My analysis is structured as follows: In the next section, I will lay out spontaneous order theory, provide examples, and discuss how to distinguish between the individual and social dimensions in the normative evaluation of orders. I will base this analysis on an engagement with the works of Friedrich August von Hayek, who made the concept of spontaneous orders a centerpiece of his life work. Examples of how to evaluate spontaneous order will be provided by Martin and Storr (2008), Nozick ([1974] 2013), Olson ([2000] 2001), and Schelling (1969). This is followed by a deeper descriptive look into the "tale of the two crimes," good and bad smuggling, and, finally, an invisible-hand analysis of selected smuggling practices in the Mediterranean. The conclusion summarizes the results and the benefits of using invisible-hand explanations when studying the normative evaluation of illicit orders.

Approaching the Normative Evaluation of Spontaneous Order

Spontaneous order theory approaches social phenomena not from a bird's-eye view but from the perspective of the individual. In short, it is concerned with the individual decision-making process and the institutions that govern it. Robert Nozick, a pronounced advocate of spontaneous order theory, posits that

> there is a certain lovely quality to explanations of this sort. They show how some overall pattern or design, which one would have thought had to be produced by an individual's or group's successful attempt to realize the pattern, instead was produced and maintained by a process that in no way had the overall pattern or design "in mind." (Nozick [1974] 2013, Ch. 2)

This section develops the argument that invisible-hand explanations can aid the normative analysis of illicit orders by (1) detaching the overall appearance of an order from the actual intentions and actions, (2) pointing attention to the procedural rules that govern an order, and (3) putting emphasis on the evolutionary process during which rules are adapted to achieve superior equilibria.

Key Definitions

Economic ordering is an indirect response to human imperfection. Without order, individuals would be helplessly trapped in social dilemmas (Ostrom 2010). Humans cannot know everything, and they cannot trust each other unconditionally (Pennington 2011). This makes economic interaction very costly because we need to gather and process as much information as possible and protect ourselves against opportunistic behavior from others. The resulting transaction costs are the decisive limits of human cooperation (Coase 1937; Demsetz 1968; Williamson 1979). However, cooperation between individuals is the very source of progress and wealth (Hayek 1988; Smith [1776] 1993). Whether it be the division of labor, trade, or science, without cooperation, most accomplishments of human civilization would be unthinkable. Hence, humanity has devised institutions that coordinate individual activities in a way that facilitates cooperation (North 1992). However, what exactly is an order?

Turning to Hayek ([1973] 2013, 36), he writes that an order is the resulting

> state of affairs in which a multiplicity of elements of various kinds are so related to each other that we may learn from our acquaintance with some spatial or temporal part of the whole to form correct expectations concerning the rest or at least expectations which have a good chance of proving correct.

This definition has three key elements: First, an order is based on the interrelations of "elements." This means that participants in an order can identify and set rules that trigger certain repeated interactions, a mechanism that we are so used to that we tend to overlook its complexity. In market order, for example, most trades follow a set pattern. Sellers make an invitation to potential buyers to make an offer, which is in civil law known as "*invitiatio ad offerendum*." For example, a sign in a coffee shop that displays various drinks and prices. Based on this, customers can make a corresponding offer to buy drink *x* for price *y*. The shop owner can decide to accept, decline, or make a counteroffer, for example, if a certain product is sold out. If both parties agree, the transfer of the product follows concurrent payment, and often within seconds, buyer and seller have concluded civil contact with each other without realizing its many layers.

Such an order is maintained through institutions. Institutions are the formal and informal rules and norms that govern social exchange (Crawford and Ostrom 1995; North 1991). Institutions define the social environment in which we operate by tackling human imperfections. They limit the scope for opportunistic behavior and facilitate access to information. They can be endogenous to an order (and deliberately created by the involved individuals), or they can be exogenous (and set by actors outside the order). To illustrate this: The simple act of buying coffee is governed by a myriad of formal and informal institutions. The most basic one is the rule of trading: in exchange for x amount of money, the buyer gets the product y. Unlike, for example, an idealized socialist society, in which goods are allocated based on pre-defined needs and not through an exchange. Then there are the formal exogenous rules of civil law outlined above. And there are the public laws that only apply to the seller such as hygiene and advertising standards. Beyond that, seller and buyer observe a multitude of informal rules, such as tipping culture, lining up, or even writing the seller's name on the coffee cup to facilitate serving.

That we rarely realize the complexity of orderly interaction is due to the other two key concepts in Hayek's definition of order: learning and forming expectations. The interrelation of elements creates repetitive institutional patterns that allow us to learn. Returning to the coffee shop thought experiment, someone completely new to the market would certainly struggle on the first attempt to acquire a coffee. For this, it is already enough to transact outside the usual institutional framework, as Europeans who struggle with US tipping culture vividly demonstrate. However, this person would quickly realize that most day-to-day market interactions follow a similar pattern and learn how to behave in transaction situations, no matter if they were a coffee or a burger. It is not even necessary that the person know the formal legal sequence laid out above to form expectations about how potential counterparties might behave. In essence, an order is like an unspoken language that allows its participants to efficiently transact, exchange, and cooperate without having to know the counterparty beforehand. Similarly to the law, one does not need to know exact grammatical rules to speak a language perfectly. In essence, every pattern of interrelations that allows participants to form informed expectations is also an order.

A Typology of Ordering

Not all orders are the same (see table 8.1). One basic distinction is between spontaneous orders and planned orders. Spontaneous orders are not purposefully designed by a central entity but instead the product of the evolutionary

TABLE 8.1
Typology of Ordering

	Spontaneous Order	*Planned Order*
Legal	Market Economy	States
Illicit	Black Market	Mafias

Source: Created by Florian A. Hartjen

interaction between individuals that gradually seek to improve their position. The defining element of spontaneous orders is the absence of a particular intended purpose (Hayek [1973] 2013, 38). Spontaneous orders are, as the Scottish philosopher Adam Ferguson put it, "the result of human action, but not the execution of any human design" (Ferguson [1767] 1980). The example of market orders, as the prime instance of spontaneous orders, illustrates their character. Markets comprise a plethora of human-purposeful planning and institutions, such as contract law, money, and societal norms. The resulting specific market prices and allocations, however, are not intended by anyone. This must not be confused with the general expectation that the market order will provide some prices and an allocation mechanism.

Neither should one confuse order with legality. Orders can arise in line with the formal rules of society and outside the law. Illicit orders, in general, seem to be an excellent case study for spontaneous order theorizing. The omnipresent use of violence in the underworld does not contradict the existence of order (Campana and Varese 2013). In the absence of available state enforcement, transaction costs in criminal markets are high. It is significantly more likely that a fellow criminal will behave opportunistically, and acquiring reliable information without exposing oneself to prosecution is more costly. Thus, examples of illicit institutions that facilitate cooperation are plentiful: Prison gangs regulate black markets for contraband (Skarbek 2014), pirates create constitution-like rules that provide checks and balances for crews (Leeson 2007), and mafias and warlords may provide public services and take on state-like characteristics (Gambetta 1996; Shortland and Varese 2014). These illicit institutions allow participants to form expectations about what follows from their actions and, thereby, create order. It transforms anarchy into various kinds of repeated games that make the outcomes of illicit activities predictable (Dixit [2004] 2006). With one major exemption, illicit orders are also spontaneous orders. They act as what Hayek ([1960] 2011, 40) calls "an adaptation to a large number of particular facts which will not be known in their totality to anyone." The exemptions are large mafia-like organizations that strive for a territorial protection monopoly (Varese 2017). Mafia governance, as illegitimate quasi-state governance, may either result in planned orders or rather resemble firms where basic market functions are internalized. Examples of the latter are the Central- and Southern American drug cartels that were led like international corporations.

Many of the above examples of illicit ordering are synonymous with the threat of violence and, at times, actual harm. Nonetheless, illicit ordering also has a track record of producing beneficial economic results for most of those trading inside it because it allows predictable, orderly, and cost-sensitive behavior (Becker 1974). Buchanan (1979, 131–132) argues that by minimizing competition between criminal actors, *organized* crime minimizes the output of "social bads" in the same manner as monopolies on legal markets reduce output:

> Freedom of entry, the hallmark of competition, is of negative social value here, and competitiveness is to be discouraged rather than encouraged. . . . It is not from the public-spiritedness of the leaders of the Cosa Nostra that we should expect to get a reduction in the crime rate but from their regard for their own self-interests.

Defining Perverse Spontaneous Orders

But orders can also fail. The question is what failing, in fact, means. Is a successful trade between drug cartels without any casualties a beneficial (market) order because it creates trust for future transactions? And is a casino a perverse order because, in the end, the bank always wins and all other participants lose? This shows we need not only to distinguish between planned and spontaneous orders but also between the social and individual results an order produces. In *Why Most Things Should Not Be for Sale*, the philosopher Debra Satz makes a similar argument. She aims at identifying "noxious" markets and argues for prohibiting them. Examples of noxious markets would be those for child labor or transplant organs. Satz defines the term noxious as markets that cause "widespread discomfort and, in the extreme, revulsion" (Satz 2010, 3). Indeed, it seems that the terms noxious and perverse can be used interchangeably in a way that perverse means "turned away of what is right or good." Both describe a vague feeling that something is off with an order. Therefore, it is crucial to identify who exactly benefits or suffers from a perverse order.

In her book, Satz distinguishes between two categories of 'harmful' outcomes a noxious market can produce. Those "that are deleterious, either for the participants themselves or for third parties" (Satz 2010, 94) are perverse on the individual level. As examples, she puts forward market exchanges that fueled a genocidal war or that erased personal wealth, for example, at a (manipulated) stock market. Effectively, the individual dimension comprises two sub-categories: (1) direct participants of an order, and (2) third parties that are directly influenced. To this, Satz adds markets that "undermine the social framework needed for people to interact as equals, as individuals with equal standing" (Satz 2010, 95). Here, Satz has societal concepts such as democracy in mind. It is hard to reconcile this dimension with the methodological individualism that spontaneous order theorizing is based on. A potential translation could be that this category concerns longer-term and indirect negative externalities that an order produces. For example, air pollution caused by car traffic can (directly) impact the health of individuals living on a heavy traffic road and indirectly affect individuals living on other the sides of the globe because of emission-induced climate change. To conclude, using Satz's works as a systematic basis, an order can have three groups of affected individuals: direct participants and noninvolved individuals that are spatially and temporally *directly* or *indirectly* affected.

However, the reception of Satz's works also displays how challenging the normative evaluation of spontaneous orders is. In his response, "Why Most Things Should Probably Be for Sale," Pennington (2015) demonstrates how prone analyzing especially the social dimension of orders, is to fall for the "Nirvana fallacy" (Demsetz 1969). This means comparing actual orders with idealized alternatives that would only, in theory, produce perfect outcomes. Looking at Satz's case studies, Pennington (2015) concludes that

> a comparative institutions account exploring the likely effect of alternatives under the same non-ideal conditions points towards a strong presumption in favor of largely unfettered markets. . . . A robust refutation will, however, need to evaluate markets on a symmetrical basis with other institutional possibilities and not continue to judge them against standards that have rarely been applied with due symmetry to "social democratic" alternatives.

This exemplifies that we need to be explicit not only about those affected by a perverse spontaneous order but also about evaluating an order in light of the actual feasible institutional alternatives.

This point is exemplified by a case study done by Martin and Storr (2008). The authors concentrate on the "social" dimension and present two case studies for not socially beneficial, that is, perverse, spontaneous orders: A negative belief system in Bahamian folklore that hampers social progress and a specific nonviolent protest that turned into a violent mob. The example of the mob is particularly interesting because it contains everything that has been discussed so far: a vague sense of perversion combined with the unclear roles of those involved creates the potential for a Nirvana fallacy. In brief, this protest was caused by stark differences in pay between local workers from the colonial Bahamas and workers from the US. After marching to the Colonial Administration Offices, "one of the workers threw a bottle through a nearby window and, without anyone issuing a command, the rest of the crowd marched down Bay Street 'smashing as they went'" (Martin and Storr 2008, 80). Breaking storefronts and even looting shops should fulfill the condition of being the outcome of a perverse order.

Interestingly, though, "there was also a feedback mechanism at work during the riot. Rioters signaled to one another which stores they should leave untouched, and which stores to loot. Beyond signaling, rioters would actively protect certain stores, forming blockades and turning away their fellow rioters" (Martin and Storr 2008, 81). Given that the march that the authors describe "became an outlet for a variety of frustrations with the social order that existed in the Bahamas during that period" (Martin and Storr 2008, 81), it seems rather remarkable that some form of beneficial order existed that limited externalities. And it demonstrates that this protest was indeed an order based on rules and not just an anarchic accumulation of frustrated people.

The authors are explicit about analyzing the social dimension of perverse spontaneous orders. But they miss defining this more thoroughly. Considering the above, the study focuses on the negative externalities produced by the order. Directly influenced are the owners of the destroyed and looted shops. Beyond that, one could speculate about wider negative implications for Bahamians in relation to the British authorities. But the shop owners are the focus here. However, is this perhaps a case of the Nirvana fallacy because a violent mob missing the rules that protected at least some of the stores would probably still have marched but destroyed even more property? Under the given circumstances, the order of the mob might have rather prevented worse and, hence, should be preferred over having a violent mob go wild without any boundaries. Or is this a case of a "could have been worse fallacy" and the mob was what the authors describe it to be: a perverse spontaneous order that brought destruction instead of an ordered expression of opinion? Social scientists very rarely find conditions that allow for controllable natural experiments (e.g., Klick and Tabarrok 2005). The 1942 Bahamas riot is not such a case, and while the authors describe the positive feedback mechanism, they do not account for it in their normative verdict. Furthermore, it would be fascinating to examine the perspective of those inside the mob. If they felt safe and managed to protect their friends' property and direct violence against their enemies, there is nothing perverse about the spontaneous order from their point of view.

What does this indicate for the normative evaluation of spontaneous orders? The riot was a singular event with relatively visible effects. Nonetheless, the results are up for scrutiny. This is mainly because the authors were not explicit about who exactly was negatively affected by the order and what the alternatives would have been. The larger an order becomes, the more crucial it is to be upfront about the affected individuals. Based on the above, perverse spontaneous orders can be divided into two subgroups that do not contradict each other: (1) Orders that produce direct or indirect negative externalities and (2) orders where the individual results deviate significantly and negatively from the participants' original intentions and preferences. Orders can be socially and individually perverse at the same time or produce negative effects on just the participants or non-participants. The study of negative externalities has a long tradition (Coase [1960] 2013) and is crucial for questions of environmental pollution, such as emission-induced climate change. However, what about spontaneous orders that produce perverse results on the individual level?

Spontaneous Orders that Are Perverse for the Participants

Robert Nozick ([1974] 2013) touches on this question in his seminal work "Anarchy, State, and Utopia." In his response to John Rawls's influential "A Theory of Justice," Nozick commits to showing how a stable minimal state can arise out of the terrifying Hobbesian state of nature without infringing individual rights. Thereby, he opposes the Rawlsian theory of distributive justice, which would impose a large-scale, designed order. In Nozick's thought experiment, individuals would over time form protective associations that would fulfil all necessary judicial and protective tasks. Out of efficiency, competition would then lead to a single protective agency being a de facto state. The exact process is not of interest here; however, what is of interest is the question of what happens if a protective agency abuses its powers: "But one 'protective association' might aggress against other persons. Relative to Locke's law of nature, it would be an outlaw agency. What actual counterweights would there be to its power?" (Nozick [1974] 2013, Ch. 2).

Such an outcome would seem to satisfy the conditions for a perverse spontaneous order. Out of mere human action and rational decision-making, without any central planner or intention behind it, an order arises that the individuals contributing to it with their actions would have never wanted in the first place. So, even for Nozick, one of the most influential advocates of invisible hand processes (Nozick [1974] 2013, Ch. 2), such an outcome is thinkable. However, he also thinks that perverse spontaneous orders differ from planned orders in their instability:

> If the "outlaw" agency simply is an *open* aggressor, pillaging, plundering, and extorting under no plausible claim of justice, it will have a harder time than states. For the state's claim to legitimacy induces its citizens to believe they have some duty to obey its edicts, pay its taxes, fight its battles, and so on; and so some persons cooperate with it voluntarily. An openly aggressive agency could not depend upon, and would not receive, any such voluntary cooperation, since persons would view themselves simply as its victims rather than as its citizens. (Nozick [1974] 2013, Ch. 2)

This is in line with Mancur Olson's ([2000] 2001) famous thought experiment on state building. He argues that under circumstances of anarchy, groups of "roving bandits" would steal and plunder from people until they were stopped by "stationary bandits," who, out of self-interest, provided genuine services to citizens like security in order to extract higher amounts of taxes. Self-interest, over time, leads to the defeat of the perverse roving bandits and the natural development of states.

In short, Nozick contends that spontaneous orders can indeed produce perverse results for the direct participants, and he supports the intuition regarding the lower stability of perverse spontaneous orders compared to their planned counterparts. However, how do such orders appear beyond the mere thought experiment?

This is demonstrated by Schelling (1969) in his brief analysis of racial segregation in the US. He demonstrates how individual choice, over time, leads to color-segregated neighborhoods. The driver of the process is a pure choice based on the preference to live among people from the same (ethnic) group. Interestingly, to analyze perverse spontaneous orders, Schelling contends that a high preference for living segregated (i.e., among people of the same skin color) is not a prerequisite for a segregated outcome:

> The results do not depend on each color's having a preference for the absence of the other. We can equally suppose that most blacks and most whites prefer a color mixture and reinterpret their tolerances as merely the upper limits to the ratios at which their preference for integrated residence is outweighed by numerical imbalance. (Schelling 1969, 493)

So, even if both whites and blacks originally prefer a mixed neighborhood, just a minor in-group preference dynamically leads to individually motivated segregation. This exemplifies that the perverse nature of spontaneous orders does not necessarily imply perverse motivations on the sides of the participants. Such as the stationary bandits from Olson do not necessarily need to have the greater good on their mind, participants in perverse spontaneous orders can have good intentions and nonetheless contribute with their individual decisions to an overall perverse outcome.

Lessons for Analyzing Illicit Spontaneous Orders

What Can We Learn from This for the Analysis of Criminal Orders?

First, and most importantly, things are not always as they seem. Often, we attribute planning and intention to outcomes that are just the consequence of human action. Segregation must not necessarily be the consequence of racial policies or even racial aversion but can happen spontaneously. Invisible-hand explanations, such as Nozick's or Schelling's, yield a greater understanding of the hidden dynamics in an order that would otherwise stay disguised. As Nozick puts it:

> An invisible-hand explanation explains what looks to be the product of someone's intentional design, as not being brought about by anyone's intentions. We might call the opposite sort of explanation a "hidden-hand explanation." A hidden-hand explanation explains what looks to be merely a disconnected set of facts that (certainly) is not the product of intentional design, as the product of an individual's or group's intentional design(s). Some persons also find such explanations satisfying, as is evidenced by the popularity of conspiracy theories. (Nozick [1974] 2013, Ch. 2)

This knowledge is of great importance when analyzing criminal orders. Especially crime is often attributed to being concerted by callous mafia organizations in the shadow of society while being in fact the product of "ordinary" individual human action. It may be because imagining the reigns of the underworlds is more fascinating or because, for many, it is not imaginable that human cooperation can function outside the regulating arms of the state and fostered by "criminals." Furthermore, observed hardship and violence do not necessarily depend on the participants of an order to necessarily intend them. Invisible-hand examinations detach the overall appearance of an order (e.g., intense racial segregation) from the actual intentions (e.g., moderate in-group preference).

The second important lesson is that detail matters. The term perverse, such as the term noxious, is the expression of a vague discomfort with an order. Often, in democracies, business models are turned into victimless crimes because the electorate experiences this discomfort. Good examples are the prohibitions on sex work, certain drugs, or, in earlier times, homosexuality. Spontaneous order theory can disentangle the vague assessment from the actual outcomes of an order, but only if it is specific regarding those that are affected and the possible alternatives. Hence, we need to distinguish between orders that are perverse for the participants and those that produce negative externalities. And to be meaningful, the results must be put in relation to other feasible institutional alternatives.

This leads to lesson number three: rules matter for the outcome of an order. Individuals make decisions based on their preferences and intentions, the available information, and the options. Rules set the boundaries for these decisions and incentivize certain behavior. Something that Hayek also had in mind when it came to the normative evaluation of spontaneous orders. He suggested that "for the resulting order to be beneficial, people must also observe some conventional rules, that is, rules which do not simply follow from their desires and their insight into relations of cause and effect, but which are normative and tell them what they ought to or ought not to do" (Hayek [1973] 2013, 45).

Prima facie, it seems plausible that if participants act according to some standard of morality, which Hayek seems to be having in mind here, the overall order should also be beneficial. However, this is not convincing for two reasons. First, as Martin and Storr (2008, 78) reply to Hayek's quote: "the existence or nonexistence of normative rules which curb desire and shape perceptions do not by themselves determine whether the resulting order is beneficial." One of many historic incidents that underline the skepticism against Hayek's suggestion: During the 1938 nationwide pogrom against the Jewish population in Germany, looting and murdering mobs marched, and hundreds were killed as a just result of the Nazi ideology serving as a conventional rule. The mobs were a spontaneous order that produced outrageous negative externalities but were not perverse for those individuals that participated directly. The results were in line with what they believed was right and what they expected. And second, it is the beauty of spontaneous orders, like the market, that individual causes can be reconciled without the need for a common normative background. On a market, the intentions or goals of the seller of a good or service do not matter to the buyer as long as the trade is mutually beneficial. In line with Martin and Storr, I suggest that the prerequisite for mutually advantageous exchange is not necessarily a common normative understanding but procedural rules that incentivize cooperative behavior and minimize transaction costs. This means rules that mitigate the knowledge problem (Hayek 1945) and the threat of opportunistic behavior (Ostrom 2005).

From this follows a fourth important lesson for the study of illicit spontaneous orders. For Hayek, spontaneous order and evolution are "twin ideas" (see, Schaefer 2021), implying rules that not only guide individual behavior but similarly gradually improve the overall quality of the order itself: "The process of adaptation operates, as do the adjustments of any self-organizing system, by what cybernetics has taught us to call negative feedback: responses to the differences between the expected and the actual results of actions so that these differences will be reduced" (Hayek [1973] 2013, 125). Here, Hayek reinforces that the "expected results of actions" are a good basis for a normative verdict on specific spontaneous orders. And he points attention to the evolutionary process. Rules do not only produce feedback on individuals' behavior but also vice versa. In spontaneous orders, participants aim to adapt the rules to maximize their expected utility, a mechanism to look out for when assessing illicit ordering.

In the following section, I introduce the business model of migrant smuggling and its participants. As outlined in the introduction, current research on migrant smuggling differs strongly from the assessment in media and policy. This gap has large-scale consequences for policymaking and public perception. In order to address this in section 4 using spontaneous order theory, I will have a look at the roots of the perceived perverse nature of migrant smuggling.

The Perverse Image of Migrant Smuggling

Definitions and Numbers

Two million four hundred seventy-eight thousand eight hundred thirty-eight. This is the number of irregular migrants that reached the borders of the European Union between 2009 and 2019, according to official numbers by the European border agency Frontex (2020). Irregular migration is one of the hot topics in international politics, not only in Europe but also in the United States, Africa, Central Asia, and the South Pacific. The United Nations (2000a) defines an irregular migrant as a person who crosses borders "without complying with the necessary requirements for legal entry into the receiving State." Irregular migrants flee from war, economic despair, or unlawful prosecution but do not or not yet qualify for legal entry. It involves overcoming man-made and natural borders, vast deserts, dangerous waters, and high walls. Often far away from their homes and not familiar with local conditions, languages, and rules, migrants seek the help of specialists. This is the birth of migrant smuggling as a business model (Salt and Stein 1997).

And this business model appears to have created one of the largest illicit markets in the world. If every migrant that reached the EU in the past decade paid just $1,000 to smugglers, this would constitute an illicit market worth more than $2.5 billion just in the Mediterranean. And $1,000 is just the lower end of what a journey from Northern Africa to Europe can cost (European Commission, DG Migration & Home Affairs 2015, 45). The core business of migrant smugglers is far more than just transporting migrants. It also involves the supply of shelter, jobs, forged documents, and financial services. Sellers of all these different services and irregular migrants interact on a large black market for smuggling services that is ordered by informal rules and competitive prices. This market is mostly unregulated and evidently not controlled by a large state-like mafia (Campana 2017). Neither migrants nor their service providers can impose an intended outcome on the market. Hence, it fulfils the condition of spontaneous order.

Prima facie, the illicit nature of migrant smuggling seems to dictate the conditions: Information between migrants and service providers is distributed highly unequally (Bilger, Hofmann, and Jandl 2006), creating a classic lemons problem (Akerlof 1970), and trust between migrants, who risk not only their lives but also a small fortune, and their smugglers is low in the absence of any formal law enforcement. And once on an overloaded rubber boat on the open sea, irregular migration becomes a gamble for life. Frequently, this ends with death. The International Organization for Migration's Missing Migrants Project has registered more than 20,000 migrants who died trying to cross the Mediterranean since 2015 (International Organization for Migration 2019). Undoubtedly, many deaths in the Mediterranean remain undetected and thus do not appear in the official statistics.

Conceptually, migrant smuggling needs to be distinguished from human trafficking, as these two crimes are often confused by the public. The latter is defined by the United Nations (2000b) as the coercion of persons for the sole purpose of exploitation. Essentially, this makes trafficking a business model that does not involve the migrant as an individual. It is a crime against the individual who is traded between the traffickers and third parties. Migrant smuggling, in turn, is defined as an offense against the states whose borders are illegally crossed (Campana 2019; United Nations 2000a). This makes agency the core difference between smuggling and trafficking (see table 8.2). In theory, an irregular migrant chooses to migrate based on the available information and the motive and makes individual decisions about timing, routes, and smugglers. The trafficked migrant has almost no agency and is merely forced to participate in another noxious market abroad, such as forced prostitution or slavery.

Perverse Images of Migrant Smuggling

This concept of high-agency smuggled migrants stands in stark contrast to the public image of migrant smuggling as a perverse market. Tragic events such as the death of the three-year-old boy Alan Kurdi, who drowned in

TABLE 8.2
Migrant Smuggling vs. Human Trafficking

Features	*Smuggling*	*Trafficking*
Commodity	Illegal entry into a country	Control over an individual
Actors involved in the exchange	Smuggled persons and smugglers	Third-parties and traffickers
Offense against	State's immigration law	Person
Level of agency of the smuggled person	High	Absent or nearly absent

Source: Created by Florian A. Hartjen; Adapted from Campana and Varese (2016)

September 2015, reinforce the image of helpless migrants who are fully at the mercy of ruthless smugglers (Triandafyllidou 2018). And viewed from the other side of the Mediterranean, following this perverse market narrative makes sense: Smuggling operations seem to be highly profitable, and at the same time, thousands of migrants drown in the Mediterranean. Travel conditions are reportedly bad, and migrant stories in the media portray the ideal image of helplessness. Why should rational individuals, who have agency over their actions, freely commit to this market? Nonetheless, a significant strand in migrant smuggling research is questioning this narrative, drawing a picture of cooperation, choice, and smart strategies to minimize risk (see, section 4). This view, however, has not yet reached the public. And most notably, the European Commission recently built its "EU action plan against migrant smuggling (2021–2025)" without regard to newer research. This document will be used to explore the perverse order narrative.

For the EU Commission, the market for migrant smuggling is perverse in every sense. First and foremost, it is deemed to create extreme harm for the direct participants, namely the migrants who are forced into the hands of organized crime. The action plan consistently describes migrant smugglers as pure evil. The sentence "smugglers put people's lives at risk, offering false perspectives and causing serious harm to migrants" (European Commission 2021, 3) is not only highlighted, but it also exemplifies an extreme black-and-white image of the relation between smugglers and migrants. This is very much in line with the public fascination for strong images and personal stories in the media. The migration researcher Mainwaring (2019, 9) finds that "the spectacle of shipwreck renders migrants into helpless victims exploited by unscrupulous smugglers, so desperate that they take unfathomable risks."

In this sense, for the EU, it is not an informed decision that makes migrants choose smugglers but "disinformation and the false narrative of smugglers, attracting migrants to embark on perilous journeys with promises that do not match reality" (European Commission 2021, 3). Added to this would be push factors such as "demographic growth with the accompanying socioeconomic difficulties and lack of job opportunities, discrimination, instability, conflicts, environmental degradation and climate change, the perception of the EU as an economically, politically, socially and environmentally more stable region" (European Commission 2021, 3) that drive migrants into the arms of smugglers. Once on their way to Europe, they were "exposed to violence, extortion, exploitation, rape, abuse, theft, kidnapping and even homicide" (European Commission 2021, 3). And everything would be run by "smuggling networks," which "are able to rapidly adapt their offer of illicit services" (European Commission 2021, 3). The latter claim is especially staggering, as Campana (2017, 481) years ago came to the conclusion that

> . . . rather than being internalized within a single organization, activities are segmented and carried out by localized and rudimentary hierarchies with a small number of high-centrality actors operating at various stages along the smuggling route. Coordination is more likely to occur vertically than horizontally, indicating that higher-level smugglers are largely independent and autonomous.

Overall, the EU action plan displays a very simplistic image of the migrant smuggling markets in the Mediterranean. And while citing some field research, not a single source that could convey a more nuanced or up-to-date view is mentioned. Neither is a feasible institutional alternative discussed beyond "eradicating" migrant smuggling. The main concern communicated is that smuggling causes extreme harm for the migrants. Negative externalities are only a side note. Among these is the "increasing role of State actors in facilitating irregular migration and using human beings to create pressure at the EU's external borders" (European Commission 2021, 1). And that "organized crime structures capable of carrying out sophisticated operations that cover the full range of migrant smuggling services along the entire route constitute a high risk to Europe's security, in particular the individuals in the higher echelons of these criminal organisations." In short, for the EU, the Mediterranean markets for migrant smuggling are perverse because they directly harm irregular migrants. Whether putting the migrant into focus and leaving out other potential externalities, for example, on the domestic labor market, is a political move to sell activities as humane is not decisive. It reflects what the public believes and serves as a basis for the EU policy framework.

Consequences and Way Forward

Indeed, for policymakers, the perverse market narrative is a welcome excuse because it renders the ongoing humanitarian tragedy into a fight with callous smuggling operations. It makes the European governments "bystanders" "whose only role is to rescue victims from the hands of traffickers" (Campana and Varese 2016, 101). In other words, it is not the closed border strategy executed by the EU that is responsible for thousands of deaths, but the irrationality of migrants and the ruthlessness of large smuggling rings. Based on this, the EU can sell its international deals with partners like Turkey or Niger that are paid billions to stop irregular movements (Vogt 2020).

Literature on migrant smuggling has made remarkable progress in drawing a more nuanced picture over the past years. It portrays irregular migrants who indeed have agency over their actions and smugglers who are in competition with each other and provide genuine services. Nonetheless, the public image persists. A convincing narrative is missing that connects the observations and addresses the "tale of the two crimes," good and bad smuggling. I suppose that observations that make the migrant smuggling markets seem perverse and high-agency migrants do not contradict each other. For migrants, smuggling is a "rational gamble." Migrants know about the risks and the life-threatening conditions. But they also know that the vast majority of those who try will sooner or later reach the EU. And they actively try to increase their chances with institutions that minimize risks. I suggest that on the individual level, the markets for migrant smuggling are not perverse because the outcomes this order produces do not substantially and negatively deviate from the expectations of the majority of migrants. In the following section, I will explore the narrative of the rational gamble based on three basic misconceptions the EU's action plan conveys: (1) migrants are helpless, (2) smugglers trick migrants into the market, and (3) eradicating smuggling will help migrants. Based on the lessons from spontaneous order theory, I will put special emphasis on distinguishing individual intentions from a seemingly intentional design.

This analysis can only provide snapshots of many different smuggling markets and patterns over a time frame of ten years, as displayed in the literature. This has the disadvantage of providing just a granular view of regions and time-specific conditions, something that is at length covered by an organization such as the IOM, though. The purpose of this analysis is instead to use spontaneous order theorizing to reach an informed and structured normative verdict on migrant smuggling in the Mediterranean.

Migrant Smuggling: A Rational Gamble

For a long time, the perverse market narrative also prevented migrant smuggling research from advancing toward a better understanding of the relation between smuggled migrants and their service providers. It implied assessing the order based on its general appearance rather than based on the individuals' intentions and expectations. Sanchez (2017, 20) contends that "as part of these narratives, the public is told that clandestine migration is under the control of transnational criminal organizations that exploit migrants and the displaced, prey on their desperation, exploit them financially, and victimize them physically, sexually, and emotionally." Recently, however, a new strand of research has advanced to fill this gap (e.g., Achilli 2018; Campana and Gelsthorpe 2021; Sanchez 2017). These and further studies rely on extensive qualitative fieldwork and discover some fascinating self-enforcing institutions that trigger positive feedback loops while not denying that irregular migrants in the area nonetheless face victimization and violence.

In general, these studies conclude that migrant smuggling can create a beneficial relation between irregular migrants and their aides. Campana and Gelsthorpe (2021, 19) conclude that "interactions underpinning the smuggling market are more complex and nuanced—and in many ways similar to those taking place in other markets, both legal and illegal." In this market, similar to other markets, acting in good faith is economically rewarded, and genuine cooperation is observable. Achilli (2018, 92), based on his extensive fieldwork, concludes that he

> . . . came to recognize the complex system of moral values surrounding smuggling and the strong bonds between the smugglers and migrants. . . . Media reports constantly point to the brutality of smugglers and the plight of migrants, but they fail to account for the brutality caused by states' efforts to enforce border controls and neglect to acknowledge the ability of smugglers to help people navigate the unequal geographies of mobility.

Overall, this literature has revolutionized the view of migrant smuggling. It depicts irregular migrants who know well about the risks of using smuggling services but who take their chances because it allows them to reach countries and opportunities they otherwise would have been excluded from. And it paints an alternative picture of smuggling aid, one based on economic thinking rather than on exploitation and, sometimes, even empathy and the willingness to provide a genuinely helpful service. What this new strand is missing, though, is a systematic political-economic framework.

Of course, smuggling can still go terribly wrong, and migrants can be cheated and end up in the hands of traffickers. However, in general, the markets seem to deliver on the expectations of migrants and smugglers, which contradicts the idea of a perverse spontaneous order. The "Missing Migrants Project" by the IOM reports seven deaths per 1,000 migrants that safely crossed the Mediterranean (2019). While this still translates into thousands of probably unnecessary deaths, it also means over 99 percent of those that try do not die, something that is not at all considered by the EU Commission which is exemplified in the "hidden hand" explanation that still dominates the public.

Misconception 1: Smugglers Trick Migrants into the Market

The perverse order narrative revolves around the information and power asymmetry between migrants and smugglers. Prima facie, this is indeed prevalent because information is the very service migrants seek from smugglers. Migrants require information about safe routes, the activities of border guards, weather conditions, modes of transportation, jobs, and safe houses. At the same time, irregular migrants that reach the smuggling hubs in Northern Africa are often already far away from home and potentially without the legal right to stay in the respective country. On this basis, it seems logical that smugglers have an easy time tricking migrants into inferior agreements.

Campana and Gelsthorpe (2021, 10) find that "the majority of the migrants we interviewed were rather upfront about their (low) expectations with regard to the trustworthiness of smugglers." In general, there seem to be low trust levels between migrants and smugglers. Interviewee 1 states that "what they were not really prepared for is the hunger and the thirst and these basic things. But the rest? Oh yes." At first glance, low trust seems to indicate a perverse order. But, in fact, it highlights that migrants are well aware of the information asymmetries. And the literature demonstrates various patterns of strategies that moderate it.

There is good evidence that African irregular migrants travel from hub to hub and acquire new information about work opportunities and smugglers at every stage (Nissling and Murphy-Teixidor 2020). Acquiring reliable information in a potentially hostile and unknown environment is associated with considerable costs. This creates a demand for institutions that provide orientation for the newly arrived migrants and ideally deal with local information and potentially some form of third-party contract. In legitimate markets with stark information asymmetries between buyers and sellers and a high degree of localized knowledge, this opens up opportunities for specialized brokers.

Do such "brokers" of migrant smuggling services exist? Yes, but often they have not been identified as such. There is evidence from all major routes in the Mediterranean of the existence of brokers. However, their importance as transaction cost optimizers for migrants has so far been overlooked. Rather, brokers are often depicted as being part of the callous smuggling mafia. Lucht (2013, 179–180) reports of "pushers" who perform the role of brokers in the infamous smuggling hub Agadez in the Saharan country of Niger:

> The newcomers give the name of the "ghetto" in Agades in which they prefer to stay while awaiting further transport to Libya, and the pushers say "no problem," they'll make sure they get there without any confusion. They are in daily contact with the halfway houses in the desert . . . . In fact, since their colleague on the bus has already informed them which "ghetto" the boys have in mind, the pushers have already talked to the boss and told him to get ready to pick up three guys at the police checkpoint outside of town.

The pushers not only broker for ghetto bosses who operate safe houses in which migrants wait for their next leg of the journey to start but also for the Nigerien bus company. From the latter, they receive 1,000 CFA per migrant, and from the ghetto operators, up to 10,000 CFA (approximately $15) (Lucht 2013).

In line with this, for Libya, there is evidence that brokers "advise migrants on which smuggler to use or take migrants to locations where they can connect with samsars" (Malakooti 2013, 52) where "samsars" refers to aides working for a specific smuggler. Similar arrangements are reported by Campana and Gelsthorpe (2021, 16) in interviews with smuggled migrants. Six interviewees mentioned that they used brokers in their interactions with smugglers. In addition to information, these brokers also provided other institutional solutions, such as escrow services, which will be discussed below.

Generally, migrants' demand for information and third-party enforcement leads to a specialization in the Mediterranean migrant smuggling markets. That intermediaries act as the first point of contact makes sense, especially in illicit markets. Smugglers must fear prosecution in almost any transit state and hence keep a low profile. Brokers, in contrast, can openly advertise their services as accommodations for migrants. And, most importantly, they build a reputation for providing genuine services among generations of migrants that report their experiences back home to new potential clients. Interviewees reported to Campana and Gehlsthorpe (2021, 13):

> There are a lot of smugglers . . . good and bad, those who steal. So I got this one through the recommendation of my friends. I asked around about him and asked 3 or 4 people and they said he is good. . . . He was well-known for having good behavior in his work.

On the other side, there is evidence that smugglers are also concerned about their reputation. Campana (2017, 495) reports a wiretapped conversation between two smugglers discussing the sinking of a smuggling boat in the Mediterranean causing hundreds of deaths:

> [Yusef] continues saying that his fellow countrymen trusted him, and he is extremely sorry for what happened; contrary to other organizers, he had personally notified the families who have lost somebody in the shipwreck, and he had even sent 5000 dollars to his village and to the village named "Adi Hargets" for the relatives of the victims from these areas.

Of course, the victims' families would have had no formal recourse to demand compensation for their loss. However, the smuggler Yusef seems to fear future losses if he gets a reputation for being a dangerous smuggler.

Of course, this requires that the information be processed between experienced migrants and those who aspire to or plan their journeys. For this reason, the role of social networks cannot be underestimated (Campana 2019). A study conducted by Dekker et al. (2018) found that 80% of a group of 51

Syrian migrants consulted social media networks (Facebook and LinkedIn) before the journey, and 38% of a sample of 47 Syrian migrants consulted these networks along the route. Beyond social networks, the internet offers many other possibilities for minimizing transaction costs. Sixty-six percent of the migrants along the route used map services (such as Google) and "voice over IP," and instant messaging services (WhatsApp, Viber) facilitated direct information transmission between migrants and between migrants and smugglers (Dekker et al. 2018).

From a transaction cost perspective, social media networks fulfil two distinct roles: transmitting information and facilitating bargaining. Migrants exchange information about service providers and routes, even share feedback, and, in addition, get in touch with smugglers who offer their services through social media networks (Roberts 2017). This exemplifies the Hayekian idea of order that is behind the migrant smuggling markets: sharing information allows participants to form expectations that are likely to be met. For Libya, Sanchez (2020, 20) reports that for migrants:

> Finding facilitators was not difficult, fees and payment terms were clear. Several participants did report having been given false information at the time of the negotiation (for example, facilitators lied regarding the length of time the journey would take or had promised a larger boat and not a dinghy), and invariably indicated that crossing the Mediterranean was not something they would attempt again. However the negotiation phase was not described as problematic as the period of time that preceded the departure.

The fact that migrants do not per se trust smugglers and actively seek information, combined with the vertical competition for reputation between smuggling service providers, allows for feedback loops to be built. Word about reliable brokers can be passed on more easily, and brokers have the incentive to search out trustworthy smugglers that they work with. This creates repeated interactions on a market, usually characterized by one-shot interactions. What seems perverse because of low trust levels allows for evolutionary competition that, over time, sorts out opportunistic providers of services. In line with this, Interviewee 2 reported that bad actors are typically flushed out of the market within a few months (also, Interviewees 1 and 3).

Misconception 2: Migrants Are Helpless

However, what if something goes wrong along the route? Migrants invest a substantial amount in their journeys, collect resources from families and friends, and often have to work along the route for months to finance the next leg. Is all this lost if, for example, the transport is intercepted by officials?

From the outside, migrants seem to be entirely helpless when confronted with opportunistic behavior. But the main reason that smuggling in the Mediterranean looks different from the inside is to be found in the institutions that govern the markets. Procedural payment rules create positive feedback loops that reward cooperative behavior and limit transaction costs, and migrants even found ways to keep information "hostage" in order to protect themselves against excessive violence.

To signal trustworthiness, an unobservable but crucial feature migrants look out for, credible smugglers alter payment modalities. This includes accepting down payments and paying on arrival (Bouteillet-Paquet 2011, 96), offering warranties (Bilger, Hofmann, and Jandl 2006, 85), or using third-party escrow services (European Commission, DG Migration & Home Affairs 2015, 47). All these payment modalities have two things in common: They emit a credible signal to the migrants about the quality of the service, and they create repeated interaction. Accepting down payments and the final sum only on successful execution signals to the migrants that the smuggler is confident about the success of the smuggling operations and willing to bear losses in case something goes wrong. Both parties need to interact once more after the successful smuggling operation, which minimizes the incentive for opportunistic behavior through direct reciprocity. However, who should enforce alternative payment modalities? This can hardly be done by either side of the service agreement, which hence creates the demand for third-party governance.

A common system used by smugglers and migrants is the "Hawala" system (see Schaeffer 2008). The hawaladar, the local operator of the system, is trusted by both the migrant and the smuggler(s) and would release funds along the route to pay for services (Campana 2019). For both sides, hawaladars are known providers of financial services. Furthermore, they are independent of the smuggling industry and, as such, do not provide illegal services. For migrants, this means that the risks of opportunistic behavior by the hawaladar are relatively low. This risk is further minimized by the involvement of family members. Triandafyllidou and Maroukes (2012, 138) report that typically

> "the migrant phones his relatives/friends back home and gives, through a code known only to him and the guarantor, his permission for the agreed sum to be released by the guarantor to the smuggling broker in the country of departure. The money is then forwarded to intermediary smugglers across the transit countries."

The discussed third-party money services serve an important role in minimizing both parties' transaction costs and creating direct reciprocity. Even though migrants have to pay a premium for the services, this practice seems to be efficient for minimizing risks.

Over time and along all major routes, surprisingly sophisticated rules govern the interaction between smugglers and migrants. Besides the direct feedback mechanisms, the sum of institutions, ideally, creates evolutionary competition that, over time, improves the efficiency of the markets. This is particularly the case when demand and supply are high. In an interview, an international field officer, for example, spoke of the "Golden Times" for migrant smuggling, meaning the year 2015 in Afghanistan, when thousands were on the move to Europe around the same time. During this time, there is even evidence of written smuggling contracts between smugglers and migrants that set out the terms of the journey (Interviewee 1).

However, there is an elephant in the room. All this should not mask the fact that this market is prone to the use of violence and threats (Baird and van Liempt 2015). Irregular migrants are not only treated badly, but often they are deprived of their freedom of movement, their passports, and their cell phones. How can this be reconciled with markets that supposedly improve the situation for migrants and that are based on competitive institutions?

First of all, extreme violence is rare on the Mediterranean migrant smuggling markets—it goes against the "work ethic" employed by smugglers (Achilli 2018, 87). Rare off-equilibrium behavior does not indicate the collapse of the entire set of market institutions. In the underworld, violence and the threat of using it are legitimate means to align interests (Campana and Varese 2013) and signal sincerity (Gambetta 2009). The "moderate" use of violence can most likely be attributed to disciplining efforts by smugglers to minimize their own risks. Smugglers not only have to fear being revealed to the authorities by their clients but also need to minimize the risks of being detected during the clandestine smuggling operation. In particular, when smugglers and migrants agree on deferred payment schemes, the threat of violence (also against migrant families) serves the purpose of enforcement.

However, threats are not only used by smugglers. In their most recent study, Campana and Gelsthorpe (2021, 17) describe how migrants keep compromising information about the smugglers as "hostage." One of their interviewees suggests the regular and successful use of this strategy to keep the smugglers aligned:

> We had the number of the smuggler and called him and told him this happened with us and the boat was broken and we did not tell the police about you and because of that we want a new trip or we will return to the police. You are this person and one of the men said that "I have a photo of you. I took a photo of you. Believe me I will publish the photo if you don't bring us another boat and we also have children and women with

> us so behave with us" and he [the smuggler] said "okay, okay, tomorrow I will get you a new boat and will send you on a new trip. (Campana and Gelsthorpe 2021, 17, quote by Interviewee 17)

If we want to understand why the markets for migrant smuggling persist notwithstanding foreign interventions and bad travel conditions, the rules of the game are crucial. Migrants are not entirely helpless against opportunistic smugglers. Demand for protection has led to institutions that alter the power asymmetries between service providers and migrants. However, these institutions work particularly well in markets with high evolutionary competition and the need for reputation building. Conversely, this indicates that disruption makes migrants more vulnerable.

Misconception 3: Eradicating Smuggling Will Help Migrants

A meaningful invisible hand analysis compares actual institutional settings and their outcomes with feasible alternatives to avoid nirvana fallacies. The EU action plan intents to eradicate migrant smuggling, mostly with activities in migrants' home and transit countries. One such activity in the town of Agadez in Niger allows for the study of how trying to eradicate migrant smuggling markets alters the relation between migrants and smugglers.

Agadez had long been an infamous smuggling hotspot when EU-sponsored Nigerian authorities decided to crack down on the openly operating smuggling industry here towards the end of the 2010s. A set of articles published in the Washington Post between 2015 and 2017 portray the resulting institutional changes. They underscore how a disturbed rule system significantly deteriorates the conditions for irregular migrants. This emphasizes the positive impact rule-based illicit markets have on migrants' journeys across Northern Africa and the Mediterranean. In 2015, Agadez was described as one of the world's "human-smuggling capitals," from which every Monday a military-protected and organized smuggling convoy brought migrants across the desert and the border to Libya (Sieff 2015). Businesses could openly advertise their services and gain a reputation for safe passage among generations of migrants, just as described above. A passage to Libya costs between $150 and $300, and operators could make a fortune by building up a reputation for good services that were passed down through generations of migrants. Sieff (2015) reports on the migrant Konissa, who

> . . . had stepped off the bus in Agadez the previous night, just after 11 o'clock. He had been traveling for three days from the Ivory Coast and his legs felt stiff and heavy. When he walked through the parking lot,

> men started approaching him, his small black backpack giving him away as a migrant. "You going to Libya?" they asked in French and Hausa. "You need some help?" But Konissa, 25, already had a contact in Agadez. His uncle had traveled to Libya last year.

There were hundreds of thousands of migrants traveling through the dangerous Sahara from Agadez, and to them, it almost felt like relying on a legitimate and experienced travel business.

Then the EU decided to crack down on the smuggling industry with the help of local militias (Massalaki 2015; Vogt 2020). With the government crackdown, a lot changed: "Impoverished migrants are grappling with sharply rising fees. Growing numbers are being transported on riskier routes. Many are being sold to Libyan militias and criminal gangs" (Raghavan 2017). Established smugglers were either arrested or subsidized by an EU program to leave the business. This created opportunities for new smugglers to enter the market, but these did not know the desert as well. And while demand for smuggling services through Agadez was still high, the established rules and institutional learnings of the past disappeared with the old guard of smugglers. And with it, the feedback mechanisms that had gradually made the market more efficient and safer. Raghavan (2017) observes a new business model instead: "Traffickers now routinely sell migrants to credit houses... The smugglers may be trying to recoup some of their own costs: With increased border patrols, they must pay more bribes to corrupt military and police. In some cases, the credit houses even send trucks to Agadez and buy unsuspecting migrants from smugglers." Those migrants would either be kept hostage until payment or sold into Libyan camps for forced labor. Meanwhile, "community leaders and smugglers in Agadez predict the E.U. measures will ultimately fail to stop the trade. In interviews, disgruntled former smugglers said the one-time E.U. incentive payments, of about $2,700, were far from enough to start new careers" (Raghavan 2017).

In this period, outcomes clearly deviated from what the migrants expected from their endeavors. The provoked disorder led to a transitionary, perverse market. However, the incentives to provide genuine services are still in place. And other routes through the Maghreb and across the Mediterranean are ready to be reactivated—nothing new, as the highly fluctuating numbers of irregular migrants distributed on the three main routes demonstrate (Frontex 2020). It can be expected that the market will adapt to this new reality. In the meantime, it leaves thousands of irregular migrants in despair, though. Trying to eradicate the markets for smuggling services around the Mediterranean may have short-term effects on the numbers of smuggled individuals and especially the travel conditions. Though they do not seem to provide a long-term solution to ending death in the Mediterranean.

Conclusion

The market for migrant smuggling in the Mediterranean is not perverse for the participants. A prerequisite for this would be that outcomes negatively and categorically deviate from what migrants expect when they enter the market. They do not. There is good evidence that migrants willingly decide to rationally gamble. The benefits of reaching the EU outweigh the nonetheless low (< 1 percent) risk of death and the hardships of the journey. The order may be perverse because it produces negative externalities, for example, brain drain in migrants' home countries and disruption of labor markets in host countries, but this question requires another approach and is not in the stated focus of the EU action plan.

This section demonstrated that migrants have reasonably low expectations about smugglers and traveling conditions because they are well informed by former generations of migrants and by brokers who specialize in the provision of information. If something goes wrong, though, migrants are not helpless. They can make use of financial institutions, such as the hawala system, and risk-minimizing strategies to alter power relations and protect against opportunistic behavior. Finally, intervention can lead to transitional perverse circumstances because the current generation of migrants does not get the outcomes they expect. However, even the EU itself recognizes that migrant smuggling markets are highly adaptable and thereby resilient against intervention. Over time, new institutions that accommodate environmental challenges, such as government crackdowns, or other routes again gain prominence.

The question remains if the snapshots provided are a mere possibility or a systematic tendency. A definitive response would require a comparative analysis of different smuggling markets across the globe—another example of where research is needed. However, anecdotal evidence, for example, provided by Sanchez (2014) on the US-Mexican border shows similar mechanisms across the Atlantic. And, in fact, it should not be underestimated how large Northern Africa is. This chapter has provided evidence from various unconnected regional migrant smuggling markets that all show similar institutions and mechanisms. Hence, my preliminary verdict would be that there is a systematic tendency for smuggling markets to provide beneficial outcomes on the individual level. Since, in many ways, migrant smuggling markets do resemble other legal and illegal markets, this makes sense because markets are generally seen to provide efficient and mutually beneficial allocations of goods and services.

Policy Response Should Not Be Structured Around Perceived Perversion

Things are not always what they seem. And, in reality, the markets for migrant smuggling in the Mediterranean are not what they seem to the EU

Commission. The current EU action plan follows a hidden-hand explanation that exaggerates market failures, overlooks functioning informal institutions, and attributes too much to non-existent large smuggling mafias. It is the key advantage of spontaneous order theory that it allows looking behind the veil of perception. It directs attention to the details: What are the benefits/harms? Who is influenced? What are the rules that govern social interaction? What feedback do they trigger? How do they evolve over time? If the authors of the EU action plan were more careful in answering these questions, they would have come to a different conclusion. Instead, they structure a massive policy response, impacting millions of lives, around a perverse market perception that has been refuted in the up-to-date field literature for years.

This chapter offers three important contributions to the different academic questions: (1) It provides clarity for the analysis of perverse spontaneous orders. It is crucial to distinguish orders that produce negative externalities from orders that produce outcomes that negatively deviate from the participants' expectations. Discussing supposedly perverse spontaneous orders without being explicit about this harms its validity substantially. (2) Most importantly, this chapter offers an explanation of how vastly differing observations and explanation patterns on the issue of migrant smuggling can be reconciled. "The tale of the two crimes," good and bad smuggling, is, in the end, just a tale. The perverse market narrative is firmly established and believed by the public, which is why one of the most powerful organizations in the world still employs it. Only by looking at the individual motivations behind the perceived outcomes of an order, the rules, and the feedback they trigger, as well as their evolution, can the true nature of the relationship between migrants and smugglers be discovered. In short, using a hidden-hand explanation for a spontaneous order disguises the reality of things, namely the rational gamble migrants are willing to accept. (3) Lastly, this analysis indicates that, in light of feasible alternatives, current policy intervention to eradicate migrant smuggling markets does more harm than good. It is not a good idea to build massive policy interventions on public narratives of perversion without scrutinizing them carefully. This short case study demonstrates how useful spontaneous order theory can be for the study of illicit order. It provides a framework of questions and, thereby, guidance toward a nuanced normative evaluation.

Note

1. List of interviews
    1. Fieldworker with significant experience in Maghreb and Afghanistan
    2. International NGO project coordinator

3. Security Advisor for Libya
4. Regional NGO project coordinator
5. Regional NGO project coordinator
6. Fieldworker with significant experience in Eastern Europe

References

Achilli, Luigi. 2018. "The 'Good' Smuggler: The Ethics and Morals of Human Smuggling among Syrians." *The Annals of the American Academy of Political and Social Science* 676 (1): 77–96.

Akerlof, George A. 1970. "The Market for 'Lemons': Quality Uncertainty and the Market Mechanism." *The Quarterly Journal of Economics* 84 (3): 488–500.

Baird, Theodore, and Ilse van Liempt. 2015. "Scrutinising the Double Disadvantage: Knowledge Production in the Messy Field of Migrant Smuggling." *Journal of Ethnic and Migration Studies* 42 (3): 400–417.

Becker, Gary S. 1974. "Crime and Punishment: An Economic Approach." In *Essays in the Economics of Crime and Punishment Volume*, edited by Gary S. Becker, and William M. Landes, 1–54. New York, NY: National Bureau of Economic Research.

Bilger, Veronika, Martin Hofmann, and Michael Jandl. 2006. "Human Smuggling as a Transnational Service Industry: Evidence from Austria." *International Migration* 44 (4): 59–93.

Bouteillet-Paquet, Daphne. 2011. *Smuggling of Migrants: A Global Review and Annotated Bibliography of Recent Publications*. Vienna: United Nations Office on Drugs and Crime.

Buchanan, James M. 1979. "A Defense of Organized Crime?" In *The Economics of Crime and Punishment: A Conference Sponsored by American Enterprise Institute for Public Policy Research. 3rd ed.*, edited by Simon Rottenberg, 119–132. Washington, DC: American Enterprise Inst. for Public Policy Research.

Campana, Paolo. 2017. "Out of Africa: The Organization of Migrant Smuggling Across the Mediterranean." *European Journal of Criminology* 15 (4) 481–502.

———. 2019. "Migrant Smuggling." In *International and Transnational Crime and Justice*, edited by Mangai Natarajan. Cambridge and New York, NY: Cambridge University Press.

Campana, Paolo, and Loraine Gelsthorpe. 2021. "Choosing a Smuggler: Decision-making Amongst Migrants Smuggled to Europe." *European Journal on Criminal Policy and Research* 27 (1): 5–21.

Campana, Paolo, and Federico Varese. 2013. "Cooperation in Criminal Organizations: Kinship and Violence as Credible Commitments." *Rationality and Society* 25 (3): 263–289.

———. 2016. "Exploitation in Human Trafficking and Smuggling." *European Journal on Criminal Policy and Research* 22 (1): 89–105.

Coase, Ronald H. 1937. "The Nature of the Firm." *Economica* 4 (16): 386–405.

———. [1960] 2013. "The Problem of Social Cost." *The Journal of Law and Economics* 56 (4): 837–877.

Crawford, Sue E. S., and Elinor Ostrom. 1995. "A Grammar of Institutions." *The American Political Science Review* 89 (3): 582–600.

Dekker, Rianne, Godfried Engbersen, Jeanine Klaver, and Hanna Vonk. 2018. "Smart Refugees: How Syrian Asylum Migrants Use Social Media Information in Migration Decision-Making." *Social Media + Society* 4 (1): 205630511876443.

Demsetz, Harold. 1968. "The Cost of Transacting." *The Quarterly Journal of Economics* 82 (1): 33–53.

———. 1969. "Information and Efficiency: Another Viewpoint." *The Journal of Law and Economics* 12 (1): 1–22.

Dixit, Avinash K. [2004] 2006. *Lawlessness and Economics: Alternative Modes of Governance.* New Delhi: Oxford University Press.

European Commission. 2021. *A Renewed EU Action Plan Against Migrant Smuggling (2021–2025).* Accessed November 20, 2022. https://home-affairs.ec.europa.eu/renewed-eu-action-plan-against-migrant-smuggling-2021-2025-com-2021-591_en.

European Commission, DG Migration & Home Affairs. 2015. "A Study on Smuggling of Migrants: Characteristics, Responses and Cooperation with Third Countries." Accessed October 2, 2020. https://ec.europa.eu/home-affairs/sites/homeaffairs/files/what-we-do/networks/european_migration_network/reports/docs/emn-studies/study_on_smuggling_of_migrants_final_report_master_091115_final_pdf.pdf.

Ferguson, Adam. [1767] 1980. *An Essay on the History of Civil Society.* New Brunswick, NJ: Transaction Publishers.

Frontex. 2020. "Detections of Illegal Border-Crossings Statistics." Accessed August 6, 2020. http://frontex.europa.eu/trends-and-routes/migratory-routes-map/.

Gallagher, Anne T. 2008. "Human Rights and Human Trafficking: Quagmire or Firm Ground-A Response to James Hathaway." *Virginia Journal of International Law* 49 (4): 789–848.

———. 2015. "Exploitation in Migration: Unacceptable but Inevitable." *Journal of International Affairs* 68 (2): 55–74.

Gambetta, Diego. 1996. *The Sicilian Mafia: The Business of Private Protection* (1st ed.). Cambridge, MA: Harvard University Press.

———. 2009. "Signalling." In *The Oxford Handbook of Analytical Sociology* [eng]. *Oxford Handbooks in Politics & International Relations*, edited by Peter Hedström, and Peter Bearman, 168–194. Oxford: Oxford University Press.

Hayek, Friedrich A. von. [1944] 2007. *The Road to Serfdom: Text and Documents; The Definitive Edition* [eng]. Vol. 2 of *The Collected Works of F. A. Hayek/ed. by W. W. Bartley.* Chicago, IL: University of Chicago Press.

———. 1945. "The Use of Knowledge in Society." *The American Economic Review* 35: 519–530.

———, ed. [1960] 2011. *The Constitution of Liberty: The Definitive Edition* [eng]. *The Collected Works of F. A. Hayek v. 17.* Chicago, IL: University of Chicago Press.

———. [1973] 2013. *Law, Legislation and Liberty: A New Statement of the Liberal Principles of Justice and Political Economy* [eng]. Hoboken, NJ: Taylor and Francis.

———. 1988. *The Fatal Conceit: The Errors of Socialism, edited by W.W. Bartley III* [eng]. v. 1 of *The Collected Works of Friedrich August Hayek*. London: Routledge.

International Organization for Migration. 2019. *Calculating "Death Rates" in the Context of Migration Journeys: Focus on the Central Mediterranean*. https://publications.iom.int/system/files/pdf/mortality-rates.pdf.

Klick, Jonathan, and Alexander T. Tabarrok. 2005. "Using Terror Alert Levels to Estimate the Effect of Police on Crime." *The Journal of Law & Economics* 48 (1): 267–279.

Leeson, Peter T. 2007. "An- arrgh -chy: The Law and Economics of Pirate Organization." *Journal of Political Economy* 115 (6): 1049–1094.

———. 2017. *WTF?!: An Economic Tour of the Weird* [eng]. Stanford, CA: Stanford University Press.

Lucht, Hans. 2013. "Pusher Stories: Ghanaian Connection Men and the Expansion of the EU's Border Regimes into Africa." In *The Migration Industry and the Commercialization of International Migration* [eng]. Vol. 69 of *Routledge Global Institutions*, edited by Thomas Gammeltoft-Hansen, 173–189. London: Routledge.

Mainwaring, Ċetta. 2019. *At Europe's Edge: Migration and Crisis in the Mediterranean*. Oxford: Oxford University Press.

Malakooti, Arezo. 2013. *Mixed Migration: Libya at the Crossroads: Mapping of Migration Routes from Africa to Europe and Drivers of Migration in Post-Revolution Libya*. Translated by Tahar Benattia. Paris: Altai Consulting.

Martin, Nona P., and Virgil Henry Storr. 2008. "On Perverse Emergent Orders." *Studies in Emergent Order* 1 (1): 73–91.

Massalaki, Abdoulaye. 2015. "Niger Passes Law to Tackle Migrant Smuggling, First in West Africa." *Reuters*, May 12. Accessed August 11, 2020. https://www.reuters.com/article/us-europe-migrants-niger/niger-passes-law-to-tackle-migrant-smuggling-first-in-west-africa-idUSKBN0NX1M020150512.

Merriam-Webster.com. 2022. "'perverse'." Accessed November 14, 2022. https://www.merriam-webster.com/dictionary/perverse.

Nissling, Simon, and Ana-Maria Murphy-Teixidor. 2020. "What Makes Refugees and Migrants Vulnerable to Protection Incidents in Libya? A Microlevel Study on the Determinants of Vulnerability." In *Migration in West and North Africa and Across the Mediterranean: Trends, Risks, Development and Governance*, edited by International Organization for Migration, 175–188. Geneva: International Organization for Migration.

North, Douglass C. 1991. "Institutions." *The Journal of Economic Perspectives* 5 (1): 97–112.

———. 1992. *Transaction Costs, Institutions, and Economic Performance*. San Francisco, CA: ICS Press.

Nozick, Robert. [1974] 2013. *Anarchy, State, and Utopia*. New York, NY: Basic Books. .

Olson, Mancur. [2000] 2001. *Power and Prosperity: Outgrowing Communist and Capitalist Dictatorships* [eng]. New York, NY: Basic Books.

Ostrom, Elinor. [1990] 2015. *Governing the Commons: The Evolution of Institutions for Collective Action*. Cambridge: Cambridge University Press.

———. 2005. *Understanding Institutional Diversity*. Princeton, NJ: Princeton University Press.

———. 2010. "Beyond Markets and States: Polycentric Governance of Complex Economic Systems." *American Economic Review* 100 (3): 641–672.

Pennington, Mark. 2011. *Robust Political Economy: Classical Liberalism and the Future of Public Policy. New Thinking in Political Economy*. Cheltenham: Edward Elgar.

———. 2015. "Why Most Things Should Probably Be for Sale." *Georgetown Journal of Law & Public Policy* 13: 251–274.

Raghavan, Sudarsan. 2017. "This African Migrant Dreamed of Reaching Europe: A Phone Call Changed Everything." *The Washington Post*, December 31. Accessed October 19, 2018. https://www.washingtonpost.com/world/africa/this-african-migrant-dreamed-of-reaching-europe-a-phone-call-changed-everything/2017/12/30/cdabbae4-d951-11e7-a241-0848315642d0_story.html?utm_term=.fa93079261e4.

Richman, Barak D. 2017. *Stateless Commerce: The Diamond Network and the Persistence of Relational Exchange*. Cambridge, MA: Harvard University Press.

Roberts, Zoe. 2017. *Information Exchange between Smugglers and Migrants: An Analysis of Online Interactions in Facebook Groups*. MPhil dissertation, Institute of Criminology, University of Cambridge.

Salt, John, and Jeremy Stein. 1997. "Migration as a Business: The Case of Trafficking." *International Migration* 35 (4): 467–494.

Sanchez, Gabriella. 2014. *Human Smuggling and Border Crossings* [eng]. *Routledge Studies in Criminal Justice, Borders and Citizenship*. Hoboken, NJ: Taylor and Francis.

———. 2017. "Critical Perspectives on Clandestine Migration Facilitation: An Overview of Migrant Smuggling Research." *Journal on Migration and Human Security* 5 (1): 9–27.

———. 2020. "Beyond Militias and Tribes: The Facilitation of Migration in Libya." Accessed November 10, 2020. https://cadmus.eui.eu/bitstream/handle/1814/66186/RSCAS_2020_09.pdf?sequence=1&isAllowed=y.

Satz, Debra. 2010. *Why Some Things Should Not Be for Sale: The Moral Limits of Markets* [eng]. *Oxford Political Philosophy*. New York, NY: Oxford University Press.

Schaefer, Alexander. 2021. "Hayek's Twin Ideas: Reconciling Methodological Individualism and Group Selection." *Cambridge Journal of Economics* 45 (6): 1209–1226.

Schaeffer, Emily C. 2008. "Remittances and Reputations in Hawala Money-Transfer Systems: Self-Enforcing Exchange on an International Scale." *Journal of Private Enterprise* 24 (1): 95.

Schelling, Thomas C. 1969. "Models of Segregation." *The American Economic Review* 59 (2): 488–493.

Shortland, Anja. 2019. *Kidnap: Inside the Ransom Business*. Oxford: Oxford University Press.

Shortland, Anja, and Federico Varese. 2014. "The Protector's Choice." *British Journal of Criminology* 54 (5): 741–764.

Sieff, Kevin. 2015. "A Smugglers' Haven in the Sahara." *The Washington Post*, July 20. Accessed October 19, 2018. https://www.washingtonpost.com/sf/world/2015/07/20/a-remote-city-of-smugglers/?utm_term=.e1c220c77e53.

Skarbek, David. 2011. "Governance and Prison Gangs." *The American Political Science Review* 105 (4): 702–716.

———. 2014. *The Social Order of the Underworld: How Prison Gangs Govern the American Penal System* [eng]. Oxford: Oxford University Press.

———. 2016. "Covenants Without the Sword? Comparing Prison Self-Governance Globally." *American Political Science Review* 110 (4): 845–862.

Smith, Adam. [1776] 1993. *Wealth of Nations: Hackett Classics*. Indianapolis, IN: Hackett Publishing Company Inc.

Triandafyllidou, Anna. 2018. "A 'Refugee Crisis' Unfolding: 'Real' Events and Their Interpretation in Media and Political Debates." *Journal of Immigrant & Refugee Studies* 16 (1–2): 198–216.

Triandafyllidou, Anna, and Thanos Maroukēs. 2012. *Migrant Smuggling: Irregular Migration from Asia and Africa to Europe* [eng]. *Migration, Diasporas and Citizenship*. Basingstoke: Palgrave Macmillan.

United Nations. 2000a. *Protocol against the Smuggling of Migrants by Land, Sea and Air, Supplementing the United Nations Convention against Transnational Organized Crime*, 15 November 2000, available at: https://www.unodc.org/documents/middleeastandnorthafrica/smuggling-migrants/SoM_Protocol_English.pdf [accessed 5 October 2023]

———. 2000b. *Protocol to Prevent, Suppress and Punish Trafficking in Persons, Especially Women and Children, Supplementing the United Nations Convention against Transnational Organized Crime*, 15 November 2000, available at: https://www.ohchr.org/en/instruments-mechanisms/instruments/protocol-prevent-suppress-and-punish-trafficking-persons [accessed 5 October 2023]

Varese, Federico. 2001. *The Russian Mafia: Private Protection in a New Market Economy*. Oxford: OUP.

———. 2017. "What is Organized Crime?" In *Redefining organised crime. A challenge for the European Union?*, edited by Orsetta Giolo, Stefania Carnevale, and Serena Forlati, 27–56. Oxford, UK: Hart Publishing.

Vogt, Richard. 2020. "Niger: The Other EU-Financed Migrant Hub of Africa." May 22. Accessed October 8, 2020. https://www.law.ox.ac.uk/research-subject-groups/centre-criminology/centreborder-criminologies/blog/2020/05/niger-other-eu.

Williamson, Oliver E. 1979. "Transaction-Cost Economics: The Governance of Contractual Relations." *The Journal of Law and Economics* 22 (2): 233–261.

9

Hayek on the Origins of Moral Sentiments

Biological versus Cultural Mechanisms for the Evolution and Transmission of Human Morality

Edgar V. Cook

Moral psychology has grown substantially as a field of study over the last twenty years. A key supposition of most theories is that moral reasoning is ubiquitous and represents a key, defining feature of human nature (Haidt 2012; Tomasello 2019; Janoff-Bulman and Carnes 2013; Enke 2019; Henrich, Heine, and Norenzayan 2010). This perspective is not new, of course. Charles Darwin, the original progenitor of the theory of evolution, saw morality as a core aspect of human nature and argued that morality emerged through a process of cultural evolution based on group selection, which he did not attribute to biological mechanisms of evolution but rather the imitation and widespread adoption of beneficial social and technological innovations (Darwin 1871, Chapter II). Friedrich Hayek, to whom this collection of essays is dedicated, similarly argued that human morality arose through a process of sociocultural group selection of acquired normative behaviors and beliefs (Hayek 1988, 25). Hayek believed that cultural evolution operated independent of biological selection but that biologically evolved instincts and emotions—such as the universal capacity for empathy and imitation—provided the cognitive bedrock upon which human morality was able to develop in the first place.

Biological versus Cultural Evolution

The key theoretical debate this chapter focuses on is thus over whether biological or cultural evolutionary processes—operating at the level of the individual in the former and at the group level in the latter—are primarily responsible for the development of human morality. While moral psychology may seem like a niche topic to study from an evolutionary perspective, morality was seen as a key feature of human nature by early evolutionary theorists (Darwin 1871, Chapter II). Social theorists, including Hayek, have long recognized that human morality raises intriguing questions about the limits of our understanding of evolutionary processes. If moral diversity cannot be attributed to genetic variation in the human population, then how do we explain the emergence of moral behaviors and the diversity of moral beliefs and practices that we observe across groups, cultures, and nations? For Hayek, as well as Darwin, the answer to this question necessarily lies *outside* the scope of biological evolution and instead involves a spontaneous process of emergent social order and group cohesion based on informal rules. As we will see, Hayek and Darwin were largely in step with modern evolutionary explanations for moral behavior, although the key aspects they appear to have missed include the capacity for *shared intentionality*—which facilitates the ability to cooperate intentionally and infer others' motives—as well as the influence of exogenous factors such as geographical variation in natural resource endowments (Diamond 1999), environmental threats (Gelfand 2019; Gelfand et al. 2011), and changes to religious proscriptions around marriage within extended families (Henrich, Heine, and Norenzayan 2010).

At the outset, it is important to distinguish between two key mechanisms for evolution: biological evolution, which operates at the level of the individual through gene mutation and natural selection, and cultural evolution, which operates at the level of the group through socially acquired normative behavior. It is important not to conflate biological and cultural mechanisms for human evolution with the "units of selection" at which these mechanisms operate. Evolutionary theory identifies multiple levels at which selection could occur, including genetic change across generations at the level of the individual and genetic change at the level of groups across generations (Wade et al. 2010). However, a consensus has emerged that natural selection via gene mutation of heritable characteristics only operates at the level of the individual rather than at the level of groups within species (Gardner and Welch 2011; Dawkins 1981). This does not rule out the possibility that group selection can account for the "evolution" of social norms and altruism—a point that both Hayek and Darwin stressed in their own work and which is further elaborated below.

Biological evolution is described by Darwin as a process that operates at the level of inherited biological mutations among individual members of a species, whereby biological mutations lead some individuals to be better suited to their environment than others, making those members with the beneficial mutation more likely to survive, reproduce, and pass on their genes to future generations (Darwin 2004). Modern evolutionary theorists have defined biological evolution similarly, arguing that microevolution (genetic changes *within* species) and macroevolution (speciation) arise through mutation, genetic drift, and sexual fitness, which operate at the level of individuals (see, for instance, Richard Dawkins in *The Selfish Gene*, 1978).

Group selection, on the other hand, was conceived of by both Darwin and Hayek as being largely unrelated to genetic variation in the population and thus independent of biological mechanisms of evolution. Although Darwin is most well-known for the theory of biological evolution he outlined in *The Origin of Species* (Darwin 2004), in his later work, *The Descent of Man, and Selection in Relation to Sex* (Darwin 1871), Darwin argued that the origins of human morality and other beliefs and social practices could only be explained by cultural evolution based on group selection of acquired beliefs and social norms. This process, as originally formulated by Darwin, operates *within* species through group selection, such that practices and beliefs that allow some groups to more efficiently cooperate and make use of their environment are more likely to be imitated by other groups and passed down through subsequent generations. In short, cultural practices and beliefs that enable groups to make better use of their natural, social, and environmental resources lead to population growth and an ability to outcompete and grow more quickly than groups with cultural practices and beliefs that are less well-suited to the environment (Darwin 1871).

However, many contemporary theorists, including Richard Dawkins (Dawkins 2016), argue that evolution only operates through biological processes of natural selection based on genetic mutations. A key criticism Dawkins and other proponents of biological evolution make of theories of cultural evolution is that speciation only arises through genetic mutation and differentiation, so cultural evolution based on group selection, which does not stem from underlying genetic mutations in the population and therefore cannot lead to genetic differentiation, cannot be considered a form of evolution on principle.

More fundamentally, however, Dawkins argues that morality and other cultural practices and beliefs (including religion) are transmitted through memetic imitation, whereby ideas and practices are adopted and propagated from one person to the next like a parasite taking over a host (Dawkins 2016, Chapter 11). According to this view, whether a belief or practice is adopted by other individuals within and between groups is entirely unrelated to whether these cognitions and behaviors confer social advantages on groups, allowing them to make better use of their environments and overtake other groups. Instead, Dawkins' account would appear to grant agency to beliefs, attitudes, and norms themselves, which act as a contagion, hopping from one host to another, regardless of their usefulness—or harmfulness—to the host.

Many scholars also view group selection as logically and empirically incompatible with methodological individualism, although Hayek vigorously disagreed (Hayek 1988). Specifically, some scholars argue that the benefits of free riding outweigh the benefits of engaging in altruistic behaviors, which should create strong incentives for individuals to abandon altruistic behaviors that arise socially without genetic mutation (Dawkins 2016).

However, despite the continuing debate over the appropriateness of using group selection as an explanation for the development and transmission of moral sentiments, Darwin's own account of human morality explicitly argues for a dual role of biological and cultural adaptation in shaping human behavior—a phenomenon scholars have labeled gene-culture coevolution (Fehr and Fischbacher 2003). Research in the field of development psychology offers evidence that would seem to confirm that human morality depends on both biologically evolved cognitive capacities for shared intentionality and imitation as well as social interaction, and social learning (Tomasello 2019).

In the chapter that follows, I first provide a more in-depth summary of Darwin's and Hayek's complementary perspectives on the evolution of human morality, showing that both saw dual roles for biological and cultural evolution in shaping moral behavior and cognitions. I then bring three contemporary lines of research on moral psychology under the spotlight, comparing their findings and theoretical developments to Darwin's and Hayek's initial accounts and delineating what I see to be both the biological substrates of moral development and the social processes that lead them to flourish.

Early Enlightenment Accounts of Moral Reasoning

Darwin's theory was built on early efforts to explain the origins and function of moral reasoning by enlightenment thinkers. Descartes argued that humans possess a unique capacity to reason, which is independent of their external experiential learning, and thus believed that moral principles are derived a priori and are entirely independent of experience and human senses (Marciano 2009).

According to Scottish Enlightenment philosophers such as Hume (Hume 2006) and Adam Smith (Smith 2010), however, what makes humans unique are their *experiences*. Hume and Smith posited a "sensual" theory of human nature, whereby human knowledge is entirely dependent upon sensory information gained from cumulative experiences. Thus, Hume and Smith viewed reason as constrained by sensory experiences, in that reason alone cannot generate knowledge independent of information gleaned from observation and experience. The mind stores and updates knowledge structures based on sensory impressions and is thus *acquired* over the lifespan.

Hayek and Darwin on Cultural Evolution and Morality

Hayek agreed with Hume and Smith that reason is not exogenous to human experience. The mind, according to Hayek's (2012) early work on psychology, uses abstract categories, or "schema," to interpret sensory information, and every abstract category in the mind is first built upon sensory experiences. Therefore, though humans exhibit what appears to be an innate capacity to reason about empirical phenomena, this capacity arises from cumulative sensory experiences. According to Hayek, the differences we observe in cognitive capacities between children, adults, and other species are a function of the different accumulated sensory experiences that each has acquired throughout their life.

However, Hayek, as well as Darwin, still believed that biologically evolved instincts play an important role in laying the groundwork for social behavior. However, they did not believe these instincts could explain the variation in morality between species *or* between groups within a species (Caldwell 2000). Specifically, Hayek and Darwin argued that biologically evolved moral emotions such as sympathy (Darwin 1871) and altruism (Lavoie 1990; Hayek 1988) facilitate the social development and transmission of moral sentiments but did not believe these emotions distinguish humans from other species. Rather, many species possess the same innate capacity for emotions as humans, but it is the unique condition of human social life that leads emotions like sympathy to develop into moral norms and beliefs about what is right or wrong (Marciano 2009).

Hayek's and Darwin's conceptions of evolution are thus based on the fundamental premise that species only evolve through biological processes, but that morality evolves *within* species through group selection (Marciano 2009), whereby norms and beliefs that confer advantages on groups are more likely to be adopted and spread via imitation (Hayek 1988).

Thus, Hayek and Darwin argue that morality cannot be reduced to biologically evolved instinctual responses. Instead, similar to Haidt's (2012) claim that inherited genes work in concert with socialization to shape behavior, Hayek and Darwin viewed diversity in moral sentiments as an indicator that moral emotions give rise to the capacity for moral reasoning, but that social experience itself guides the development of higher level cognitions about morality.

Hayek and Darwin, similar to Smith and Hume, believed that human (as well as nonhuman) reasoning relies on the use of abstract categories to organize and understand sensory information (Caldwell 2000). Darwin went so far as to claim that there are no meaningful innate differences in mental capabilities between humans and other species.

> [T]he difference in mind between man and the higher animals, great as it is, certainly is one of degree and not of kind. We have seen that the senses and intuitions, the various emotions and faculties, such as love, memory, attention, curiosity, imitation, reason, etc., of which man boasts, may be found in an incipient, or even sometimes in a well-developed condition, in the lower animals. (Darwin 1871, Chapter IV, para. 52)

According to Darwin (1871), as soon as a species gains information about particular phenomena in the world through sensory experience, they are able to reason about that phenomenon using abstract categorization. Indeed, Hayek and Darwin both believed that any apparent difference in reasoning capacity between humans and other species is simply a function of the different accumulated experiences humans gain as a result of their social interactions and physical adaptations to their environment (Darwin 1871, Chapter II; Hayek 1988, Chapter 1).

The theoretical perspectives advanced by Smith, Hume, Hayek, and Darwin all share a common supposition that human sociality is a natural, intuitive feature of human existence that has always existed and did not need to develop or be built from the ground up (in contrast to Hobbes's state of nature (Hobbes 1967)). In this sense, social behavior is neither innate nor "learned"; humans have simply always been social animals and did not need to "learn" how to live in groups. As Hayek put it, "the savage is not solitary, and his instinct is collectivist" (Hayek 1988, 11).

Thus, Hayek and Darwin argued that morality exists because of both biologically evolved intuitions common to all humans and a process of group selection, whereby moral beliefs and values that lead some groups to cooperate more effectively and to outcompete other groups are more likely to survive. The last piece of the puzzle for Hayek and Darwin was explaining how moral values and practices are transmitted across individuals and groups. Hayek—similar to Darwin's earlier arguments in *The Descent of Man* (1871)—argued that moral norms and beliefs are transmitted through *imitation* and are thus acquired rather than inherited: "although biological theory now excludes the inheritance of acquired characteristics, all cultural evolution rests on such inheritance—characteristics in the form of rules guiding the mutual relations among individuals which are not innate but learnt" (Hayek 1988, 25). Individuals and groups naturally imitate one another, and moral practices that allow groups to more efficiently coordinate social life are more likely to be adopted by others over time, simply by virtue of the fact that the groups adopting these behaviors will experience faster population growth than the groups that do not.

Synthesizing the accounts offered by Hayek and Darwin above, we end up with a basic framework that allows us to delineate which aspects of human morality can be attributed to biological versus cultural evolution. Firstly, because biological evolution tends toward *between* species variation, it cannot explain variation in moral practices between cultures and groups. Rather, biological evolution can be used to explain how humans developed the cognitive capabilities needed to engage in moral reasoning as a species. On the other hand, cross-cultural variation in moral practices can only be explained by cultural evolution based on group selection of acquired behaviors and norms. Thus, determining the evolutionary origins of morality depends fundamentally on identifying the cognitive and emotional factors that shape moral judgments and then determining whether those factors derive from evolved capacities common to all humans or are a product of institutions developed through social interaction. With this framework in mind, we proceed to evaluate the evolutionary accounts of human morality offered by contemporary theories of moral psychology.

Contemporary Accounts of the Origins of Morality

Two of the most prominent theories at the forefront of moral psychology are the moral foundations theory (Haidt 2012; Graham et al. 2013; Koleva et al. 2012) and the theory of dyadic morality (Gray, Waytz, and Young 2012). Both theories allow for biological and cultural processes to shape human morality, but they differ in their interpretations of the psychological factors that drive moral reasoning and the extent to which cultural variation in moral beliefs and practices stems from culturally evolved adaptations or innate, biologically evolved intuitions. Whereas moral foundations theory (hereafter, MFT) argues that moral values arise from "moral intuitions," which are genetically inherited and *vary* within the human population (Haidt 2012), the theory of dyadic morality (hereafter, TDM) argues that morality instead arises from a universal "harm-based" cognitive schema, which allows for cultural variation in moral norms and beliefs without relying on genetic variation between groups. Instead, TDM argues that moral judgments arise in situations where individuals observe a conscious agent intentionally causing harm to a vulnerable, innocent victim (Gray, Waytz, and Young, 2012). Human moral reasoning is therefore dependent upon a shared cognitive ability to infer others' motives (i.e., intentions), which is an ability unique to the human species and thus one that necessitates biological evolution but which facilitates social learning of diverse forms of moral reasoning.

Moral Foundations Theory

Moral Foundations Theory was originally developed by Jonathan Haidt (2012) and his coauthors (Koleva et al. 2012; Graham et al. 2013) to explain variation in moral practices and beliefs across cultures. Building on the work of the anthropologist Richard Sweder, Haidt argues that humans exhibit five unique moral "foundations" or types of moral values, which each arise from distinct biologically evolved "intuitions" and emotions (Haidt 2012). These five moral foundations include:

1. Harm/care, which refers to concerns about protecting innocent victims from harm and empathizing with victims;
2. Fairness/cheating, which encompasses moral principles related to equity, reciprocity, and fairness;
3. Ingroup/loyalty, which includes moral concerns related to protecting one's ingroup and being loyal to family and friends;
4. Authority/respect, which consists of moral dictates about respecting social hierarchies and authority figures;
5. Purity/sanctity, which refers to moral precepts about chastity and physical and spiritual purity;

Research employing survey measures of the five foundations proposed by MFT finds that liberals and conservatives in Western democracies endorse each foundation to varying degrees, with liberals (both classical liberals and progressives) subscribing to the two "individualizing" foundations of harm/care and fairness/cheating most strongly and conservatives endorsing the three "binding" foundations of ingroup/loyalty, authority/respect, and purity/sanctity more strongly than the harm/care and fairness/cheating foundations (Clifford et al. 2015; Koleva et al. 2012).

According to Haidt (2012), the diverging endorsement of individualizing and binding moral foundations between liberals and conservatives leads to political polarization, especially in the United States, where voters have sorted along ideological lines into the Democratic and Republican parties. Indeed, research finds that differences in scores on the moral foundations questionnaire strongly predict policy preferences among liberals and conservatives (Koleva et al. 2012). More recently, research on "moral reframing" has found that framing messages around an individual's moral values to argue in favor of policies they typically oppose can lead conservatives to support liberal policies such as gay marriage and environmental regulations and liberals to support conservative policies such as making English the official language of the United States and increasing military spending (Feinberg and Willer 2019). Thus, there is evidence that the endorsement of distinct moral foundations varies across groups and that moral values appear to predict diverging political preferences. However, the validity of MFT as an explanation for the emergence of morality depends on whether moral values arise from distinct, biologically evolved, and genetically inherited intuitions, as the theory suggests.

MFT is based on the premise that each moral foundation stems from a distinct set of emotions and "intuitions," which are genetically determined, located in different regions of the brain, and lead to different emotional reactions to moral violations (Graham et al. 2013). For instance, endorsement of the purity/sanctity foundation supposedly arises from disgust sensitivity, with actions that trigger disgust reactions being more likely to be moralized, regardless of the objective harmfulness of the action (Haidt 2012). According to Haidt (2012), individuals who subscribe more strongly to the purity/sanctity dimension do so because they are higher in "disgust sensitivity." This is illustrated by the fact that conservatives tend to score higher on both measures of disgust sensitivity and measures of support for the purity/sanctity foundation (Koleva et al. 2012). Similarly, liberals, who tend to score more highly on measures of empathy, are more likely to endorse the harm/care foundation (Haidt 2012). Thus, it would appear that Haidt's theory is based on the claim that cultural diversity in moral practices is due to both socialization and genetic differences between groups.

In particular, Haidt's account of the development of human morality argues that the capacity for moral reasoning relies on biologically evolved, genetically inherited "intuitions" (Haidt 2012). However, in departure from Hayek and Darwin, Haidt appears to argue that diversity in moral beliefs and values stems from group selection *based* on genetic diversity *within* species in addition to sociocultural processes of behavioral adaption and imitation.

This claim is controversial, and recent research has called into question much of Haidt et al.'s hypotheses about the influence of distinct genetically determined intuitions on moral reasoning. For instance, research has found little evidence that judgments of actions that violate particular moral foundations correspond to emotional responses in distinct parts of the brain (Schein and Gray 2018). Moreover, other work has found that moral judgments are better predicted by the perceived harmfulness of actions rather than differing levels of support for the five foundations (Schein and Gray 2016).

MFT is thus left on shaky ground, both because the evolutionary account Haidt proposes conflates biological and cultural evolutionary processes and because more recent work has failed to find evidence that moral foundations map onto distinct emotions and regions of the brain (Schein and Gray 2018). Hayek would likely view Haidt's claims about genetic differences in moral intuitions with skepticism. Hayek's and Darwin's accounts of moral evolution argue that biological and cultural mechanisms are fundamentally independent of one another, with the former granting humans the emotional capacity needed to engage in moral reasoning and the latter selecting which moral practices and beliefs persist and are transmitted across groups.

The Theory of Dyadic Morality

The Theory of Dyadic Morality (TDM), in contrast to MFT, argues that morality is based on a universal "harm-based" cognitive schema, which is composed of six necessary but individually insufficient cognitive elements/perceptions: an *intentional* perpetrator → *causing* harm → to a *vulnerable* victim (Schein and Gray 2018). In order for individuals to view an action or event as immoral, they must perceive all six elements to be present—specifically, they must perceive that a conscious agent is intentionally causing harm to an innocent victim capable of feeling pain (Gray, Waytz, and Young 2012; Schein and Gray 2015). The more an observer perceives that an action has caused intentional harm, the more likely they are to feel outrage and to morally condemn the perpetrator of the act.

According to Schein and Gray (2018), this harm-based schema enables diverse moral practices to develop across cultures and groups based on differences in the perceived harmfulness of acts. The more something is viewed as harmful (e.g., disrespecting your elders, stealing property from another person, or having sex with siblings), the more likely it is that the act will be "moralized," and moral norms will arise to proscribe similar behaviors. Importantly, this harm-based schema is not theorized to be based in distinct regions of the brain but rather to be a universal cognitive framework upon which humans form moral judgments and develop moral values.

Research testing the predictions of TDM has found that perceptions of the harmfulness of acts and the intentionality with which perpetrators engage in acts predict moral judgments better than scores on moral foundations (Schein and Gray 2018). Moreover, TDM's theory is significantly more parsimonious than MFT, to the extent that it argues moral reasoning is based on a shared cognitive schema (Schein and Gray 2015) rather than five sets of distinct intuitive emotions, which vary based on genetics between individuals (Haidt, 2012).

Most importantly, in contrast to MFT, TDM provides an evolutionary explanation for human morality that comports with Hayek and Darwin's framework for distinguishing biological and cultural evolution from one another. Gray and his coauthors argue that moral reasoning is dependent upon biological evolution to the extent that moral reasoning requires the biologically evolved ability to engage in "mind reading" of others' intentions as well as the capacity to feel empathy. But these factors only enable moral reasoning for the human species as a whole; they cannot explain cultural variation in moral practices and what people choose to *moralize* (Schein and Gray 2015). However, Schein and Gray are less specific about the extent to which group selection pressures might determine whether certain "moralized" norms are more likely to survive and be socially transmitted than others.

Becoming Human: A Synthesis of Biological and Cultural Accounts of Morality

Michael Tomasello's research on developmental differences between humans and apes provides a more detailed account of the unique contributions biological and cultural evolution make to human morality. Similar to Hayek and Darwin, Tomasello (2019) argues that human morality is the product of both biological and cultural processes. Specifically, biologically evolved cognitive capabilities enable moral reasoning, but sociocultural experiences shape moral norms and practices. Moreover, Tomasello argues that moral reasoning *is* in fact a uniquely human capacity that derives from biologically evolved differences in cognitive abilities between humans and other species. Based on research comparing early childhood development between chimps and human children, Tomasello argues that humans' biologically evolved capacity for *shared intentionality* enables them to engage in moral reasoning in ways that chimps (and other species) cannot.

Humans develop the ability to engage in "joint intentionality" at an early age (first with individuals at age 3 and then with groups at age 9), whereas chimps and other species never develop this ability. Joint intentionality allows humans to engage in *perspective-taking* and to intentionally coordinate with others based on abstract goals and shared "imagined" realities (Tomasello 2019). Chimps (and other species), on the other hand, exhibit little to no ability to engage in perspective-taking or to coordinate with other group members in a premeditated way. When chimps work with other group members to achieve a goal (usually related to food), they are using the others as tools rather than cooperative partners. In other words, chimps are hardwired to compete rather than cooperate, whereas humans are hardwired to cooperate (Tomasello 2019).

The biologically evolved capacity for joint intentionality then interacts with the unique conditions and challenges of human social life to give rise to moral norms and beliefs. As children gain the capacity for shared intentionality, they develop moral beliefs and practices through their repeated interactions with peers and by imitating trusted adults. At a cultural level, moral practices are ultimately shaped by the unique social-coordination problems groups face based on their environment and group size. Thus, in line with Hayek and Darwin, Tomasello's research suggests that morality is enabled by biologically evolved abilities but that moral practices are ultimately the result of spontaneous interactions in social groups and the persistence of acquired behaviors that confer advantages on the group as a whole.

Kinship, Environmental Threats, and Resource Endowments

Despite offering insight into the role that biological and cultural processes play in shaping moral sentiments broadly, MFT, TDM, and Tomasello's theory of human ontogeny still cannot explain the variation we observe in moral sentiments across cultures. Instead, what we have is a careful delineation of the nature of moral reasoning in humans and the extent to which moral sentiments can be attributed to biological or cultural evolution. But these theories offer little insight into the *environmental* origins of differences in moral systems across cultures. Hayek's explanations for the origins of morality also left unanswered the question of why some cultures develop individualistic moral sentiments whereas others cling to traditionalism and "binding" moral values.

Hayek argued that modern societies can be differentiated based on the extent to which they exhibit either an "extended order" of liberal moral values based on protecting individual rights and liberties or traditional moral values that prioritize communal sacrifice, social order, and redistribution (Hayek 1988). According to Hayek, this moral divide reflects a tension between humans' innate "collectivistic" instinct toward parochial altruism, which he viewed as part of humans' evolved psychology, and the liberal moral values that characterize modern democracies, which are "evolved" rules that arose through a process of group selection. Still, the question remains as to why some societies have moral sentiments that are more "collectivistic" in nature while others have moral beliefs that are more reflective of the individualistic "extended order" described by Hayek. Though he was referring to the conflict between socialism and capitalism that characterized world politics at the time he was writing, Hayek's depiction of the tension between these two types of morality is reflected in contemporary work on "individualizing" and "binding" moral values across cultures (Graham et al. 2013; Enke 2019).

Survey measures of moral foundations, aggregated at the county level, strongly predict vote choice across states in the United States (Enke 2020), with "binding"/communal moral values being more common in rural areas. Moreover, in a separate article, Enke finds that the extent to which societies endorse universal/"individualizing" moral values over "binding"/communal moral values is explained by the strength of kinship ties at the country level, with kinship ties referring to "the extent to which people are embedded in extended family networks" (Enke 2020, 954). Using data from countries surveyed for the World Values Survey, Enke (2020) finds that countries with historically tighter kinship ties are more likely to rely on communal moral values to regulate social behavior, whereas societies with looser kinship networks are more likely to rely on universal/individualizing moral values as well as the belief in an external moralizing god to regulate behavior. Thus, the strength of kinship ties potentially explains how the universal psychological features of human moral psychology give rise to the variation in moral values we observe across cultures. Enke's results suggest that "systems" of moral sentiments develop in order to solve "the different economic needs that arise due to variation in the structure of extended family relationships" (Enke 2020).

More recently, Joseph Henrich, in his book *The Weirdest People in the World*, has argued that much of the variation in kinship ties and individualizing versus traditional/binding moral values stems from seemingly arbitrary changes to the Catholic Church's policies regarding marriage within extended families, specifically marriage to cousins, in the fourteenth century. By prohibiting within-family marriages, the Church began a process of loosening kinship ties in areas of Europe where the Church had a stronger presence. The areas that first adopted these new proscriptions around kin marriage still, to this day, have populations that score more highly on measures of individualizing moral values.

Thus, Henrich's work offers convincing evidence that seemingly exogenous shocks to kinship networks affected the rate at which communities developed individualizing moral norms. However, there are other factors that may have similarly affected the development of moral systems across cultures that future work should pay greater attention to. Resource endowments—both in terms of the crops, livestock, and other natural resources available within a particular geographic setting as well as the amount of available resources between groups—very likely shaped how groups interacted with their environment and other groups. Recent evidence has found that conflicts between hunter-gatherer groups during the late Pleistocene and early Holocene would have been frequent and deadly, which likely would have selected groups that exhibited especially altruistic, cooperative behaviors in the face of threats from other tribes (Bowles 2009). Areas with scarce resources would likely have proven especially fertile grounds for intergroup conflict, which could similarly explain the variation in the prevalence of binding versus individualizing values across cultures. Lastly, recent work on "tight" versus "loose" societies finds that cultures in geographic regions prone to natural disasters, disease, and conflict with rival groups exhibit a "tighter" adherence to social norms, with people obeying social norms more stringently (as well as a greater number of punitive, proscriptive norms) in such places (Gelfand et al. 2011).

Conclusion

In closing, it is worth noting how prescient Hayek's account of the cultural evolution of moral sentiments was for its time. In step with most contemporary work, Hayek attributes the development of human morality to a process of cultural evolution, with group selection selecting for moral norms/rules that enhance the groups' competitive advantage and population growth. As we have seen, Hayek overlooked a number of important historical factors that may have shaped moral beliefs differently across cultures, and future work should expand on our theoretical understanding of how these historical processes shaped morality. Yet fundamentally, his distinction between biological and cultural evolution as explanations for the diversity of moral sentiments we observe across cultures was both revelatory and consistent with recent advances in moral psychology and evolutionary theory. To better understand how systems of moral values develop over time, researchers should seek to explain how exogenous features of early humans' environments incentivized moral behavior in diverging ways around the globe.

References

Bowles, Samuel. 2009. "Did Warfare Among Ancestral Hunter-Gatherers Affect the Evolution of Human Social Behaviors?" *Science* 324 (5932): 1293–1298.

Caldwell, Bruce. 2000. "The Emergence of Hayek's Ideas on Cultural Evolution." *The Review of Austrian Economics* 13: 5–22.

Clifford, Scott, Jennifer Jerit, Carlisle Rainey, and Matt Motyl. 2015. "Moral Concerns and Policy Attitudes: Investigating the Influence of Elite Rhetoric." *Political Communication* 32 (2): 229–248.

Darwin, Charles. 1871. *The Descent of Man, and Selection in Relation to Sex*. New York, NY: D. Appleton.

———. 2004. *On the Origin of Species, 1859*. London: Routledge.

Dawkins, Richard. 1981. "In Defence of Selfish Genes." *Philosophy* 56 (218): 556–573.

———. 2016. *The Extended Selfish Gene*. Revised impression. Oxford: Oxford University Press.

Diamond, Jared M. 1999. *Guns, Germs, and Steel: The Fates of Human Societies*. New York, NY: Norton.

Enke, Benjamin. 2019. "Kinship, Cooperation, and the Evolution of Moral Systems." *The Quarterly Journal of Economics* 134 (2): 953–1019.

———. 2020. "Moral Values and Voting." *Journal of Political Economy* 128 (10): 3679–3729.

Fehr, Ernst, and Urs Fischbacher. 2003. "The Nature of Human Altruism." *Nature* 425 (6960): 785–791.

———. 2019. "Moral Reframing: A Technique for Effective and Persuasive Communication across Political Divides." *Social and Personality Psychology Compass* 13 (12): e12501.

Gardner, Andy, and John J. Welch. 2011. "A Formal Theory of the Selfish Gene." *Journal of Evolutionary Biology* 24 (8): 1801–1813.

Gelfand, Michele. 2019. *Rule Makers, Rule Breakers: Tight and Loose Cultures and the Secret Signals That Direct Our Lives*. New York: Scribner.

Gelfand, Michele J., Jana L. Raver, Lisa Nishii, Lisa M. Leslie, Janetta Lun, Beng Chong Lim, Lili Duan, et al. 2011. "Differences Between Tight and Loose Cultures: A 33-Nation Study." *Science* 332 (6033): 1100–1104.

Graham, Jesse, Jonathan Haidt, Sena Koleva, Matt Motyl, Ravi Iyer, Sean P. Wojcik, and Peter H. Ditto. 2013. "Moral Foundations Theory." *Advances in Experimental Social Psychology*, 47: 55–130.

Gray, Kurt, Adam Waytz, and Liane Young. 2012. "The Moral Dyad: A Fundamental Template Unifying Moral Judgment." *Psychological Inquiry* 23 (2): 206–215.

Haidt, Jonathan. 2012. *The Righteous Mind: Why Good People Are Divided by Politics and Religion*. New York: Vintage.

Hayek, Friedrich. 1988. *The Fatal Conceit: The Errors of Socialism*. Abingdon: Routledge.

———. 2012. *The Sensory Order: An Inquiry into the Foundations of Theoretical Psychology*. Chicago, IL: University of Chicago Press.

Henrich, Joseph, Steven J. Heine, and Ara Norenzayan. 2010. "The Weirdest People in the World?" *Behavioral and Brain Sciences* 33 (2–3): 61–83.

Hobbes, Thomas. 1967. *Hobbes's Leviathan*. Рипол Классик.

Hume, David. 2006. *An Enquiry Concerning the Principles of Morals: A Critical Edition*. Vol. 4. Oxford: Oxford University Press.

Janoff-Bulman, Ronnie, and Nate C. Carnes. 2013. "Surveying the Moral Landscape: Moral Motives and Group-Based Moralities." *Personality and Social Psychology Review* 17 (3): 219–236.

Koleva, Spassena P., Jesse Graham, Ravi Iyer, Peter H. Ditto, and Jonathan Haidt. 2012. "Tracing the Threads: How Five Moral Concerns (Especially Purity) Help Explain Culture War Attitudes." *Journal of Research in Personality* 46 (2): 184–194.

Lavoie, Don. 1990. "Introduction to F. A. Hayek's Theory of Cultural Evolution: Market and Cultural Processes as Spontaneous Orders." *Cultural Dynamics* 3 (1): 1–11.

Marciano, Alain. 2009. "Why Hayek Is a Darwinian (After All)? Hayek and Darwin on Social Evolution." *Journal of Economic Behavior & Organization* 71 (1): 52–61.

Schein, Chelsea, and Kurt Gray. 2016. "Moralization and Harmification: The Dyadic Loop Explains How the Innocuous Becomes Harmful and Wrong." *Psychological Inquiry* 27 (1): 62–65.

———. 2018. "The Theory of Dyadic Morality: Reinventing Moral Judgment by Redefining Harm." *Personality and Social Psychology Review* 22 (1): 32–70.

Smith, Adam. 2010. *The Theory of Moral Sentiments*. New York: Penguin.

Tomasello, Michael. 2019. "Becoming Human." In *Becoming Human*. Cambridge, MA: Harvard University Press.

Wade, Michael J., David S. Wilson, Charles Goodnight, Doug Taylor, Yaneer Bar-Yam, Marcus A. M. de Aguiar, Blake Stacey, et al. 2010. "Multilevel and Kin Selection in a Connected World." *Nature* 463 (7283): E8–E10.

Index

Aristotle, 117; kingship, 126; law, 123–24, 126; politics, 125–26
artifact: constitutions as, 80; embodiments of fact and value, 79; human action, 79; immaterial, 80; materials, 82; words, 80–81
artisanship, 77–78; contestation, 77–78; goals of, 83; Ostromian, 75, 81; process of, 76
Austrian economics, 16; aggregate production function, 16; culture, 151; equilibrium, 28; feminism, 157–58

Benton, Lauren: legal logic, 138
Berry, Wendell, 89; art of the commonplace, 96; environmentalism, 96–102; great economy, 103; health, 105; hubris, 97; theology, 103–6
black market, 184
Buchanan, James M.: on competition, 185–86; on creativity, 74
Burke, Edmund: on personal liberty, 116

Canada, 39
Caribbean: Bahamas, 153, 187; Barbados, 159; Jamaica, 162, 165; microenterprise development in, 150, 161–74; Trinidad and Tobago, 161
central planning, 14, 30; and development, 154–55; of environmentalism, 95; microenterprise, 150; morality of, 106; rent-seeking and, 155
Chamlee-Wright, Emily: on community recovery, 153; on Zimbabwe, 167
Chimpanzee, 223
Christianity, 96
civilization: artifacts of, 70; and culture, 67; discipline of, 69; and freedom, 68; production of, 72
Cobbs-Douglass Production Function, 20
COVID-19, 170–71
culture: as an interpretive lens, 151–52; as norms and attitudes, 151

Darwin, Charles, 213; *The Descent of Man*, 218; on morality, 215
Dawkins, Richard: *The Selfish Gene*, 215
Debeck, E. K., 54
Deenan, Patrick: on human nature, 91
Descartes, Rene, 216
de Tocqueville, Alexis, 70; apprenticeship of liberty, 71

Easterly, William: on foreign aid, 154; on international funding bodies, 155–56
economic development, 154, 159, 166–67
economists: assumptions of, 22, 24, 94–95; on memory, 46; monetary, 38
egalitarianism. *See* equality
England: common law of, 131–33, 135–37, 140–44; King Edward I, 139, 143; King Henry II, 133; King John, 137–38; Norman conquest of, 135; Parliament of, 135; Tudor and Stuart Monarchs, 135
entrepreneurship, 12, 23–25; Austrian, 73–74; COVID-19 Vaccine, 25; craft breweries, 108; culture of, 153, 174; female, 159–60, 163–65, 171; incentives, 29; the iPhone, 25; microenterprise, 149, 160, 171; microfinance. *See* entrepreneurship, microenterprise: skills, 167–68; western methods of, 149
epistemology, 3; humility and, 107
equality, 6; and First Nations, 43
European Commission, 195
European Union, 181, 193
evolution: biological, 214–16; cultural, 214–16; feedback responses, 192; gene-culture coevolution, 216; by group selection, 215; memetic imitation, 215–16; moral, 4; of moral instinct, 217; as spontaneous order, 192
excludability: of ideas, 15
externality, 95, 101, 206

farming: industrialized, 95, 104, 106; monocropping, 102; small-scale, 89–90, 108; subsidization of, 98; theology of, 105; topsoil erosion, 98
feminism: gender relations, 157; and top-down development, 150, 156–57
Ferguson, Adam, 70; on dominance, 73; governance, 72
First Nations, 37, 167; and disease, 53

Geertz, Clifford, 152
Gerald of Wales: and ethnogenesis, 138–39
German historicism, 122
Goodman, Paul, 76
government: by prison gangs, 180; purpose of, 113
The Great Depression, 19

Haidt, Jonathan: moral foundations theory, 219–22; political psychology of, 220–21
Hamowy, Ronald: common law, 135–37; legal history, 135
Hayek, F. A.: The Abuse of Reason Project, 2; archaeological thought, 79; aristocratic principle, 118–19; business cycle theory, 19; capital intensity, 17; classical political philosophy, 114, 117, 125–26; on coercion, 115, 124–25; complex phenomena, 1–2; *The Constitution of Liberty*, 3, 65, 113, 135; constitutions, 82, 84; *The Creative Powers of a Free Civilization*, 65; cultural evolution, 67, 84, 192; currency, 56; economic calculus, 21; economic growth, 17, 155; as economic historian, 20; emergency powers, 125; on the entrepreneur, 74; on environmentalism, 89, 92; on equilibrium, 5; and the extended order, 224; free civilization of, 67; on Hamowy, Ronald, 135–37; on historicism, 29–30; on human action,

68; on idealism, 120–21, 123; on individualism, 81–82, 114, 120; the knowledge problem, 4, 19–20, 156; *Law, Legislation and Liberty*, 3, 134; on metaphysical freedom, 114–15; on moral evolution, 213–14; nobel prize address, 93–94; and order, 26, 66, 72, 182–83, 201, 214; on political freedom, 114; pretense to knowledge. *See* Hayek, F. A., the knowledge problem; on prices and production, 21; psychology, 217, 226; *The Road to Serfdom*, 106; on rule of law, 7, 113, 121–22, 132, 146; *Scientism and the Study of Society*, 22; on the Socratic Maxim, 117; systems theory of, 1; on technological progress, 16–21
Henrich, Joseph: on kin marriage, 225; *The Weirdest People in the World*, 225
Horwitz, Steven, 157
Hudson Bay Company, 42
human trafficking, 194
Hurricane Katrina, 153

industrial revolution, 13
innovation. *See* entrepreneurship
institutions: analysis of, 137; barriers to, 143; as complex orders. *See* institutions, spontaneous orders; conflict and, 140; of culture, 54, 151; externally imposed, 156–57, 206; framework of, 24–25, 28; gendered, 158, 164–65; of law, 134; of liberty, 132, 137; of the market, 93; organic development of, 68; power concentration, 29; rules of, 183; of smuggling, 205; social functions of, 53; and spontaneous orders, 11, 52, 132, 197; stickiness of, 54, 154, 156–57
Ireland: Brehon Law, 139–40; colonial, 132; defamation in, 141–44; Nine Years War, 144; Parliament of, 139–40; Rauth, Adam, 142; Robert de Trym, 141; Simon de Cromhal, 143; Sir John Davies, 144–45; William Grane, 144; William the Merchant, 144

Jobs, Steve, 25
justice: and distribution, 18, 119, 124

Kirzner, Israel: knowledge, 169
knowledge: communication of, 28; cultural, 152; division of, 93; of farming, 90, 99; generation of, 15; individual, 25; institutions, 68–69; limitations on, 19, 81, 115–16; local, 99, 153, 167; memory, 47; metis, 156; pretense to, 97, 106; price, 93; scientific, 23; sensory, 217; storytelling as, 50; tacit, 39, 55, 169; transfer of, 50

Laudabiliter, 139
Lavoie, Don: on neoclassical economics, 151
law: Brehon, 139–40, 145; canon, 139–40; certainty, 124; character of command, 119; civil, 184; common law, 135–37, 143–44; defamation, 141–44; ecclesiastical, 142; emergent, 131–32; impartiality, 124; intellectual property, 15, 25; King's Court as, 136, 138; legal positivism, 3; March Law. *See* law, Brehon; murder, 141–44; Natural Law, 3–4, 122; pluralistic, 140; task of, 121
liberalism: ethos of, 107; and human nature, 91; humility and, 120; market-oriented, 89; moral values of, 224; political economy of, 90
Libya, 200
Life Yard, 169–71; ROSCA, 172–74
Locke, John: on property, 100; rule of law in, 113, 123
London, 37

mafia, 185
Magna Carta, 65
mainstream macroeconomics. *See* Neoclassical Economics

Marx, Karl, 12, 29
Mbiti, John: philosophy of, 173–74
McGinnis, Michael, 69
Mediterranean, 180
Menger, Karl, 52
methodological individualism, 66, 186, 216
Miller, Eugene: on rule of law, 120–22
Mises, Ludwig von, 28; on entrepreneurship, 73
money: gifts as, 48; ledger. *See* money, receipts; memory, 40, 45, 48–49; receipts, 47; supply of, 18; transaction costs and, 37
monopoly: patent law and, 15
morality: communal, 225; coordinating function of, 219; disgust sensitivity and, 221; dyadic, 219, 222–23; evolution of, 4, 213–16; farming, 105–6; harm-based, 222; imitation and, 218; instinct for, 217; of migrant smuggling, 198; moral foundations theory, 219–22; moral psychology, 220, 225; order of, 192; psychology of, 213; reasoning, 216–18; and Shared Intentionality, 223–24

Native American. *See* First Nations
Nazi Germany, 192
Neoclassical Economics, 12–13; and equilibrium, 28; Growth Theory of, 154; as static, 151; top-down development and, 156
Nirvana Fallacy, 187, 204
Nisbet, Robert, 82
Nozick, Robert: *Anarchy, State, and Utopia*, 189; hidden hand explanations, 191, 207; protective agencies, 189; Spontaneous Order Theory of, 182, 190

Olson, Mancur: on bandits, 189–90
order: competitive, 28, 31; of Creation, 96; criminal, 190–93; ecological, 95, 98; economic, 183; emergent. *See* order, spontaneous; equilibrium, 27; externalities to, 188, 206; illicit, 179–80, 186–90; mobs as, 188; monocentric, 26; polycentric, 26, 66; rules for, 191–92; spontaneous, 27, 67, 72, 101, 131, 169, 180
Ostrom, Elinor, 7; artisanship and, 66, 74; collective action and, 75; Rules-in-Use, 44
Ostrom, Vincent, 74–75; archaeological thought of, 79
Overlapping Generations Model, 45

Pacific Northwest, 53
Pennington, Mark: environmental policy of, 95; Nirvana Fallacy, 187
Pericles: and the Aristocratic Principle, 118–19; *The Funeral Oration*, 117–18
Plato, 117
Polanyi, Karl: on cultural institutions, 151
post-colonialism: development, 166; third world, 166
potlatch, 38; ban on, 39, 44–45, 55; free-riding and, 38–39, 46, 50–51; as gift-giving, 42; host of, 49; reasons for, 40–44, 48; and redistribution, 42
price: coordinating function of, 26, 29; generation of, 18, 93; spontaneous, 28; value, 104

Quesnay, Francoise, 20

rational choice theory, 53
Rawls, John, 189
Romer, Paul M.: Endogenous Growth Theory, 25; on technological progress, 14–15, 23

Saint-Simon, 12
Satz, Debra: on noxious markets, 186–87
Schelling, Thomas: on segregation, 190
Schumpeter, Joseph, 12–13, 20, 29; on entrepreneurship, 73
science: merits of, 25

Smith, Adam, 20, 217
smuggling: and agency, 194–95; good *versus* bad, 181; harmful, 196; Hawala, 202; information asymmetries, 199; of migrants, 180–81, 193; North Africa to Europe, 193; rationality of, 197–98; reputation and, 200; social media and, 201; transaction cost optimization, 199, 202; transaction costs, 183; trust and, 202; violence and, 203
social change: emergent, 4–5
Solon, 119
Solow, Robert: on business cycles, 20; on economic growth, 15; Growth Model of, 20; on technological progress, 13–14
Storr, Virgil: on the Cunning Spirit, 153; on the Enterprising Spirit, 153
Strauss, Leo: *The Natural Right of History*, 116
Sweder, Richard, 220

technological progress, 11, 29; exogenous, 22
Thucydides: *History of the Peloponnesian War*, 117
Tomasello, Michael: on human ontogeny, 223–24

Washington Post, 204
Weber, Max: on Ideal Types, 122
Wilson, Peter: on culture, 158–59
Wobst, Martin M., 79–80

About the Editors

Dr. **Peter J. Boettke**, professor of economics and philosophy, George Mason University; director, F. A. Hayek Program for Advanced Study in Philosophy, Politics, and Economics, Mercatus Center at George Mason University.

Dr. **Erwin Dekker**, senior fellow, F. A. Hayek Program for Advanced Study in Philosophy, Politics, and Economics, Mercatus Center at George Mason University.

Dr. **Chad Van Schoelandt**, associate professor of philosophy, Tulane University.

About the Contributors

Jaime L. Carini, PhD student in musicology and DM candidate in organ performance and literature at Indiana University Bloomington.

Edgar V. Cook, PhD student in political science at Duke University.

Dr. **Lachezar Grudev**, research associate in the Department of Contextual Economics at the University of Siegen.

Florian A. Hartjen, PhD student in political economy at King's College London.

Craig Lyons, PhD student in history at Cornell University.

Casey Pender, PhD student in economics at Carleton University.

Samuel Schmitt, PhD student in political science at the University of North Carolina at Chapel Hill.

Dr. **Abigail Staysa**, postdoctoral research fellow in politics at Princeton University.

Kayleigh Thompson, PhD student in social anthropology at York University.